HOLIDAY * NEWFOUNDLAND

LABRADOR

Strait of Belle Isle

Gulf of St Lawrence

St. Anthony

ATLANTIC OCEAN

HENSALL PUBLIC LIBRARY

Horse Is.
Cape St. John
Tilt Cove
Snooks Arms
Seal Cove
Fogo  Joe Batts Arm
Twillingate
BAY of EXPLOITS

Rattling Brook

Humber River

Botwood

Curling
Corner Brook

Deer Lake
Badger

Buchans  Grand Falls

Gander

C.N.R.

Bonavista

TRINITY BAY

Sandy Point
St. George's

CONCEPTION BAY
BELL ISLAND

BAY
St. GEORGE

Codroy

C.N.R.

Belleoram  Hearts Content
Milltown
BAY d'ESPOIR
Burgeo  Pushthrough

Carbonear
Harbour Grace
Bay Roberts

St. JOHN'S

Brigus
Bay Bulls

ort aux Basques  Ramea

Francois
FORTUNE BAY

Placentia

Ferryland
Aquaforte

Cabot Strait

Grand Bank

Miquelon Is.

Burin

PLACENTIA
BAY

Avalon Peninsula

Renews

St. Pierre Is.

Trepassey

Cape Breton Is.

Grand Banks

NEWFOUNDLAND HOLIDAY * NEW

HOLIDAY * NEWFOUNDLAND

OUNDLAND HOLIDAY * NEWFOUNDLAND

# NEWFOUNDLAND
# HOLIDAY

# NEWFOUNDLAND
# HOLIDAY

J. HARRY SMITH

THE RYERSON PRESS — TORONTO

3267

# CONTENTS

vi                          CONTENTS

# LIST OF ILLUSTRATIONS

# NEWFOUNDLAND
# HOLIDAY

# 1

*Mostly Introduction—With Some Comment on History
and Why It Comes into a Story Such as This.*

A MEANDERING tale this—the story of a summer spent travelling across Newfoundland and up, down, and along its east and south coasts—a journey undertaken because of a wish to see and know something about Canada's tenth and newest Province. Having such knowledge of the other nine and their peoples, as might be derived from living in two of them, and making many short visits to the rest, it seemed highly desirable to round out a close acquaintance with one's own country by going to the Island Province, walking its streets and roads, and talking with its people.

Back somewhere in mind, perhaps, was a special interest in that land born out of a love for ships and sea, awakened by meetings with Newfoundlanders for whom I took a liking, but found curiously reticent about their own country. Newfoundlanders are like that—at home or abroad—never will you find one of them loudly proclaiming the beauty of his island home, the importance of its contribution to world food supplies, or the fine qualities of its people. So far do they go in this matter of reticence as to say little or nothing about their history. Yet, on all this continent there is no community with a history more fascinating, or forming a more important part in the record of discovery, and settlement, and the preservation of Anglo-Saxon existence than this rugged island off the North American shore.

Through four hundred years, life for the Newfoundlander never has been easy.  The North Atlantic is seldom a placid sea, and its climate is anything but soft.  Newfoundlanders are seamen, and most of them through all the years have lived by fishing—the most toilsome, rigorous and dangerous of sea-going occupations, and one in which periods of depression have occurred with unfailing regularity and paralyzing effect.  Over most of the time war and oppression have embittered their way of living.  But they have met and endured adversity with the same stubborn persistence with which they face and ride out raging seas and Arctic gales.  Such manner of life over generations could not but develop a Newfoundland type of character—strong, reserved, on the surface uncompromising, stubborn in defence of what seems right and fitting and, above all, kindly—hard living has made them kindly and hospitable.  Canadian and American service-men stationed among them in war-time can tell about that, and gratefully they do.

Practically all of its third of a million people are shore-dwellers.  A thousand miles long is the journey round the three sides of this triangular island—about three hundred miles on each side—but the shore-line, following deep bays and fiords, upon which some thirteen hundred villages and outports lie sheltered from the sea, runs to six thousand.  It is the existence of these bays and fiords, offering safe anchorage to any and all ships afloat, that has made the Island a bastion of naval power and guardian of the North Atlantic.

Fish made Newfoundland important from earliest days.  To European governments seeking wealth and sea-power it became coveted territory, and its varied and violent history is closely woven into that of battle for North Atlantic mastery.  Since the end of the fifteenth century Newfoundland has played a part in every war Britain has waged.  Between the Armada and Trafalgar her coastal waters were the scene of constant fighting, and her shores continually were harassed by enemy forces.  Both great naval battles had important results, re-affirming and more solidly establishing her place as the first over-seas colony and foundation stone of the later-to-be built British Empire.

Little doubt there is that on both occasions Newfoundland fishermen and Newfoundland seamen were among those present.

Stoutly and stubbornly they fought for their land through the French wars. One cannot but wonder if the whole history of North America, and particularly that of Canada, might not have moved along vastly different avenues had not Newfoundlanders so tenaciously maintained their place behind the rock walls of their island homeland.

When Newfoundland men stood staunchly beside Britain's best in naval engagements of two Great Wars, they were carrying on in the tradition of their fathers built up through four centuries. After Dunkirk, when British Commonwealth forces stood alone to face a victory-flushed enemy, when Europe was closed to their ships, and Mediterranean ports were threatened, it has been stated authoritatively that Newfoundland alone then stood as a mighty naval fortress, possession of which secured Atlantic Ocean control, and went far to make possible final triumph over the submarine menace.

"Too much history about this, for a travel book," says one or, perhaps, several readers.

Sorry, my friend, but it has to be that way. We discussed that round a dinner table in St. John's. Said one: "You cannot know Newfoundlanders of today if you don't know something about their history."

"Nonsense!" said another. "Everybody knows what's worth knowing of our unhappy history—and most people are not interested in history anyway."

The philosopher at the foot of the table shook a finger emphatically. "The man who has no interest in history can have no foundation for any faith in the past, no reasoning estimate of the present, and only dog-like hope for the future. These Newfoundlanders you see today, are, most of them, the descendants of the very people who first settled here."

He was right, I think, and over and above that stands the fact, that the history of no other part of North America offers a more fascinating tale, or one with better claim to widespread understanding, particularly at this time of recently consummated federation.   Most of those who call the Island "Home" are direct descendants of men and women of the sea who settled it, fought for it, and carried it through adversities and prosperities, joys and sorrows that have made them the distinctively New-foundlandish kind of people they are.   They bear the stamp of the rugged nature of the land they have lived in, its early, out-of-the-world isolation, and the kind of life it has imposed upon them.   There has been no immigration into Newfoundland for a century and, to an unusual degree, original national char-acteristics have remained unvaried by infusion of racial strains unrelated to their own.   Through history they have been kinsmen to those who founded North America's first white settlements, both French and English, and they still are.   As a people, no finer contribution could be worked into the varied-coloured tapestry of Canada's pattern of racial origins now swiftly taking form.

Newf'ndland—that's the way they say it—the word run together with the accent on last syllable, and few foreigners seem to know it—is a pleasant land in which to wander in summertime. In the near future it will be much better known than now. Improved facilities for holiday travel will open up its lonely hamlets and magnificent scenery to motor traffic.   Even now a huge, modern passenger and automobile-carrying steamer is building to take care of fast-increasing travel from mainland to the Island, and much work is going forward on Island roads.   A trans-island highway now under construction will run six hundred miles from Port aux Basques to St. John's, and, as travel grows, suitable accommodation for tourists and others will be established at convenient and interesting points.   This is one of several phases of island development to which the new Provincial Government has committed itself.

And this brings us to a point suggesting that, perhaps, we had better get on with our journey and its wandering story—told pretty much as a tale is told round a fire-side at night by a garrulous and discursive gossip telling what he has seen, and telling it truly as he saw it, or as it was told to him.

# 2

*We Make a Landing—Port aux Basques—Over the Barrens to Codroy Valley—Newfoundland's Loveliest and Best Agricultural Country.*

NEWFOUNDLAND does not flaunt the varied beauties of her scenery, or her undeniable charm, in the face of those approaching her southern shores from the Canadian mainland. Harbours awaiting passenger-carrying steamers lie behind a setting sometimes formidable, now and again grim, but often uncompromisingly austere and forbidding. Mountainous rock cliffs face the sea and behind them, apparently, is a waste of brown, treeless hills promising nothing of the warmth of kindly welcome awaiting the visitor whose courage carries him through that rugged line of defence, and whispering no hint of the widespread panoramas that shall delight his eyes as he journeys across and about the Island.

The comfortable night-boat from North Sydney, Nova Scotia, sights Newfoundland's south-western corner somewhere about dawn on a mid-June morning. Full daylight reveals a rolling line of red hills, and far in the blue behind them more and higher hills with splashes of last winter's snow still clinging to their sides. Bleak and bare enough it looks, calling to mind tales of barren lands, wind and fog-swept, wastes of rock and bog peopled by caribou and bears, where human kind exists on only an outer fringe grasping a meagre living from a turbulent and grudging sea. One wonders if dreams of a kindlier and happier land are to dissolve into disappointing realities.

5

The first vision of Port aux Basques is not altogether reassuring. Seen from sea, it is a group of several hundred square-built, flat-roofed wooden houses huddled together on a narrow strip of rock running out to the sea. Their builders, happily, have not spared paint for each has followed his own fancy as to colour, creating a patchwork quilt-like result suggesting one of those so-called modern paintings that strive towards stark reality rather than beauty. We enter the snug harbour that runs well back into the hills and tie up at a stout dock where freight trains soon are busy exchanging loads brought from far across the Island for those that have come with us across the sea. This it is that makes Port aux Basques more important than size, population, or history would seem to warrant. Here is the western terminus for the trans-island railway, and the busiest year-round port for travel between Newfoundland and the North American continent. The railway is narrow gauge, and a first glimpse at its comparatively tiny engines, coaches and freight cars has been known to inspire amusement, later replaced by respect when one becomes acquainted with the tough job this little, but long, railway has to contend with, and how well it does it.

This shall be our journey's first stopping place—a day or two here to get something of the lay of the land and meet its people. No hotel offers lodgings—but something just as good is suggested by the taxi-driver—a house in the town's centre, customary accommodation for passing commercial men, or any other of the few travellers who have reason to stop over. Clean and comfortable it is, with satisfactory meals and rates that are reasonable enough.

Out along the peninsula winds the town's one street. Homes, weather-tight and tidy, crowd either side, allowing room for a movie, open once or twice a week; the Town Council Hall; the Orange Hall for preservation of the "Pious, Glorious and Immortal Memory of the Battle of the Boyne," brought to this land by men from Northern Ireland; and a Salvation Army barracks. These are town features second only to two churches, a huge Church of England frame edifice standing by the sea at road's end, and a smaller United Church not far away. A Protestant town this—they say there is one Roman Catholic family somewhere about but no one seems to know quite where. About three-quarters of the people are Church of England and the rest United, except fifty or so Salvationists. Schools in this country are organized on denominational lines and here are two—English Church and United. Their buildings are surprisingly large; they have to be. If you like children in the mass, and some do, this would be an interesting place in which to live. To the visitor their number is amazing. Total population is about twenty-six hundred, and twelve hundred of them are school-going youngsters. If those too young for school, and those recently finished, were added, the total percentage of youth would be high. Of the Island's 335,000 population over half are eighteen years of age or younger—a significant indication of hopeful outlook toward the country's future. Sturdy, bright, well-fed looking youngsters they are, and if pleasant manners and engaging approach to strangers have any relation to their schooling, the latter would seem to have admirable qualities.

There are two towns here, or rather two villages which make one town. Port aux Basques is well up the harbour, nearer to docks and railway station. Here it was in earliest days Basque fishermen made annual spring visits in search of cod, dried and salted their catch on the shore, and packed it for sale in France or Spain. To them the place was a fishing station, and sole trace or relic of their ever having been here is the name as it stands on charts drawn by the earliest navigators to reach these waters.

Present settlement dates back something over a century, not so long but that memory of early days is kept alive by old men whose grandfathers were among the first to arrive. A healthy if rigorous climate this, for there seems to be many of them. On a fish-dock I joined a group watching a ship that looked like a converted sub-chaser unloading rock-hard blocks of frozen herring into cold-storage for later use as cod-bait. Gossiping they were, and quite disposed to let a stranger in on the conversation. They knew much about town history, but soon agreed that the best authority was old Tom Connley, to be found down street somewhere around the Council Hall.

"You'll not miss 'im. 'E's a little man, all skin and grief. 'E knows it all and 'e'll tell you."

I found him—a keen little man, hawk nose, bright of eye, happy in talk, and showing no sign that much grief had troubled any of his eighty years. Not only would he tell me, he'd show me. So away we walked a short mile or so down the road to Channel, the town's other village.

The English came later than the Basques, and they settled. One by one a few families drifted along the coast from the east, liked the look of this well-protected harbour, and were followed by others, until in time population was large enough to justify a place-name. They called it Channel, being alongside the harbour entrance. That trees on low-land and hill-sides gave the place a more inviting look than now, seems likely, but all these home-seekers required was a safe harbour and an ocean full of fish outside. By 1800 quite a settlement had gathered here. Already it had some trade with Nova Scotia, and the appearance of a church and cemetery was evidence of advancing civilization. Of these, nothing now remains but a few stones where the church once stood, a mossy, undecipherable memorial to the Rev. Wm. Le Gallois or Legally, the settlement's first clergy-man, who with his son was lost at sea while on a parochial journey to other settlements along the coast, and a few frag-mentary headstones, the oldest readable one commemorating Henry Pike, buried in 1853, and for whom some friend composed the following gloomy if pious epitaph:

> Then let the worms demand their prey,
> The greedy grave my reins consume.
> With joy I drop my mouldering clay
> And rest till my Redeemer come.

Of Pikes we shall learn much as we go along. I am told that in this country there are as many of that name as there are Smiths in, well, anywhere. And they all come down from battling days, when most able-bodied fellows carried pikes in

war or were the smiths who made them. The Pikes have made
their mark on Island history. The first of them, a gallant
seaman, was rescued from pirates and married an Irish princess—
a story that must be looked up when we get over to the east
coast where it happened.

Inspection of two other small graveyards establishes the fact
that, with few exceptions, settlers here were of English origin.
They or their immediate forebears had come in fishing or
fighting ships from Devon or Dorset, happy to found homes in a
new land where prospects of independence and freedom out-
weighed climatic and other disadvantages. Some, perhaps,
came for other reasons. Naval deserters were among them, and
fugitives from law; but all were stout men who knew how to
make a living by the sea. Since those days practically no people
of other origin have moved in amongst them and their descendants have retained their original manner of speech and habit
of thought to a remarkable degree. The on-coming generation
speaks the English of today; the old people, that of south-coast
England of Elizabethan days, slowly spoken, softly uttered and
altogether pleasant to the ear. Tom Connley has it.

We had to go to see the new English church, built about
twenty-five years ago and successor to several others long gone
by way of time, storm or fire.

"Aye zur," said Tom. "Oi 'elped build 'ee, and a prime job
it were. Oi dug out cellar, a big un too. 'Ee's a big church,
'olds over a thousand."

A big church it is. I looked at the solid, soilless rock on
which it stands.

"You dug it out?" I asked.

"Aye, wi dynamite, and used enough to blow all zinners in
Channel straight t'ell."

That is Tom's job in life, official "blaster-outer" of cellars,
when any are needed. Most houses have none. Rock is
everywhere—no trees, no gardens, no flowers—just a patch of
grass here and there, but very little. About town centre is a
hill of rock worth the short climb for the view. Soft, boggy,
moss-covered soil and a wide, deep fresh-water pond lie over its

top. As light fades toward summer evening, the patchwork town, set in a frame of green-shot blue sea and radiant sky, assumes unexpected charm. Colours blend and sweet-lined fishing schooners tied to the docks or moored in surrounding waters lend graceful form to a pleasant scene. They say the town is growing fast and one wonders where. Hardly room for one other small house is discernible from this point. It must have been tiny before the railway came in 1896 to make this a busy year-round port for other than fishing boats, large and small. Railway and docks give employment. The only other industry is fishing, and here the word "fish" means cod and nothing else. With fishing good, and the price obtainable fair, the town is prosperous. At other times, as now, when European countries have little money to spend on food, conditions are not so happy. But these people are thrifty and saving and have sure knowledge that good times will come again. The world will need their fish and have money to pay for it.

Always it happens so. Newfoundland has come through four hundred years of alternating prosperity and depression, mostly brought about by varied situations attendant upon war and peace. War has touched this place many times. Two monuments are here, one commemorating townsmen and women who went to the first Great War and did not return, the other a shaft of granite crowned by a bronze caribou and inscribed: "To the glorious memory of the brave officers, crew and passengers of the S.S. Caribou who were destroyed by the enemy October 14, 1942." The ship was torpedoed an hour or so after leaving this port and all on board were lost. Somehow, the poignant simplicity of this inscription is characteristic of Newfoundland and its people.

Other than by sea or railway, Port aux Basques dwellers have no way of reaching the outer world. No road yet crosses the barren waste and hills separating it from the rest of the country, though one now is building to reach into Codroy Valley farming lands. The town street runs a mile or two on the hill up the harbour, then rounds a mountain and ends at the village of Grand Bay.

At the turning, all Grand Bay lies before you, and a wide stretch of sea it is, running far back into a plain of brown, tundra-covered rock and bog reaching to faraway blue hills. The village is a cluster of homes standing on an acre or two of shore. Little over a century ago two families from eastern Newfoundland came in by sea to a spot surely as uninviting as any that might be found. But the sea offered a never-failing harvest, and here and there were spots of solid ground for growing hay, potatoes or cabbage. Perhaps Port aux Basques around the corner was getting a bit too crowded for their taste. Solitude seems to have been something these sea-going pioneers found desirable in new home-sites. But first comers were not long alone. Others followed so that now fifty-five families are here, each contributing to a respectable total of ninety school-going children. Some of their homes are on a small island lying a few hundred yards off shore where early settlers built, and there stay their descendants even though school, tiny church, public hall for meetings and parties, and most of the community are across the water.

The centre of week-day doings is the village store which supplies all the varied wants of the community—very like those one used to find in mainland villages before mail-order merchandising and motor cars swept over the land, but, instead of such tools and clothing as farmers require, here are found those of the sea and its labours. Display windows are quite unnecessary with groceries and hardware on one side, and drygoods on the other, along with coal-oil for heating and lighting. Proprietor Arthur Wells likes Federation. Now that there is no duty on goods from Canada, he can sell at lower prices and meet mail-order competition.

While we are here his father drops in with a friend. They have seen the stranger arrive and scent interesting gossip. His father has had seventy-three active years and looks as though most of them had been enjoyed, while Wilton Kettle at ninety-six looks hardly more time-worn. Wells Senior came to Grand Bay as a young man, has married twice and brought up two families, now mostly scattered over the outside world. Wilton

Kettle has travelled the seas and lived in Nova Scotia, but this is home and here he is happiest.  In childhood days nothing was here—a foot-path led round to Port aux Basques and nowhere else.  Far back were trees to supply hand-sawn timbers for the home.  "I've a saw-pit now that I sometimes use," he says, and you look at him again, mentally admitting that it might be possible.  "My house," he adds, "is more than half built from a wreck that came ashore a few miles up, and good timber it is."

Kettle's father came from Devon to settle at Grand Bay. Settlement was not encouraged in those days.  War with France brought trouble all along those coasts and, moreover, tales of good fishing in the west had appeal for adventurous spirits. Thus it was that this west coast received its earliest English inhabitants.  There came also a flow of Acadian French from Cape Breton, where, to even things up, the British were making it clear that their room was more welcome than their company. Here French and English got along pretty well together, largely, perhaps, by happy agreement that each should have as little as possible to do with the other so that language mattered not. In time it happened as usually it does elsewhere; the French learned English while the English did not bother to learn French, and English became the spoken language.  Neither group had church or clergy for many years so that religion as a bone of contention did not exist.  Even names became anglicized. Not far off shore is Mouse Island settled by French whose English-speaking descendants still live there.  Their name was Musseau, perhaps a corruption of the word monsieur.  In any case, up and down the shore, Mouse Island was the easiest way of referring to their home.  The family name changed, too.  In time it became Musho and now, for reasons quite unknown, it has become Marshall.  On Mouse Island it was, long years ago, that a British warship far out of her course struck in a storm and was lost with all on board.  She carried money to pay the army at Quebec, and for many years the odd King George golden guinea was found in the sands, the latest having turned up about two years ago.  A belief exists hereabouts that, were dire necessity to arise, a few might still be dug out of family treasure boxes here and there.

The sea around this south-west corner of Newfoundland normally is no quiet stretch of ocean. Wide open to both south and west from whence prevailing winds come, sometimes with savage rage, it knows storm and wreck about as well as any part of the North Atlantic coast, and men and boats venturing these waters need to be good. Remains of many a shattered ship lie up and down the shore. The iron bow of a big freighter has been hanging over a rock a mile or two off Port aux Basques since 1899 and now is a well-known and useful landmark to fog-bound fishermen, so that when finally it disappears, as soon it will, they will be asking for a permanent lighthouse on the rock. Near the harbour entrance is an islet in the middle of which is a deep gulch. Flying one black night ahead of a thunderous gale, a square-rigger struck the rock and ran well up into the gulch where the crew, who had been staring death in the face for many hours, quietly stepped ashore.

Wars of long ago have left their memories here no less than those of recent days. War with France was almost continuous for generations, and, since Newfoundland was one of the prizes fought for, times were rare when the approach of a strange ship did not bring the possibility of trouble. Sometimes nothing much happened even though the visitor proved to be an enemy. There was the case of Mickey Gillan, caught when out fishing alone by a French gun-boat, for which the British were searching up and down the coast, and compelled by the enemy to pilot them into the backwaters of some convenient harbour to lie hidden for a week or two. Here the Frenchman lay snug until the coast was clear. Then he released Mickey, paid him off handsomely, and started for open sea. But he had dropped his pilot too soon. His ship ran on a sand-bar and stayed there. Mickey saw this and kept on going and, just by luck, found a British frigate in home harbour where he told as much of his story as he thought wise. In a few hours the French ship was destroyed and her crew were prisoners of war. As Wilton Kettle says: "A book as big as a Bible wouldn't hold all the stories like this you could pick up around here."

To get into Newfoundland's interior you must climb aboard the narrow-gauge railway that crosses the Island to St. John's on the eastern shore, and in an hour you are in the heart of some of the Island's loveliest scenery.  Most of that hour's riding, however, is across a stretch of barrens that surely must be typical of the country's worst.  If ever the term "blasted heath" was justified, here it is.  Between the sea on one side and far-distant mountains on the other, there seems to be nothing but a wilderness of tundra-like rock and bog—not even a foot-path, let alone a road—but that want is being attended to. The Provincial Government already has bulldozers and gangs of men blasting out the long-projected road that will connect Port aux Basques with the valley.  No light job this, with rocks to be levelled, bogs to be filled and streams to be bridged, but very likely it will be finished and open by time this book is in its readers' hands.

We draw nearer the hills.  Still there's snow on some of them up near the top where they level off to a wide plateau.  At times we run on a causeway within stone's-throw of the sea; presently scrub spruce trees are on either side.  Now and then a bit of a clearing discloses a small cottage and a fenced-in field with a cow, more likely a goat or two, certainly a few sheep and even geese—provision enough for a comfortable larder.  Soon we have passed the last stretch of heath and are coming into farming country, or, rather, woodland in process of being opened up.  Cottages are closer together here, and neat brush-picket fences around prosperous looking small fields give an air of cosy homeliness, while the soil has that look of excellent red clay that grows fine crops of fruit and vegetables in Nova Scotia and Prince Edward Island.  The rich greens of luxuriant growth and the soft blues of distances remind us of England, while tidy little farms, despite their newness, have about them an old-world look suggesting, perhaps, what England looked like in Shakespeare's day, when Newfoundland first became a factor in the history of the future British Empire.  Very likely it was from such scenes as these that many of her seamen set out to win and hold this first outpost of over-seas dominion, just as young men in recent days went from here into the fore-front of battle on sea and land in the two Great Wars.

First stop is in the Codroy Valley at St. Andrews, twenty slowly travelled miles from our start, and here we feel that we really have arrived well into Newfoundland. A valley of neat farms rolling down from the hills to quiet rivers, having snug, pretty houses scattered over it, is a heart-warming thing to see, and never more so than in early summer when fields are at their greenest and skies their bluest. The valley of the Codroy is all this, lying between the Anguille Mountains on the north-west and the Long Range to the south. It varies from three to six miles in width and is about twenty-five in length. Excellent gravel roads serve its modest-sized farms. About two thousand people dwell here with room for as many more when back areas and roads are opened up.

Two Codroy rivers water its length, the Little to the south of both railway and road, and the Grand, a wide noble stream, to the north. Both are famous for salmon fishing, and every season they are visited by anglers from far-away places in North America. The annual miracle of the salmon's return to his native river is perplexing, but in this country another quirk is added to the problem—in different rivers the fish choose different times of coming. In the Grand, mid-June usually sees them nosing up stream, each one a living torpedo leaping into the sunshine now and then and ever ready to battle long and hard for life with anything that comes along. In the Little Codroy a couple of miles away it is well into September before they show up. They are a bit bigger in size, too, sixteen to eighteen pounds or even more, and they continue running until well into autumn. There's a simple reason for this somewhere, but no one hereabouts seems to know it.

A hundred years or so about covers the story of settlement through the valley. Mike Farrell, living in the village of O'Regans, knows as much about that as anyone could. Back in 1883, being about three years old and accompanied by a

suitable assortment of parents, he landed from a small boat at
Grand Bay.   They had heard of good farm land to be found in
this neighbourhood and were out to find it.   Shore-living and
fishing had no appeal, and the difficulties of striking inland
through almost impenetrable bush, no terrors.   They came
west by sea as did all settlers to this land.   With the long-
inhabited, and somehow organized eastern coast, over-land
communication did not exist.   Five hundred miles of mountain
and forest forbade it.   "A tough, hard journey through the
woods.   It was," says Mike, "fun for the children, but hard on
men and women.   We had no horses, and all we had was back-
packed in."   The river was no help—too broken by rapids
and shallows.   But they found their place, and set up homestead
on its north bank in the midst of what now must be one of the
Island's loveliest areas.

To visit Mike you cross the river on a new and impressive
bridge a quarter of a mile long.   Gravel roads offer comfortable
driving, but speed is not likely to be great.   If the charm of
passing scenery did not slow progress, the continual presence
of nibbling road-side sheep most certainly would.   Sheep here
give an air of settled permanency to the scene.   They tell the
passer-by that he is among homes—places where people really
live on the land and love it.   Time was when every Canadian
farm seemed to have its few sheep, spots of light and life on every
broad, green landscape—but not now, and both scenery and
land are the poorer for it, and so, by the way, are the average
dinner tables and "near-wool" clothing most people buy.
The sheep we meet, having recently been shorn, are gaunt
objects, naked and looking very much ashamed of it.   There
isn't the makings of one warm sock on a dozen, and as mutton
their appearance is not appetizing.   But with every ewe there's
one if not two lambs decently woolly, and as bright-eyed as a
sheep can be—a bit adventurous in spirit but keeping close to
mother between dashes across the car's approaching front.

Mike Farrell's house, a neat, frame building, gives warm
welcome.   There are grandchildren, of course, all over the
place and a lamb, disowned by its mother, trots through the

parlour to nuzzle any friendly fingers offered. Mike was born back in St. John's in 1880, his father having come from Ireland some years before. Others had preceded them to this coast, Acadian French from Cape Breton, said to be descendants from heroes of Longfellow's "Evangeline," and others from the Channel Islands. Newfoundlanders were here, too, and a few Scottish families originally from the Isle of Barra and still preserving the Gallic for home conversation. Pioneer life here was pretty much that lived in Ontario, Quebec, Vermont or anywhere else in earliest days. Fishing called most of the settlers and they lived on the sea. For others no transportation existed. In wintertime dog-sleds carried what loads had to move, drawn, not by the far-famed Newfoundland dog whose benign countenance has gazed out from hundreds of advertising calendars keeping somewhat lazy-looking guard over a sleeping child of tear-starting beauty and unbelievable innocence. The northern huskie took over labour here, and his descendants with practically all of the huskie bred out of them still carry on with the job in many shore communities. Later on oxen came in and it is within quite recent times that the last of them gave place to the horse. Stout, heavy pullers, easily fed and placid in temperament, they were well suited to the country, and there are farmers here who would be glad to see them back again.

Food was plentiful and varied on land and sea, and for a change in diet caribou could always be had by easy hunting. They still are plentiful back in the interior and frequently are to be seen in the valley and on the hills. Moose are not native to the Island. Forty or so years ago a few were imported from New Brunswick and turned loose. They took kindly to the country, decided to stay, and set about obeying natural law so that now they are numerous enough to allow a couple of thousand to be shot yearly by those who like that kind of sport. Newfoundlanders seem to think little of them as meat. They much prefer the caribou flesh which, they say, is more tender and delicate of flavour. Caribou are far less numerous than in days gone by and hunting them more of a test of skill and endurance. At one time they moved across the country in great herds and

could be shot down with little effort.   In a book written about
thirty years ago, a "keen big-game hunter" from abroad tells of
visits made here for the purpose of taking home as many heads
of the finest stags he cunningly could stalk and kill.   If report of
his prowess be honest there must have been little room left in
his home for ancestral portraits which, of course, might have
been a no less melancholy form of interior decoration than
stuffed heads of defunct caribou gazing reproachfully from his
walls.   Mike tells me he knew a guide who once saw five
hundred does pass a river ford with not a stag among them, all
reduced to untimely widowhood by human lust for decorative
antlers.   The guide must have been a swift counter, or perhaps
he liked telling a good story as guides have been known to.
Nevertheless the idea is there and doubtless that sort of thing
did happen.   Now-a-days the caribou are properly protected
and plenty are available for reasonable, sportsmanlike shooting.
Black bears still roam the hills, coming down now and then to
carry off an unwary sheep, but they are less numerous than in
past days when a nicely roast bear ham or a broiled steak might
often be a welcome addition to the pioneer's meat supply.
Rabbits they had, as Mike says, "in galore," and they canned
them in jars for winter use—plenty of meat, and almost always
a salmon to be had for the catching.   Salmon played an important part in their economy.   Salted in barrels, they went to
Canada or the United States.   Farming folk up-river took their
share of the run, and few would fail to send to market five or
ten barrels every year, bringing in a gratifying addition to their
meagre income.   In many cases this was the only cash that
came in the year round.   Up to fifteen or twenty years ago
almost all business was done on a credit system.   Fisherman
and farmer turned their catch or produce over to the merchant
who paid for it in bait, fishing gear or merchandise and even
today each has his own opinion as to how satisfactorily the
arrangement worked out for himself.   Men born in these parts
grew to a fair age before ever they saw money.   One farmer
recalls seeing a fifty-year-old man gazing in rapture at silver

coins piled in his cupped hands—the first money he had either seen or owned.

Days of primitive, hewn-out-of-the-bush pioneering are not far behind us on this Island. Log cabins have given place to neat frame houses, but here are men and women who saw much of it, and it is not a tale of grief and almost unendurable toil they tell, but a prideful story of worthwhile accomplishment enjoyed, and something lasting to show for it. Land clearing still continues, but in a different way. As we drive down the river road we come to a huge bulldozer tearing stumps out of the ground and levelling it off. This is a government move toward opening up much-needed land for the production of increased food crops. The farmer cuts the second-growth timber, burns the slash, and calls for help; four men with bull-dozer and tractor-plow turn it into workable soil at a rate of about two acres a day and a cost to the farmer of ten dollars an acre.

Newfoundland escaped none of the disastrous effects of the world economic depression from the year 1930 on. Export prices of fish fell to half normal figures and almost one-quarter of the fishing population were reduced to living on government relief. One attempt to alleviate the situation was the settlement of four hundred families on small farms which, it was hoped, would augment fishing income. This was a highly expensive operation for a country very far indeed from being wealthy and the result was not unanimously considered to be successful. Later on a somewhat similar plan was put into effect for war veterans who were given some farm training.

One of Newfoundland's most urgent needs is more land for food production and more homes for land workers. Total arable land is small in relation to size of the Island, but opinion grows that it is larger than earlier surveys would indicate. It is possible that modern machinery and methods of soil hus-bandry would bring into fertility important areas hitherto judged useless. New roads are being constructed to join up long-settled communities and the hope is that new farming areas may be opened. Meanwhile such land clearing as we see here in the Codroy Valley is going forward elsewhere in areas where roads, schools, and other amenities already exist. In most localities, particularly in higher altitudes, the growing season is short. Root crops do splendidly. Potatoes are equal to the best, although not nearly enough are produced for home demand. At present Prince Edward Island supplies them though at prices which the Newfoundland grower says he cannot meet, but which are profitable to foreign growers because of mass production on larger fields worked by modern machinery and methods.

The sight of so many roadside, shorn sheep raises the question what happens to the wool, and farther along the road where the river begins to widen out towards the sea we find the answer. We stop at Mrs. Downey's pleasant farmhouse to see something of the weaving that, I am told, is carried on in many of the farmhouses of the valley. Mrs. Downey is at home and we see her loom set up in a very workmanlike but small shed. Although the calls of a growing family leave little time for weaving, it is an interesting occupation for odd spare hours. Her finished work is of excellent quality as to texture, design and colour. Most of it is for home use, curtains, drapes, table-covers, but samples of tweeds in lovely colourings would seem to promise long life and much stout wear.

In the earliest days many, if not most, well-established homes had spinning wheels and looms as part of the household equipment. But changing conditions brought in factory-made textiles and home-weaving almost died out. Then came the devastating depression following First Great War, and urgent need arose for supplying medical and nursing care in isolated villages all round the coast. In 1920 Lady Harris, wife of then Governor of Newfoundland, aided by leading doctors and citizens, organized an outport nursing committee which later developed into the Newfoundland Outport Nursing and Industrial Association, and part of its effort was to supply a selling agency for home knitting and weaving. In 1934 the government's Department of Health and Welfare took over all nursing services and "Nonia," as the organization had come to be known from its initials, carried on with the industrial work. It now has eight hundred and fifty workers scattered through fifty settlements and in one recent year distributed over thirty thousand dollars for work done. A shop is maintained at the Newfoundland Hotel, St. John's, and the quality of the work offered for sale is extraordinarily high. Another somewhat similar organization is the "Jubilee Guilds of Newfoundland and Labrador," somewhat more cultural in purpose and fostering home handicrafts throughout the Island. It also has a sales organization at St. John's and, like "Nonia," supplies looms and materials to a large number of workers. These organizations have given new life to home weaving now much more general than a few years ago.

As it is done here in the valley, the farmer shears his sheep, washes the wool and sometimes sorts it. In most cases it then goes to a carding and spinning mill—much of it to Prince Edward Island, whence it returns as yarn, dyed or natural, or sometimes as blankets that would give comfort to the coldest winter night. Driving on down the road, we find the local carding mill operated by the proprietor and one girl millhand. Until a year or so ago a tiny stream and water-wheel gave life to the three machines that do the work, but the gasoline age caught up and the soft chug-chug of a small engine modestly speaks of industrial development. One machine separates matted fibres and discards those too short for good yarn. The others mix the wool and deliver it in the form of short loose rolls each exactly like the others and ready for nimble fingers to feed into the spinning wheel as yarn. But progress and expansion are in the air. The proprietor regretfully fears he must put in a spinning machine to head off P.E.I. competition—and that may lead to dyeing and goodness knows what, perhaps even more sheep on the road. Later we stop at a similar mill run by brooklet and a water-wheel so small that you wonder they could turn a sewing machine, let alone the little plant it operates. The almost imperceptible village for which these two provide industrial activity is known as Millville, and, at that, it probably is a more pleasant place in which to live than it would be as the home of thousands of workers employed in a huge textile factory.

Fortune favours our ride back across the valley. We hit neither sheep nor lamb despite their frequent decisions to cross the road just as we get into fair striking distance. But there's an added complication. Late afternoon has brought bevies of happy and noisy children out of the two or three neat, up-to-date schoolhouses we pass, but the way is made more pleasant by their cheery smiles and half-shy greetings.

# 3

*Bay St. George Where Fish for Sport and Trade Abound—Corner Brook, a Town Pulpwood Built— Curling—Then across Newfoundland on a Narrow but Long Railway.*

TIME comes to move on from the valley and morning brings a welcome promise of rain after weeks of sunshine. Soft grey clouds cover the sky and wisps of fog from sea crown the hilltops. Distant views are now deep purple against sombre forest hues. The train from Port aux Basques arrives on time, seemingly a regular habit of trains in this country. As we move eastward the valley alternately narrows and widens, gradually losing its pastoral aspect. Stiff grades carry us to impressive heights presenting wide views of forest, deep, wooded ravines and noisy brooks hustling to lower levels, and every now and then another clearing with its cottage and barn.

Soon we roll into the village of St. George's, spreading itself along the shore of Bay St. George, which reaches thirty-five miles into the land and opens out into the Gulf of St. Lawrence. Except at the small village centre where a few shops, churches and dwellings are gathered, every field-surrounded home is far enough away from the next to assure that quiet and privacy conducive to long-lasting neighbourliness. Fishing and lumbering with a bit of farming are the occupations here. When one is not busy another is, and if things are quiet all round nobody worries too much—they're sure to improve with time. The village social event is meeting the daily train bringing foreigners in from Port aux Basques, or the train which comes from the east. It seems curious to the visitor that everyone whose home happens to be elsewhere than on this island is termed "foreigner." They call him that but treat him not at all in that way. A friendly smile and a genial good-day come from nearly everyone met on the road, and in no time at all one feels quite at home.

Far across the harbour the village of Sandy-Point gathers itself around a spired church and not far away is Harmon Field, an important United States army airport. Sandy-Point once was the big town of Bay St. George, but the railway came down on this side and most of its inhabitants moved across, some bringing their houses with them. It then was the seat of the Roman Catholic bishop but he, too, felt it necessary to be in closer touch with the world. So one winter day the able-bodied men of the community, Catholic and Protestant alike, had a "bee," put skids under his palace and hauled it across the frozen bay to where it now stands beside his small but interesting cathedral. The palace is not large, but even so, bay ice must have been thick that day to have borne it.

Throughout this area people of English and French origin are about equally divided in number. As far as is known, the first settler was a French naval deserter with a Cape Breton wife who landed here about 1800. For many years settlement around the bay was French and some French is still spoken in homes. But the English, with some Irish and a few Scots, came in, and stubbornly took over, as is their custom, and here again French surnames are dying out to be replaced by English equivalents, or something approaching thereto. Tom White is an instance. He is recognized as the local historian and is one who finds pleasure in passing on his lore. His family name was Le Blanc, but he's Tom White now. There's also a family of Youngs whose forebears were known as La Jeune, and so on through a long list.

Easily enough did the fisherman earn his living in earlier days. Herring, cod, salmon and haddock were to be had in abundance, particularly herring, and markets were constant.

Most of the catch went out in barrels, the fishermen being skilled in the cooper's craft. At this moment lobsters and salmon are the main sources of income and go mostly to the United States. Herring fishing has dwindled since the war due to declining markets, advanced freight rates, and high prices of salt and mill-made barrels. Some fishermen doubt if that trade will ever revive, but Newfoundland's chief industry has seen too many recurring ups and downs to be sure of any such prophecy.

Here it was I first became acquainted with the caplin, a fish practically unknown to inland dwellers and, probably, not familiar even to fishermen far away from these Island coasts. Hundreds of them lay sun-drying on a fishing boat deck, each about size of a smelt and looking very much like one, though I am assured it is a distinctly different fish. Vast shoals of them swarm into Newfoundland bays and harbours at this time of year. In full run their numbers at times have been so large that piles of them have been crowded ashore to provide excellent fertilizer for potato patches, and add to sea air an aroma better read about than experienced. Then no net is needed to take them, a pail will do, and they are gathered in by the cart-load for later use as food, bait or fertilizer.

"Are they good to eat?" I ask.

"Aye, that they be," says the young man busy turning them over so that sun might get at both sides. "My woman pickles 'em in salt and they're fine roasted in the winter."

Several times since I have eaten caplin freshly fried and I do believe him. Delicious—but if there be a difference between them and smelts it takes a more subtle taste than mine to discover it. Having in mind what a delectable luncheon tidbit the caplin could be when broiled a few moments on a piece of toast, one wonders why this tremendously plentiful delicacy is not canned for shipment to inland markets by no means embarrassed by a diversity of choice in the matter of sea food. One answer seems to be that the heat of cooking them in the can causes the oily fish to disintegrate. Maybe so, but perhaps a way will be found to can them some day.

Gradually rising hills are forest-covered a mile or so back

from the shore.   Farms are small but the soil, a reddish pebbly clay, has a look of satisfactory response to moderately skilful farming.   Many streams alternately rush and loiter seaward through these hills, and some of the country's best salmon fishing is to be found in their pools visited annually by sportsmen from many a far city.   Back farther there are trout, and plenty of them.   The kind most often encountered (with a disrespect that seems rather shocking) are called mud-trout by the natives. Results of inquiry indicate that, if not the same fish, they may be closely related to the brown trout of the mainland.   Anyway, they are a fine sporting fish.   In nearby waters they run up to a couple of pounds—back farther in the country up to five pounds—and landing them is the sort of experience fishermen sit long to talk over.   The daily catch limit is thirty-six and, they say, on a fairly good day two or three hours' fishing will bring that number.   The season opens April 15th and closes September 15th.   For salmon it runs from May 15th to September 15th and the limit is eight per day.   Should the reader be more deeply interested in this matter of sport fishing, let him drop a line to the exceedingly efficient Newfoundland Tourist Development Bureau at St. John's, and very shortly he will know all about guides, accommodation, rates and regulations, and even the most seductive kind of fly likely to tempt the sort of fish he goes after.   Miss Margaret Godden, who runs the bureau, has at her finger-tips, I imagine, more information about Newfoundland than a whole cabinet of ministers, and loves to pass it on.

In the quiet of evening when sea mists drift over the broad bay softening the brilliance of the setting sun, St. George's is a pleasant place best viewed from a point of vantage half an hour's walk up a road leading into the forested hills.   The stroll and sea-air suggest early slumber, but even were it necessary one does not need to count imaginary sheep.   Too many real ones keep passing in the lane outside the open window—lambs hysterically calling lost mothers and mothers being noisily annoyed about it.   More sheep seem to be here than back in the valley.   Sociable little things, they prefer village street to open country, and particularly favour grass by the railroad, shocking on-lookers half to death, and giving engine-drivers heart failure by dashing across the tracks in face of on-coming trains. More than once I averted my gaze to avoid witnessing a ghastly slaughter which did not happen. Those ancient and skinny ewes always got safely across to stand and bleat nonchalant derision at the passing train.

There's been a "nigger in the woodpile" here somewhere. Never have I seen so many black sheep among the white. A black ewe, haughtily disregardful of rude comment, walks the town accompanied by twins, one black and the other white. Now, I ask, is this possible?—but there it is. Even piebalds are among them. One stout youngster, black as coal, has a white face and tail, and others have white markings. This may be perfectly all right and quite in order—but never have I seen it before, and I wonder. Ponderings such as these might have brought sleep before daylight had not the boys and girls of the countryside held a dance in the community hall just across the road, where an orchestra described on a poster as "Hill-Billy" and consisting of piano, guitar, drum and some other quite melodious instrument, set pace for a night of rollicking, innocent merriment. This is mentioned only because it makes the point that Newfoundlanders miss little or nothing of what fun may be had in life, and that every community has its well-used church-hall or other gathering place and makes much use of it.

The early days for settlers up and down this western shore were greatly plagued by what is known as the "French Shore" question, one of many difficulties arising out of Newfoundland's unhappy position throughout her early history as a pawn to be fought over by warring European nations. The War of the Spanish Succession ended with the Treaty of Utrecht, in 1713, under which France recognized British sovereignty over the Island, but retained the right to catch and dry fish on almost two-thirds of its coast. This mattered little when no settlers were here to be affected. When population came there was trouble. The treaty gave both France and England "concurrent" rights, but French and English understanding of the word was vastly different. France claimed the right of complete control and her warships landed men, cut timber and threatened to burn the settlers' homes, those of British and Acadian French alike. Two hundred years this treaty lasted and during the last sixty, many a severe test was put to the stubborn courage of those who had built homes on shore or in the woods. The conflict was bitter and became more so as population increased. In 1857 France put forward claims to exclusive rights on the shore, which the British government practically recognized. Thus western Newfoundland, for any useful purpose, was not part of the colony—no administration of justice, no right of land-ownership, no roads and no schools, and apparently no friends since the British navy busied itself in seeing that treaty terms were observed. By this time England had granted Newfoundland a legislature with greatly limited powers, but the French Shore problem carried on until 1904 when England entered into a convention with France giving her territory in North Africa in exchange for all claims on Newfoundland and its fishing, thus finally disposing of the whole matter.

Island folklore is enriched by many a story of those battling days. The development of markets in mainland cities for the coast's abundant lobsters gave new impulse to the conflict. French claims that Newfoundlanders had no right to take fish brought the reply that lobsters were not fish—a puzzle good enough for years of argument, and meanwhile small packing plants began to appear. This was too much. As permanent buildings, erected within a half mile of the coast, they were illegal. Complaint brought officers of the law down on one lobster factory. Promptly rallying a few stout lads, the owner moved it about, proved that it was not a permanently fixed building, and won his case. But it remained for a St. John's merchant, Captain James Baird, to bring about a settlement of the whole question and thus immortalize himself as the John Hampden of Newfoundland. He, too, owned a lobster factory on the shore. French complaints brought a British warship and its captain ordered the factory closed. Repeated telegrams to Baird in St. John's brought the same reply, "Keep on working." The warship landed a party and closed it for him. Baird took the case to court and lost. But, being in a position to do so, and having the courage, he appealed to the Privy Council in London. His complete victory there set off something like a national celebration in Newfoundland. Much more important, it brought the whole French Shore question into British public view and forced a speedy settlement.

Away from the sea and back into the hills roams the railway line toward Corner Brook, "big city" of this western country. It is a roaming railroad much given to sudden turns along valleys and gorges, now to the left and now to the right, but more often up or down. Grunting valiantly the train mounts astonishing grades to scurry down the other side of the hill. We pass many small clearings where lumbering and pulp-wood cutting are going forward, and at a few of these we stop as though there were business to be attended to. We climb around the edge of deeper and more precipitous clefts between the hills until late afternoon when, suddenly, we round a turn and Bay of Islands and the town of Corner Brook fill a wide expanse of view far below us.

Nothing like this have I seen elsewhere except on the Pacific Coast—twenty-five miles or so of dark blue water lying between steep and high green hills, with the twin towns of Corner Brook and Curling scattered on the hillsides at the end. Smart fishing and lumber-carrying schooners crowd the docks, and an old-time touch is added to the picture by a stout weather-beaten three-master standing down the harbour under full sail. Seldom do you see a ship sailing in Newfoundland waters these days. Tall-masted schooners run in and out of every port, but sailormen and fishers here have kept up with the rest of the world. Canvas long since has been stored away and gasoline power speeds the ships on their way.

Fifteen thousand people live at Corner Brook, the Island's second largest city, and they look as though they like it. A town as modern as any on the continent, its streets run on three or four levels above the bay to a small plateau among the hills. Besides well-kept public places, trees and gardens grace pleasant homes looking fresh from the painter's brush. Perhaps they couldn't very well look otherwise—the town is not old enough. It is a young town, and seems to be peopled mostly by young people. After a time spent in some of the outports, a term applied to any settlement outside St. John's, this place has the look of a somewhat different land—perhaps not greatly different from many another North American seaside town, but newer and cleaner than most, while its people strike one as being as similar as could be to those of any other Canadian town. Many brightly dressed youngsters roam the streets, pretty girls on bicycles dash up and down and sturdy young men are busy with that part of the world's work falling to their lot. The schools, hospital, sanatorium and other public buildings look highly efficient while commercial institutions appear busy enough to arouse a feeling of guilty inferiority in the minds of loitering visitors.

This is a "company" town. The influence of the Bowater Pulp and Paper Company is paramount, and Corner Brook has all the well-kept appearance usual in that kind of community. The standard of living and physical well-being, I am told, are as high here as in any part of the Island, and in this respect the town has been taken as a model for welfare work going on in other communities. The company even runs the hotel, and does it well—for the Glynmill Inn recalls, among others, the happy memory of a delightfully cooked breakfast kipper tasty to the last mouthful—something seldom found in hotels.

Most of this town may be new, but the history of Bay of Islands goes back about as far as that of the coast generally, and is not much different. Legend says that the first settlers came from Jersey, but stayed not long, being either killed or driven away by Indians. Permanent settlement drifted in as elsewhere, and in something less than a century ago expert woodsmen from the mainland were shipping "tun timbers," three and four feet thick and so-called from their weight, to England and the United States, almost forgotten evidence that forests of great trees once covered the land. The arrival of the railway in 1895 found a prosperous community. Fish merchants and their plants predominated, but lumbering was still active and ships moved in the harbour in numbers not seen today. In 1923 came the huge paper-making industry that has modernized the town and built its population up from two thousand to its present size.

Have you ever heard a tree scream in agony? I have—a horrible sound. Beside the pulp-mill are piled mountains of short logs peeled and ready for the machines. One by one they are caught up, whirled into the mill and dropped among swiftly revolving knives. One awful shriek and the log, now small chips, has passed down the gullet of the machine to huge digesters where steam and sulphuric acid reduce it to the tiny, feathery shreds that make paper. Some of the logs are ground by fourteen-ton stones, but either way, the result is just pulp passing through pipes, automatically cleaned by one contrivance, colour-toned by another and poured on to a moving wire screen allowing its water content to drip away or be driven out by suction or pressure. Moving felt blankets carry it on over hot rollers for drying and polishing, and by the time we have come to end of the machine the log that seared our ear in protest a little while ago is winding on a roll before us as finished paper ready for printing presses and words of truth and wisdom, or what have you. This one plant consumes twelve hundred cords of wood daily and one wonders how many acres of trees that would be. It provides about a thousand tons of paper a day, for which, it is to be hoped, the world is much the better.

West Corner Brook is older, and its narrow winding street climbing along the hillside has more of the Newfoundland look, a separate municipality where ships of fish-merchants and lumbering firms came in scores when Corner Brook was a hamlet. Bay of Islands fisheries were and still are famous for herring. Pickled and barrelled, or filleted and dressed, large quantities go far across the mainland and down the coast to American cities. Originally the town was known as Birchy Cove, to be renamed in honour of an Anglican parson, Rev. J. J. Curling. Bermuda and Newfoundland in those days were linked together as one Anglican diocese with one bishop, and the churches were opening up their missionary efforts in the area.

Curling, then a naval lieutenant, and the bishop became friends, and, on the understanding that he should be posted to work here, he resigned his commission, took holy orders and spent many years in the spiritual guidance and amelioration of the rugged pioneer way of life of his people—the right man for the job apparently. Private means gave impetus to his zeal. His parish was wide and the sea its only road, but a yacht of his own carried him over it through good weather and bad, and his memory will be revered while Curling lasts.

From the main street one looks down on roofs of homes and shoreside wharves, and buildings busy with coast-wise trade in all west-coast products. Summertime sees passenger and freight steamers coming in from Newfoundland ports and the upper St. Lawrence, and great ships heavy with rolls of paper from the mill all moving seaward until the bay freezes up somewhere about midwinter. Corner Brook's sudden burgeoning has tended to modernize Curling but has taken little from its old-time appearance. War has touched it more than once. On an outstanding point of prominence, and seen from many miles up the bay or out to sea, a lighted, thirty-foot shaft of granite reminds the countryside of those who went from Bay of Islands to the Great Wars. Simply, it states: "They have been gathered and garnered in a harvest of glory."

Of earlier wars they have but faint rememberance here. Visits from the French must have been fairly frequent and almost always annoying. The American War of 1812 is not quite forgotten, for an enemy gun-boat picked up fisherman John Bagg to press him into service as a pilot. News of the war had not reached John and he had no compunctions about setting the "Yankee" on his way. Back home he was arrested on the charge of having given comfort to the King's enemies, and, on a British man-of-war, set out for St. John's with promise of as speedy and effective a hanging as could be arranged—then a simple and frequent event. The going was stormy. Bagg only just escaped being clapped into irons when he dared tell the captain he was running too close to shore for safety; but the ship carried on her course. Perhaps Bagg preferred hanging to drowning. He offered advice again and promptly was fitted with a set of manacles. Shortly after, the ship struck on rock and began to break up, with no possible help from shore and only death from the sea. Had Bagg any advice to offer now? He had—get a rope ashore. How? Somebody could swim. Impossible in that sea! But Bagg would, and did, and all ship's company was saved. The captain's wife was nearly drowned, but Bagg sprang into the sea and carried her to safety. No more irons for Bagg, now a freeman. At parting the captain asked him what he would like from England as a present. His answer was a pair of brass killickclaws which he received a year later. A killickclaw is a several-pronged anchor bound round a rock for weight and used to hold fish nets when set in the sea. I hope that story is true. Anyway, it does throw a spot of light on the men of those days and the kind of lives they lived.

Where Curling's street runs down to the shore a little stream enters a cove. Cook's Brook it is called, from a legend that credits Captain James Cook with having here replenished his ship's supply of fresh water. On this visit he charted the bay and all the west coast, and his chart has been a standard for admiralty charts ever since. An excellent copy hangs in the hotel. Cook went on to discover Australia and become world famous as the navigator Sir James.

Both Corner Brook and Curling are provided with an adequate number of churches and Salvation Army temples. Recurring fires have now and then destroyed these but they have been rebuilt larger than before. Roman Catholics are now finishing a concrete cathedral of quite fine lines and proportions. An Anglican church that must have had all the look of having been transplanted from a Devonshire village was recently burned and will be rebuilt. Both Anglicans and Catholics are moving up the hill into close quarters with the United Church, a stout, prosperous-looking building of brick. Sunday mornings will be busy thereabouts in days to come. Friendships and gossip should profit mightily.

Here again religion bars no effort for common good. It is not long since that, when one of the churches needed work done, a parish hall built, for instance, or the clergy wanted his winter supply of firewood, an announcement to that effect was made from the pulpit. A day was set apart for the work and everybody, all creeds alike, turned up to take a hand. The women came suitably armed with a five-gallon kettle for tea and ample supplies of food. A few words of prayer started the bee and by nightfall the building would pretty well be completed, or the preacher would have fuel enough to carry him through the coldest winter. The latter effort was known as a wood-frolic and, I gather, quite justified the term as a social event of uncommon interest to young and old.

The size of a horse is not necessarily entirely relative to the amount of work the animal will do, a fact emphatically established by the Newfoundland pony. You see them everywhere hauling amazing loads up staggering hills on little two-wheeled carts, and getting along with the job very comfortably. They run in stature from that of a largish Shetland pony up to a pint-size or pint-and-a-half-size horse. They are hardy, easy to feed, willing workers and are a feature of almost every village or town scene. Presumably, like most of their owners, they came from England—maybe from Dartmouth moors—and over the years they must have made a large contribution to working life here. It is comforting to record that invariably they have the appearance of being well fed and decently cared for, which seems to be what you would expect from the kindly sort of people met with in this country. Horses of a larger size are beginning to take their place where the motor truck has not ousted both, but I imagine it will be long before the last pony has hauled his final load over winding village streets.

Life in these towns must be pleasant for young folk. There's so much to do when work is over or on one of their many holidays. All games are played enthusiastically, football in particular and hockey and skating on the frozen bays or rinks in winter. Thirty years ago a Scotsman introduced skiing, and with hill succeeding hill in every direction, he couldn't have found a likelier place in which it might become popular. Golf they have, of course, and if hills add interesting hazards to a course and zest to a game, players here should be quite happy.

Newfoundland had to have a Humber River. All over the world you'll find them. In every case, most likely, some Englishman roaming afar has come across a stream that pleased him or reminded of home, and it has become another Humber. On point of beauty alone, few can have better claim to the name than this which empties into the extreme end of Bay of Islands. Pulpwood operations have had a diminishing effect upon vast numbers of salmon that crowded its banks in years gone by. But its upper pools are still famous for the size and fighting vigour of fish to be taken there. Through the surrounding country are many less-publicized streams and almost in any one of them salmon or trout await a well-cast fly.

Over many miles of varied scenery up along the Humber Valley lies the start of our four-hundred-mile journey to St. John's, a long trip, dull only to the unobservant or the unsociable. If passing scenes seem to lack interest, companions in your sleeping-car most probably will provide plenty. The car couldn't be large on a narrow-gauge railway such as this, and between early spring and late autumn it is sure to be fully occupied. From outside, each car appears diminutive and the engine tiny. You look at the hills ahead and wonder. No need to worry. The gallant little demon snorts its way up the stiffest slopes, a little slowly, perhaps, but it makes up for that on the downward scoot, and scoot is just the right word here. Freight trains we pass are long and appear heavy, so that one discovers a new respect for the power of a very small amount of live steam.

Newfoundlanders themselves don't seem to know where all the passenger traffic comes from. The daily trans-island train from Port aux Basques, mostly referred to as the "foreign train," does its best to accommodate all boat passengers from the main-land, and usually succeeds. Day-coaches take any overflow from sleepers as well as the local traffic which is sure to include several children. Never are you short of company whichever way you ride. It's a varied company—chatty and friendly enough, with as many Newfoundlanders among it as others.

For their country they have a deep and fierce affection, but you'd never guess it. It peeps out only now and then from behind an astonishing veneer of apparent dissatisfaction with almost everything within it. They are quite willing to talk about it—after you have told them where you're from and why, but, being a modest people, they make sure its less happy features are brought into view. If you believe all you hear from some, the land is too poor to grow anything; were it good the climate would not permit; fisheries are dying out and never will come back; general trade is petering off; and the government is terrible. Of course, as a newspaper friend of mine used to say, "It just ain't so, that's all, it ain't so." But such information is a bit disconcerting to the stranger, and after hearing much of it, like the gentleman in *Twelfth Night*, moved almost to tears by the serio-comic tragedy of "Pyramus and Thisbe," he's tempted to say, "This and the loss of a dear friend would go far to make a man sad."

Most "foreigners" on the train are referred to as tourists, though most seem to be Newfoundlanders now living in foreign parts like New England, Quebec or Ontario, coming back to spend their summer holidays among relatives and familiar scenes. I am assured that more Newfoundlanders and their descendants live in the United States and Canada than exist in all the Island, which may easily be true, and surely is one of this country's occasions for sad thought. Toronto alone is said to be home to thirty thousand. Having lived in that city many years without knowledge of this leavening of nice people in its midst, one only can suppose that native modesty prevents them from bragging about the land of their origin.

Decidedly smaller though it be as compared with those of standard size, you have no feeling of being crowded in the narrow-gauge sleeper. Berths seem to be the same length and width. There are fewer of them, a matter of no concern to the traveller wise enough to have secured early reservation. The only noticeable difference is the narrower passage-way between, and complaint on that score could only come from a traveller whose girth approached the unseemly. We had two such aboard with us, and in the otherwise than stilly watches of the night, each discovered business to be attended to at other end of the car. Lights were out and visibility low. Sounds of the first concussion dissolved in whispered apologies. The contestants backed away each to an end of the car and politely waited for the other to come through. It was one of those stage-waits that hold an audience spellbound. The second exchange of apologies seemed to lack something of the spontaneity and sincerity of the first, and on the third attempt there were no apologies at all, rather the reverse, if you know what I mean. Then came that sustained silence marking the apex of drama, and after that a rugged male voice, "Look ye, m'am, I'm waitin' here till ye come through, and, g'dammit, I'd be obliged if you'd hurry." The lady hurried; a ripple of something like applause brought a satisfactory conclusion to the incident.

Long before nightfall we have swung far into the ocean of forest and hills that covers much of the interior. Often the valley broadens out and presents evidences of what seem to be farming possibilities. The river widens and becomes Deer Lake. Here the valley is wide, miles wide, and at its eastern end is the village of Deer Lake, just a hamlet scattered in the woods, its dusty main street—like hundreds of others throughout northern North America—presenting to the view a row of stores, churches, a movie house, and homes, and always children. Out of every door they run, hang on every fence, or add shrill clatter to station-platform greetings and good-byes.

Half an hour or so later we touch the northern end of Grand Lake, largest of the Island's countless lakes and ponds. Seen from the air, they say, Newfoundland appears to be half water, innumerable rivers having falls suitable for hydro-electric development. Grand Lake extends sixty to seventy miles back into the plateau. We leave it where Sandy Lake River enters, and cross on a wide dam, part of the installation supplying power to Corner Brook and surrounding country. After that comes more climbing to higher levels of the great plateau that forms central Newfoundland; half rock-strewn soil with a scattering of timber, and half bog and tundra. Beyond that again we find deep forest in every direction until we run into a group of mountains marking the height of land on this cross-island journey. The highest of these is Maintopsail, eighteen hundred feet, and not far away are Gafftops'l and Mizzentops'l, named, doubtless, by some imaginative sailorman either for their height or for some freakish formation seen from far away. They have a genius for unusual and imaginative place-names in this country, and the good enough sense to leave unchanged those that have come through the years from historic or fanciful origins.

Somehow these rugged, heavily wooded hills have a familiar look. We climb along mountain ledges, pass between walls of rock through gorges, and remember a similar journey through the Selkirks that offers many a nerve-tingling moment for the traveller between the Rockies and the Pacific coast. Someone has said, that every phase of scenery in Canada is to be found in Newfoundland on a smaller scale—and here is one excellent example. It is smaller, perhaps half size, but it thrills just the same. The prospect of a possible drop of two or three hundred feet is probably just as exciting to the imagination as one of fifteen hundred, and one is willing, without experiment, to grant that the results of such a mishap would be similarly unpleasant in all important points. That sort of thing does not happen. Short of equipment, like many others these days, this railway is doing a good job handling a heavy volume of summer passenger traffic. Sleeping-cars are clean and well attended, and the dining-car service excellent. In winter, railroading here must be as tough as anywhere on the continent, but it seems to carry through in a satisfactory manner.

Was it courage or foolhardiness that seventy-five years ago set this country's small and scattered population to planning and constructing this difficult and costly piece of work? First steps were taken in 1875, when the government of the day undertook a general survey as to a likely route and industrial possibilities awaiting development. Promise of copper mining, lumbering and farming land encouraged the project, and those were prosperous days, perhaps most prosperous of the Island's history.

Money was borrowed in England on a bond issue and the first sod was turned in 1881. About sixty miles of it were built when the project went bankrupt. Doubtless the country was as little qualified and equipped to undertake the task as any such small group of people could reasonably be. The total population then numbered less than two hundred thousand—about that of a small city back on the mainland. Succeeding governments tried to carry on the scheme, but each failed in turn. In 1890 Sir Robert G. Reid of Montreal was persuaded to take over the project, and, incidentally, most of the country's natural resources. He finished the task in 1896 and set it going. Terms of agreement covering the road's operation were onerous in the extreme, and further weakened Newfoundland's already strained credit. The government that had sponsored it was defeated. Its successor modified the agreement, but adverse operating results and unsuccessful financing efforts made it impossible to carry on, so in 1923 the government had to re-assume operation. Since then the railroad has contributed heavily to cost of government, being responsible for an unduly large share of the national debt and a heavy burden in recurring periods of depression that have followed failure in the fisheries, or declines in world markets for fish.

On the ledger's other side, construction gave employment in bad times and the expenditure of too many millions was by no means all wasted. True, more than once it just about ruined the country, but the railroad had to be built if east and west were to be joined, or if the interior ever was to be opened up at all. Furthermore, it should be remembered, that its construction today under most efficient planning and management would cost far more than it did when political direction resulted in little but failure and waste.

Newfoundlanders have always believed that their country had mineral possibilities which could prove important, and there is no evidence that their belief is ill founded. Rock formations in every direction challenge exploration, and geological surveys are being widely extended. So far, iron ore at Bell Island and copper-lead-zinc properties in the Island's central interior have been the main discoveries. The latter are situated at Buchans, reached by a branching rail line from Milltown where we make a momentary stop. This is another "company" town where fifteen hundred men, women and children live in pleasant surroundings and enjoy all conveniences common to well-ordered communities of this kind. The industry has been in operation many years, and it is reported that recent exploratory drilling has indicated new bodies of ore that will extend its life many years to come.

It was along this part of the line that the stout man sitting opposite threw a ray of light on one phase of life here. He had the appearance of a comfortable sixty-five.

"I'm going home to see my mother," he said, with a decidedly Irish lilt. "It's five years since I was back and she's a bit riled about it. Sez if I don't go see her this summer she'll come and see me—and she would, too, thinking nothing of her ninety years."

"Pretty old lady to travel," I said. "Is she in good health?"

"Ah, fine. Hurt her foot this spring chopping wood for the fire, but she's all right now."

"She won't be chopping wood now," I suggested.

"I wouldn't be a bit surprised," he said. "Mebbe my sister won't let her. She's over seventy. Mother was married at eighteen and had eleven children. We had a brother drowned fishing down on the Labrador. There's two boys still fishing here, the sister at home and the rest of us went to Canada, got married and have done pretty well."

"Many grandchildren?" I asked.

"Oh, a terrible lot. I've lost track but it's well over twenty. Some married, too, and I wouldn't say but what there's as many great-grandchildren, or mebbe more."

"Eleven makes a fairly large family," I said.

Another passenger joined in. "Not far from average here. There's an old couple where I live had twenty-one. Two died and most of the rest went foreign to Canada and the States— some of them are doing well, too. The old people may be a bit lonesome, but they're healthy and well."

"Wonderful," I said, "wonderful," and tried hard to accept it as something more than just a good story. Later on I was to learn that this sort of thing is by no means unusual in this country.

In rapid succession we pass many small settlements and make our next stop at Badger, a bright, breezy townlet as much like a western prairie train-stop as any to be found east of the Great Lakes. The reason for its being is pulpwood, taken from the surrounding forest to feed another huge paper mill at Grand Falls a little farther along the line—another "company" town. Here, five thousand people, most of them young, find congenial employment and a modern way of life with all the comforting amenities. Paper making in this mill consumes another seven or eight hundred cords of wood daily. Surely forests of this Island will disappear and land erosion complete the country's ruin if effective measures of control are not put into effect and rigorously enforced. A government publication of 1950 says: "To date the government has not introduced conservation measures, but recently the two paper companies have carried out, as a joint effort, extensive silviculture research in order to keep cutting operations in accordance with the natural rate of growth in the various localities."

The year 1919 saw Newfoundland flash into world news as a place where aviation history was being made. One fine June day Captains Alcock and Brown hopped off from a spot near St. John's on the first successful trans-Atlantic flight, and since then a large share of important events in air travel have taken place here. Gander, where we pause as night falls, is one of the world's top-ranking airports. When passenger flights to Europe became practical, Gander was the natural jumping-off place, and the Second World War saw it become one of the largest and busiest of all wartime airbases on this side of the Atlantic. As a civil international airport it continues to hold that distinction. It is close to the most easterly point of North America, and planes of eight or ten airline companies are regular callers for re-fueling and service. A small army of workers has its schools, churches, hospital and all other necessities for comfortable living; modern hotel and restaurant accommodation awaits the air traveller going through. Guarded by a rugged and difficult coast, and set in a sea that has frequent uninviting moods, except for a short time in summer, the prospect of travel there has not always been encouraging. By air it is just another trip, and not a long one. This is one of many factors that is stirring Newfoundland to a new and more vigorous life.

Through the night the train arrives within touch of the east coast and dimly we see shores of bays and coves as we swiftly pass them by. Children have been asleep for hours and conversational chatter has died down to be lost in the murmur of the train moving on towards the Island's capital.

# 4

*St. John's—City of Ships, Hills and Fine Churches—
The Harbour behind the Hole in the Rock—Slums That
Are Passing.*

FOUR hundred years of history live in and about this capital city
of St. John's. Mystery and romance of all the seas; tales of
savage battle for mastery of the North Atlantic; the tragically
splendid story of a people who wrested a living from the icy sea,
and built a country under the long-lived handicap of governmental mismanagement and deliberate discouragement; these
are the threads interwoven in the vividly coloured tale of its
historic past. St. John's seems to have missed nothing that
could happen to a seaport. War, piracy, political upheaval,
destruction by fire, poverty and prosperity, all these have been
part of her experience. She has lived through them, renewed
her strength and prospered. Of all the cities on the North
American Atlantic coast she stands closest to Europe, and since
the day of her founding none other has been more intimately
concerned in European wars nor has taken a more active part
therein. We approach the city with respect, and enter it with a
deference due any scene of events having such an important
place in the history of a continent.

A fine Sunday morning it is—best of times for enjoying a
first glimpse of a strange town. Rush and rattle of daily work
is stilled, and the streets have an unexpected look of tidiness—
altogether a pleasing first impression. The railway hotel is

43

quite filled up—reservations should be made early this time of year. Balsam House proves hospitable and satisfying, and a top-floor bedroom window presents an intriguing view of the city over rows of clay chimney-pots that carry memory back to many an English town. Being comfortably settled therein, one sets forth seeking a general idea of what this city looks like.

St. John's harbour is an elongated pool lying deep in a high-walled bowl of rock, and having at its eastern end a narrow outlet to the sea. Streets and buildings fill the bowl sides, giving the town a crowded look as though early builders had been reluctant to go any farther from the waterside than they positively had to. The pool is not large—something over a mile in length, and half or two-thirds that distance across—but has plenty of anchorage for big ships; and it always appears busy, as vessels of all sizes, from little fishing schooners to huge freight and passenger steamers, move in and out of docks lining all the shore.

The entrance to the harbour appears astonishingly narrow, perhaps much more so than it is because of towering over-hanging rock cliffs on either side. It almost looks as though a reasonably strong-armed pitcher might throw a ball across, but probably two or three throws would be necessary. And yet, one wonders how, in the earliest days with the crudest of compasses and primitive navigation methods, navigators found this small doorway in the vast rock wall and safely passed through. They did it as a matter of course—brought their wind-driven ships in through fine weather, storm and fog, and thought little of it. Newfoundlanders are proud of their seamanship, and if you start talking about this sort of thing to any one of them, you are very likely to hear the story of the four Newfoundland skippers who had taken fish to Scotland and met at Dundee. They agreed to set sail for home the same day, and each to put up a barrel of rum with the first arriving in St. John's harbour to take all. Late autumn storms were due, and three chose to go by the southern and quieter route. The fourth, knowing his ship's lack of speed, struck north, and bad weather went with him. Gale followed gale. If he moved swiftly it was sometimes in hourly peril. He approached the harbour entrance in black fog, dropped anchor, and then heard familiar church bells assuring him that he was safe in port. He had won the race. This skipper could neither read nor write, but he was a master mariner, and many such as he sailed Newfoundland ships in those days. The second ship arrived within six hours and all were safe in port within twenty-four.

Any day but Sunday, St. John's sixty thousand inhabitants appear to be extremely busy people, doing most of their business in and about office buildings or large and well-stocked shops with inviting windows on either side of Water Street which runs close to the harbour docks. Modern buildings stand snugly against those of an earlier date, giving the whole street generally an old-world look that, somehow, inspires confidence in its stability. So far it has escaped the neon-lighting craze rapidly turning mainland streets into flashy imitations of west coast Chinatowns, although one newspaper has been calling on store-keepers to "light-up" and give the town a modern air. No doubt they'll do it soon enough and, possibly, decorate country roads with billboards, too. No such thing now mars the view.

Sturdy conservativism is the hallmark of St. John's business, and her businessmen are proud of it. Firms here have been in business a hundred or even two hundred years. Originally most of them were fish-merchants and shipowners, or grew to be that through prosperity in small trade. They supplied fisher-folk with all their needs, and eventually became general merchants. Through three or four generations they have formed the Island's core of credit and commercial activity. These remaining firms are those, out of a host of others, who have survived disaster, periodical economic depression and the chancey game of acquiring or losing fortune in the fisheries, and are lineal descendants of merchant adventurers who first developed the country and its trade, and of the tough seamen who made it a livable land.

At any hour of the day you cross Water Street in peril of your life. Motor vehicles on the Island now number ten thousand, most of which seem to be dashing up and down the city streets. Since most of the Island's business is done here, this is reasonable enough. But, despite pleasantly mannered direction from traffic policemen at almost every corner, these plus pony and horse-drawn carts create a turmoil bewildering enough for a city twice its size.

Hills, hills, and what hills! The hilly streets of this town deserve a chapter of their own. They are unique, colourful and dreadful. Beginning at Water Street at shore level, cross streets rise to the bowl's rim on grades that, now and then, approach the perpendicular, and are appalling to the unaccustomed pedestrian be he going up or down. In the earliest days the town ran along the shore. However, the shore-line was limited and when it grew it just had to grow upwards. In some places, alongside the tall granite courthouse, for instance, you go from one street to the next up a steep flight of steps, and are very glad indeed when you get there. Windows on upper levels look down on neighbouring roofs and on the harbour with its ships— all very pleasant, and even more so when seen from the other side of the pool where wharves, warehouses and packing plants are mirrored in the water. From there the town is a panorama set upon its edge, alive with colour and life whether bathed in sunshine or lightly veiled in mist floating in from the sea. Brick and stone business buildings stand solid behind a fringe of wharves and the graceful lace of ship masts. Homes crowd up to the sky, a background for the occasional churches and other public buildings of imposing size; at the crest the Roman Catholic cathedral assumes an air of benevolent domination.

I was standing well up on one of those climbing streets, gazing fascinated down its busy length to the maze of ship masts and running rigging, and a patch of open water with boats moving across it.

"'Tis a fine harbour we have here—but a terrible place for a city. Look at them hills."

I looked at the speaker—clearly one of the Irish who make up two-thirds of the population. He had all the look of his origin and his speech was as musical as you would hear any day on a Dublin street corner. Seventy years of life here had left him as typically Irish as was his great-grandfather stepping ashore a hundred and several years ago. Genially round of face and figure, an eye as "liquorish" as any "Wife of Bath," tidy ancient clothing, a bowler hat set on his head like an upside-down teacup on a fat, round teapot, and there you have his portrait— an engaging personality conversationally inclined.

"Look at them hills now," he said. "Did you ever see the like?"

I never had, and said so, suggesting that sometimes in winter they must be difficult to navigate.

"Ho! Terrible, terrible," he said. "On a slippery day it's as much as your life's worth to step on 'em. Would you believe it, sir, I'm told there's not another city in the world with hills like those—not one in all the world." Then I realized that St. John's hills are a matter of pride for her citizens, and it becomes the visitor to speak of them with respect. To complain of labour in climbing them is to betray a lack of physical stamina; to belittle them is bad form.

"At any rate," I said, "they give you lots of exercise. A year or two here should make a man stout of wind and limb, if it didn't kill him."

"Ah, there you've said something," and he came close to hold me with a penetrating look. "Tell me something, sir." His eye searched deep into my conscience. "Tell me, have ye noticed the beauty of our women? Of course ye have. Look at that young girl stepping out over there—twenty years old or so, eh?—and going up the hill like a ship in a fair wind. Look at the long, slim legs of her and the straight back, shoulders squared and chin up. Ain't that an elegant sight? There's a lot like that here, and it's the hills that does it. Ye can't walk up and down 'em three or four times a day and have a belly. They make elegant figures. You know," he said reflectively, "them Greeks had a word for it—calipygean, that's what they are— calipygean figures, and if you don't know what that means you'd better look it up in Mr. Webster's book of words. It's there and our girls here have got it. Even the short and thick ones are that way on account of them hills."

There was no argument. Every evidence, and there was

much of it, supported his claim.    "But they don't walk up and down much in winter," I said.

"They do pretty well, 'ceptin' when rain or mist puts ice all over 'em, but it don't last long. Now I'll tell you an astonishing thing. One winter's day I saw a little harse pulling a heavy load up one of them hills. His shoes was spiked and he was doing fine 'til he got near the top, but his driver stopped him for a breather too soon. His hind feet slipped and the cart started down hill and pulled him clear to the bottom, and him setting up on his backside all the way and lookin' as surprised as you please. And, would you believe it, sir, when he got up on his feet, the only thing wrong with him was that every hair was wore off his tail."

I bade the gentleman a respectful farewell. I was very glad indeed to have met him.

Newfoundlanders are a church-going people and city churches are notable for their size and dignity. They began building them early in city history. The Anglicans erected a large wooden church in 1720 to be replaced a century or so later by the present, fine stone cathedral. Designed by Sir George Gilbert Scott, a leading ecclesiastical architect of the time, it was destroyed by fire, in 1892, rebuilt on the old plan, and now stands as satisfying a piece of Gothic as may be found on this side the Atlantic. Plans call for a central tower, not yet built, to rise where the nave crosses the transept, the lack of which mars what otherwise would be a noble feature of the city scene. Interior proportions have the lift and grace of good Gothic. The east window is notable for its size and subdued colouring; low tones of the timbered roof and chancel furnishings complete an atmosphere as Anglican as a bishop's lawn sleeves. The services here are "sound prayer-book," about halfway between ritualistic high and evangelical low, and this practice seems to be followed pretty well throughout the Island.

Gower Street United Church holds a commanding position well up the hill and thoroughly deserves it by reason of its inspired design, its impressive size and the lovely rich colouring of its red brick—brick construction at its best. Standing on the site of the first Methodist Church, built in 1816 and burned in 1892, it may be termed the cathedral of Newfoundland's United Church and perhaps the "power plant" of its effort. Learned scholars and powerful preachers have served its pulpit. Churchmen here have a taste for sermons. They like them strong, and departure from canonically accepted theology is likely to meet an evident lack of enthusiasm. As matter of course, Continuing Presbyterians are like that, too. "The Kirk," another fine red brick building, stands near by. The first Presbyterian Church was opened in 1843. In 1939 the Congregationalists united with Presbyterians and their church, having a history dating back to the 1780's, is now Queen's Road Presbyterian.

Roman Catholicism's archepiscopal cathedral is the largest religious structure on the Island, a fact quite understandable since half the city's population is of that faith. Romanesque in type, it is built of native stone trimmed with granite from Ireland, and dates back to 1841. Excellent statuary adorns it, and under the altar lies a notable carving of Christ descended from the Cross. Not always have Roman Catholics here had privileges of churches and church services. Before 1784 celebration of the Mass was a penal offence, and so unpopular in certain quarters that mere rumour of such goings-on could start a riot. Priests were hunted as in England's Cromwellian days. Later, when the cathedral came to be built, there were difficulties about rights to purchase and own property. But reason or decent Christian charity prevailed, and the Church was granted as much land as could be fenced in a given time. The fencing was well organized, stakes and nails were laid ready and, apparently, most of the town's male population—or all those having the necessary hammer—stood ready for the signal to go. A usually reliable historian says that ten minutes later eight acres had been securely enclosed—a comfortable area for the cathedral, archbishop's palace, school, convent and other buildings now standing there.

Before coal became a general fuel, St. John's had its wood-frolics for the comfort of church-goers, but being a city the event had to be conducted on a regal scale. Ever keen for a holiday or a frolic of any kind, the citizens made this event a good one. An old engraving shows a mountain of cord-wood, the size of a three-storey house, piled on sleighs lashed together, gay with flags and bunting and lit by torches. Hauled by a small army of men (a report says up to two thousand), attached to great ship's hawsers, it moved triumphantly through the streets accompanied by bands, torch-bearers and cheering crowds. It is easy to guess that that would be one of St. John's most popular annual nights, and of such there were many in those days.

Salvation Army headquarters here centre important activities and present that busy appearance in a stout, work-a-day-looking building. The Army is a living force in the land, its blue-clad men and women forming eight to ten per cent of the population. They have their schools, hospitals and other institutions, and their brass bands here are of the kind that would brighten any dull Sunday afternoon.

Free masonry was brought to Newfoundland by army or naval officers about the mid-seventeenth century, and it has flourished with a large membership. The Masonic Hall is another fine brick building. Irish immigration came from both the north and south of that troubled land, and it was inevitable that the Orange Order came with it. It is still an important factor in community life, though less so than in times past. The Irish brought their opinions with them and in latter years seem to have kept them alive partly for the fun of having differences to quarrel over, although, it is said, that not too long ago politicians did not fail in urgent appeals to these opinions when political requirements seemed to make them expedient.

The first arrivals apparently settled at the west end of the harbour, well away from the outlet to the sea, doubtless because the land there is less rocky, and rises more gradually in the narrow valley of the little river reaching salt water at this point, for the older part of the town huddles hereabouts. A long history has left no really old buildings here as record. Wooden construction lasted only so long and fire frequently has effected a complete change of scene. There are citizens who say another blaze here would do no harm, since what they have of slum conditions lie in this neighbourhood, and they are noticeably a little self-conscious about it—a commendable thing, and all the more so since demolition is reported to be going ahead about as fast as new housing can be provided and slum-dwellers persuaded to move. Visiting newspaper writers from the mainland in search of "hot copy" have prodded this touchy spot with less than gentle comment, more than one, to my knowledge, coming from a vastly richer city with a slum area considerably larger than St. John's, and quite horrifying enough to make interesting "copy." It would be strange indeed if a four-hundred-year-old seaport, in a land where the average standard of living never was high, and often had been grimly low, had not its crowded area where housing costs held at the lowest possible level. A few streets there are of neglected, unpainted, two-storey wooden houses, and some unwholesome-looking little shops providing a meagre living for their owners—all doomed for clearance.

This west end is St. John's most colourful part. Eastward, the city is modern and business-like. Here are the reminders of Victorian, or even Georgian days, with here and there a spot left lonesome from a more remote past. Around the harbour end, past fishhouses and a modern drydock large enough to hold almost any ship coming to port, is century-old St. Mary's Anglican Church, as severe in line and solid in granite as any castle in Scotland's Highlands. War memorial chancel fittings add lustre to its age. And of the brass candle-sticks standing on each side of the Cross, the story says their advent caused half the congregation, with sharp noses for a whiff of popery, to walk out, breaking the heart of the aged parson who died shortly afterwards. But the candle-sticks remained as his memorial, and the congregation straggled back, accepting the innovation as nothing more than a renewed recognition of ancient usage, and proving that Anglicans here are pretty much alike to those elsewhere.

Our friend with the story of the little "harse" on the slippery hill, with his Irishisms of tongue and manner, could not be lonesome in this part of the town.   You'll see his like in varying age and condition of life on every corner, and the music of his speech reaches the ear from every talking group who seem to have lost little, if any, of native characteristics brought overseas by adventurous forebears.   To the east it is not so.   English and Irish have mixed at school, play and work.   Speech is becoming standardized, though each acquires from the other, and retains enough of idiom, cadence, and inflection, to make excellent spoken English—all very pleasant to listen to.   With the younger Irish much of the brogue has gone, but they've lost none of their love of a laugh, their kindliness, or their genial way of agreeing with you when there's no particular reason why they should not.   While life lasts they will hold to that maddening faculty of tremendous enthusiasm in the starting of things, or the promise of action doomed to be forgotten when something else demands its own moment of attention.   It was a St. John's Irishman told me this and I believed him.   We both were seeking information and some assistance in government offices at the time.   Many Irish are to be found in this Island's civil service.   Perhaps it all arises from a deeply generous instinct that hates to say no to a request and loves sending visitors away as happy as may be.

# 5

FIVE YEARS after Columbus made his well-publicized first trans-
Atlantic voyage, John Cabot in 1497 set up England's flag somewhere along this coast, most likely on the point of Bonavista
Peninsula, and four hundred years later, on Signal Hill, most
prominent headland hereabouts and immediately over the
harbour entrance, the Cabot Tower rose as a memorial. Never
was a memorial more happily placed. From every part of the
town it stands out against the sky, and from far out at sea it is the
only thing suggesting that a busy harbour and city lie behind
these cliffs of rock. A call here is a must for every visitor. A
motor car will climb the hill in twenty minutes, but a few
days of training in walking up and down these streets should
put one into condition to do it afoot in an easy forty-five minutes.
The Tower is as simple and direct in design as the rock on which
it stands and just about as rugged, as well it need be when
autumn and winter gales render its approach difficult, even
dangerous.

Cabot has singularly few memorials to celebrate his contribution to British history. Those honouring Columbus in both
North and South America are innumerable, and yet Cabot's
journey into the unknown was no less daring and hardly less
profitable to the nation that sent him out, than was that of

Columbus whose three ships were better manned and more generously provisioned. Columbus crossed the south seas, the far easier way; Cabot challenged the North Atlantic, its storms, ice and fog, with one small ship and eighteen companions. He found Terra Nova and got safely home. Newfoundland's codfish made England rich, and ever since have fed the hungry of western and southern Europe. Bristol, the port from which he sailed, has a memorial tower erected in honour of the merchants who grudgingly backed his venture and, as far as I know, Montreal is the only city in North America other than St. John's where his memory is marked. Montreal's memorial is a bold, larger-than-life statue of the Genoa-born navigator peering with hand-shaded eyes to the north-west, a noble gift to the city from Italy's government of the early and best days of Mussolini's regime.

Here in Newfoundland's Cabot Tower, Marconi received the world's first transoceanic radio telegraph signal in 1901, and it now is an important station of the coastal signal service. A ruined powder magazine and an old gun or two tell of early days when a battery helped guard the harbour entrance. With only an ocean between, this is North America's nearest point to Europe. Right and left, precipitous walls of bare rock fade into blue distance. A frightening precipice in front falls unbroken to the peacock-blue-green tide. The tide moves in and out through the harbour entrance between lighthouses set down where fortifications were hastily built in the mid-seventeen-hundreds as the local answer to news of war with Napoleon's France. A chain of mighty iron links lay across the floor of the channel, anchored on one side, and on the other secured to a capstan that required a thousand men to turn it on the day appearance of a French fleet outside called for chain-raising and entrance blocking. So determined a promise of unprofitable fighting proved distasteful, and the Frenchman sailed south along the shore carrying death and destruction to less well-defended settlements.

Protected from sea by the top of Signal Hill, and overlooking the channel, is Queen's Own Fort, built in 1705 and named for

England's then recently enthroned Queen Anne. Rebuilt following a French attack from the land side in 1763, and again in 1809, it remains an elderly cottage. What is left of a ruined powder-magazine (that may have survived from the original buildings) offers an interesting example of how a few stones laid mortarless but skilfully in a proper arch will defy time and the roughest of weather. Old guns on a decently preserved platform and low stone defences command the sea entrance. From here are views justifying the upward climb even though historic interest were lacking. Time-o'-day to stand here is at sunset, when long twilights add loveliness to these northern latitudes. The life-crowded rock-bowl far below that is St. John's fills with violet shadows deepening to purple in the harbour's green depths while over the tree-tops wafts of lazy blue smoke from chimney-pots speak of families round the evening meal. If you see it in late June, as I did, when one by one window lights glow forth, and a pale young moon brightens the darkening sky, you will carry away a memorable picture.

Walking back down the road offers an excellent bird's-eye view of Fort Pepperrell, a self-contained city housing United States army personnel and their families. With a nice sense of diplomacy the place is named for Colonel Sir William Pepperrell who, in 1745, led an army of New England and English troops to take Louisbourg from the French. The Fort, like the United States army dock at the harbour's west end, is one of those Newfoundland areas held as United States territory under a ninety-nine-year lease, a wartime arrangement not entirely favoured throughout the Island. Few would welcome the building in his front garden of a neighbour's garage without, at least, a by-your-leave, no matter how great the mutual advantage. The Newfoundlander feels that way about it. American authorities have handled their part of the situation with tact and courtesy. The Newfoundlander is quite aware of its power of protection in the event of a possible third world war. He also appreciates the economic value of the lease, the expenditure of large sums in maintenance and employment of many local people on civilian jobs. He gets along very well with the few soldiers and sailors seen about the city streets, mostly at evening, and often in the company of pretty girls or chatting in some convenient tavern.

Devon, loveliest of England's counties, rich above all else in the daring spirit of adventure of the men who won mastery of the seas for Elizabeth's navy, and held for England far away possessions long since grown into an Empire, is the mother-land of this Island. Merchants of Bristol may have fathered its discovery and created its commerce, but sons of Devon—such men as Raleigh, Drake, Sir Humphrey Gilbert and others of like kidney, if lesser fame—gave this land life, and set up on its people the stamp of their courage and determination to carry on through trial and tribulation when the hands of both God and man seemed against them. On the English side, men of Devon were mostly responsible for early settlement, and most of the Island's English descend from Devon stock. This is true in St. John's, and even more notably so in outports around the coasts. The farther settlements lie from the city, the more have they retained of original Elizabethan manner and speech, and general approach to life. Modern schools, radio, and the development of roads and motor travel are changing all this, but today it hardly seems possible that these, and time, could alter the kindly, straightforward and thoughtful way of life that is their happy inheritance.

Coming down from Cabot Tower, the bottom of the hill is the start of a climb back home through the town, past the interesting old garrison church of St. Thomas, a stout frame building with a history going back to 1836. Georgian royal arms tell of days when troops were paraded here to be preached at in terms suited to their rank and social position, while many memorials recall to mind men and events of past days. On Sunday mornings its memorial bells, in honour of those who fell in the First Great War, peal forth from the tower.

Much there is about the boarding-house type of stopping place that is pleasing to the traveller, who chooses to move in meandering fashion, and is in no great hurry about it. Frequenters of its table are chatty folk, ready to talk of outlying parts of the Island from which they come and how life there is lived. With a little encouragement they will offer interesting comment on current world events in relation to affairs in their homeland. Newfoundlanders in all walks of life seem well informed about what goes on elsewhere. Their newspapers serve them well, and they are consistent and intelligent radio listeners. Since most families have near relatives in Canada and the United States, news of both lands has something of a personal interest, and centuries of British trade connection, as well as political tie-up, has made news from the old land second only in importance to their own—all of which is pleasingly reflected in table-talk wherever you go.

This is a land of promise—in more ways than one—and it is in the matter of weather that generosity of promise most engagingly is displayed. This time of year—anyway, this year—certainly this month, we have more varied promises of fine weather, or the contrary, than would seem possible elsewhere. Early morning rising greets lowering clouds or fog, sunshine brightens the breakfast table, and a flurry of rain meets your outgoing. There is a coolness about it too, and you wonder when summer is coming, or if it went past in the warm fortnight natives assure you they enjoyed just before your arrival. This is "caplin scull" weather, and every year the schools of caplin bring it in when they crowd the shores on their annual visit. After that interlude summer will return. That information I picked up in a government office—astonishing what useful knowledge may be picked up in places like that.

From weather to climate is an unavoidable step. Normally Newfoundland's climate is pretty much like that of the same mainland latitudes, only less so. Around the shore it is not so cold in winter and cooler in summer, with dampness and fog to a reasonable North Atlantic extent, plenty of rain, and winds, now and then reaching gale force. A dip of the thermometer in winter below zero would be infrequent and much talked of, and seldom does it rise to a point where summer sleeping under at least one blanket is not completely pleasant. On upper levels of the interior both heat and cold go to extremes.

The summer season throughout the Island may safely be referred to as short, with the best travelling weather between the first day of June and the last day of August.

Weather-wise sea captains say recent years have brought a moderation of extremes, and also that South Atlantic hurricanes have latterly been showing a tendency to swing north, dying out in gales around this coast. September and October assume glories of autumn colouring, when days of brilliant sunshine give place to nights that welcome a glowing blaze in the fireplaces in almost every house and cottage, or perhaps to the modern oil-heater now replacing many. Through most of the year it is a pleasurable sort of climate, well suited to a rugged and hearty-living people whose life is very largely of the out-of-door variety.

Nothing is more important in this land than holidays. The dweller here has more of them than most other people, and he observes them all with something of a broadminded disregard for religious or national significance. If the Irish want to celebrate St. Patrick's Day—and they do enthusiastically—well, let it be unanimous and all go to the party. Similarly for St. George's Day and, of course, that day devoted to King William of Orange whose twelfth of July calls for bands, banners and sashes in proud parade may not be less honoured. At such times, and on fine Saturdays and Sundays, the city's plenitude of young people crowd its several spacious parks. Of these, Bowring Park, the gift of a merchant family of that name prominent for generations in city history, is a wide tract of wooded hill and glen beautifully maintained in its natural state. Three notably fine statues stand here in perfect surroundings—a replica of London's Kensington Gardens' Peter Pan, a magnificent bronze life-size caribou, the provincial emblem and memorial to war heroes of the Royal Newfoundland Regiment, and a bronze figure of a soldier in action dedicated to "The Fighting Newfoundlander."

Up the hill near the town's centre is Bannerman Park, not so large, but much favoured by children for daily recreation. Alongside it stands Newfoundland's House of Legislative

Assembly, the colonial building, to which history and age lend much interest. Built over a century ago, it has been the scene of many stirring events in the Island's greatly chequered political past. Built of stone brought from Ireland in 1850, its assembly rooms are well proportioned and amply large for the legislature's twenty-eight elected members. As a token of welcome, and marking Newfoundland's becoming the tenth Canadian Province, the other Provinces have presented furnishings of state proper to an assembly patterned like their own on Britain's Mother of Parliaments—the mace, speaker's chair, sword for the sergeant-at-arms, and so on—so that the new Provincial Parliament might conduct its business decently and in accordance with historic usage. They have a commendable liking for that sort of thing here.

Opening and closing the legislature is an orderly proceeding and a time-honoured ceremony. A marching band in the street announces the approaching guard of honour, and a smart-looking company of uniformed constabulary swings into view to take their position in front of the building. In a few moments, with Royal Canadian Mounted Police escort, comes His Honour the Lieutenant-Governor whose Windsor uniform, gold-braided coat, feathered cocked hat, and sword are fitting symbols of his office as representative of the King. The Commander of the Guard breaks the silence, "Guard, Royal salute, Present arms." A roll of drums and clash of bayonetted rifles leads into "God Save the Queen." His Honour inspects the guard, is greeted by the Premier and the Speaker of the House, and proceeds inside to deliver the speech from the throne calling parliament to action or bringing its labours to a close—all of which has been going on here in exactly the same way since representative government was granted, and the first elected legislature met in 1855. For much longer than that it has been a regular practice the world round, wherever British parliamentary institutions have been established.

Conveniently near to the legislative building and, like it, a fine characteristic bit of old-world architecture, is Government House. A century and a quarter of succeeding governors have lived here.  Since its building, in 1828, of stone brought from England by Royal Engineers, it has been the executive and social centre of the Island, and royalty and figures famous in history have been among its guests.  Entering the front door is stepping back into Regency days.  Spacious, unspoiled by over-ornamentation, it is perfect in design and offers ideal setting for a costume ball of the time of its erection, which was shortly after the Prince Regent became George IV.

For some apparently forgotten reason a Polish visitor to the Island found himself in prison.  He was an artist and decorator to whom, no doubt, prison life proved irksome.  Imagine his joyous welcome of the opportunity to break its monotony when the need arose to decorate Government House.  His work on the ceiling and walls of both dining- and drawing-rooms marks him master of his craft.  Also, it is apparent that he was given plenty of time in which to do the job to the satisfaction of his own artistic soul.  The result is something to be preserved.  We hope it won him easement of punishment but, remembering the relentless savagery of old-time law enforcement, we wonder. Later inquiry brought from one authority the suggestion that it was not Government House the Polish artist had decorated, but the legislative building.  Since Government House has decorations justifying the story, and the legislature has none, let us leave it as it is.

Policing this land would not seem to be a difficult task today. Serious crime seldom troubles officers or courts, and petty offences calling for magisterial attention are briskly and effectively disposed of.  Infringement of motoring regulations get sharp treatment.  Jail sentences are effective discouragement for drunken driving, and the authorities seem to have little hesitation in handing them out.  Throwing hot cigarette or cigar ashes from a moving car window near a fire hazard draws a fine of one hundred dollars with promise of considerably stiffer one next time.  Originally the Island's police force was patterned on the Royal Irish Constabulary, an organization reported to have had remarkable opportunities for developing efficiency and thoroughness in the business of policing (both highly necessary if its members were to enjoy long life), with the result that it became a model for newly established forces in many parts of the world. Newfoundland's constabulary kept the land in order very well, and did what they could to discourage smuggling in those merry days when the United States and Canada experimented with prohibition. Rumour reported that the Island was more or less surrounded by cargoes of illicit liquor, a situation which gave Newfoundlanders much fun and excitement and, perhaps, some considerable profit. Under Federation the force has been merged into the Royal Canadian Mounted Police, as has a corps of rangers who policed rural areas by automobile and motorcycle.

Siege, capture and enemy violence, if properly told, would crowd every lively page of St. John's earliest history, but nothing has threatened her continued existence as have frequent and devastating conflagrations. Among earliest records is one of 1816 when a blaze left a thousand people homeless. The following year, with three days between them, two visitations swept over the west end, eliminating wharves, warehouses and most of the town's homes, once again in depth of winter. Rigid rules for fire protection, and the formation of a volunteer fire-fighting brigade naturally followed in 1811. For thirty years these were effective, while the town spread eastward and up the hill, forming a new and improved half of the city doomed to desolation in June, 1846, when the homes of twelve thousand people and most of their places of work were destroyed. Half a century of freedom from any major disaster followed, to be interrupted in 1892 by the most devastating of all when sixteen hours of blaze made an ashy waste of two-thirds of the town, including cathedral, churches, public buildings and homes. No scars remain now. Wider streets and better buildings make a safer and pleasanter city, but it is no wonder that the oldest streets display no relics of picturesque and romantic past.

In the best possible place, on top of the hill about town centre, now stands the chief part of the permanent fire-fighting force that the last calamity brought into existence. The quality and amount of its equipment is impressive. Certainly, it should have little trouble in reaching any scenes of action swiftly for most of them would be downhill, calling for good brakes more than for motive power. But guiding the massive machines through these streets in winter must be a terrific test of driving skill.

We met at breakfast. He was a painter from Boston who wanted to see Newfoundland because friends had fired his desire to see this land's wealth of colour, the tremendous massiveness of its rock shore-line, and the astonishing blue-green of the ocean at rest or thunderously raging.

"Do you like it?" I asked.

"Love it," he answered. "It's the Maine coast multiplied again and again, and then something—teach you more in a month about painting colour, light and the sea than any place ever I've seen."

"How about fogs?" I asked.

"Lovely beyond words, if only you could paint it. It's a great country for painters and I like the people, but I wish they'd learn how to cook fish back in the outports, and the liquor laws are awful. You might as well be back in prohibition days."

An interesting comment this, particularly on the subject of painting, and I doubt if any visiting artist would quarrel with this judgment. The paintable qualities of this land were discovered long ago, and North American galleries have shown many examples of its wild and moody scenery and the rugged life of its fishing villages. As with everything else, the Island's interest in painting centres in St. John's. A ten-year-old art club with an active and associate membership holds two exhibitions a year, an occasional one-man show, and frequent meetings for art study. So far, Newfoundlanders have had little opportunity of seeing exhibitions of foreign paintings, a lack to which the National Gallery authorities might well give consideration.

Remarks concerning the provincial methods of liquor control invite correction, and, since we cannot know a people being ignorant of their drinking habits, it would seem well to touch lightly on the matter here. Newfoundlanders are a thrifty people and their liquor laws strongly encouraging in that direction. The sale of beer, wines and spirits is handled by a commission having three outlets for sale, two at St. John's and one at Corner Brook. Beer taverns may be licensed in any village with the approving vote of the community, but comparatively few take advantage of this provision. Every purchaser of spirits has to have a permit, costing one dollar a year for residents and fifty cents for visitors. Wherever he be on the Island, the purchaser has to send his order and money to St. John's and wait for his supply one, two or several weeks, depending on transportation facilities.

Rum is "the wine of the country," as might be expected among any seafaring folk of British origin, particularly one having had history-long trade with the West Indies. "Screech" is the somewhat puzzling name given its most popular type by American soldiers, and generally adopted by the populace, though why it is hard to imagine, unless it be a rude reflection on any outbursts of song its generous use might induce. An elderly fisherman remarked concerning a brand reputed to be "smooth as a lamb's fleece and having all the power and authority of the British navy." "Aye, lad," he said, "there's a power of good singing in a bottle o' that."

Newfoundlanders are greatly given to song, as a good-hearted people rightly should be. They have many a come-all-ye ballad, usually telling a melancholy tale of disaster at sea or the woes of a lovelorn fisher lad, and often sung to tunes far from merry and bright. They have other songs in a much more cheerful vein and love to sing them, which they do very well indeed. Such a land as this could not be without its poets and it has many. Hardly a newspaper appears without at least one set of native verses, some are of high order. Some day an anthology of Newfoundland poetry will command recognition as a notable enrichment of Canada's literature.

Every city enjoys or endures its own type of Sunday, fashioned either by the inhabitants' desire or by some insistent group of behaviour specialists. You can learn a lot about a people when exposed to one of their Sundays. No ill-natured desire for comparison influences a reference to one great and respectable community that enjoys a Sunday continentally referred to as dreadful, and another, not so far distant, where the day seems to be given more to recreation and restful pleasure. The wish is rather to make clear that Sunday in St. John's seems to lie about halfway between the two, with, perhaps, a slight tendency toward the latter.

Properly and pleasantly it opens to the music of church bells, quite a lot of them, ringing early and often but not harshly or too loudly. Then follows a motor-horn fantasia played with admirable spirit and persistence, though not quite up to the force and abandon of a normal week-day performance. Drivers here display an amazing regard for human safety. They sound warnings of possible disaster at every corner, and the good fellow crossing ahead invariably replies with a polite "toot-toot" of thank you. Busses and trucks are a bit more insistent in tone, and one genial lad has a horn sounding three or four notes, on which he plays variations, enlivening the over-all symphony. Calls for an extended effort on joyful occasions, weddings and such, are enthusiastically met, and who would churlishly withhold a horn-blast of good wishes for a bride and groom as their screaming parade goes by. Not the St. John's driver. He is a friendly and communicative soul wishing everybody well. There's talk of passing a law against this sort of thing. Maybe it will work—not, one hopes, to the extent of turning him into a morose and uncommunicative sort of person with no musical note of greeting for passers-by.

Should Sunday morning sleepiness miraculously prevail, there's the great brass breakfast gong of the boarding-house. Once it made a tremendously loud noise as casing of a huge gun-shell, but now a stout-armed lass—doubtless recruited to bed-making and meal-serving from some strenuous occupation like whaling—gives it a warlike and far-reaching voice, shaking walls and rattling windows a block away. Here one gets up and, if the day be sunny, sets forth to walk the pleasant streets and parks.

Topping the hill and continuing down beyond one passes

fine old frame houses in well-kept gardens suggesting prosperous past days cushioned by useful and amiable domestic help, easier to acquire then than now. Were it evening, undrawn curtains would permit glimpses of generous-sized rooms bespeaking a comfortable fashion of life, and if the night were chilly there'd be a blaze of warmth from the hearth. Farther along, modern architects and builders have had their way and the dignity of Victoria's days gives place to smart and lively lines and bright colours.

Sunshine seems to have brought out crowds this morning. Their Sunday-best clothes are colourful. Bright kerchiefs on young heads are effective, while more sedate hats, even bonnets, on elders mark a seriousness of purpose beyond the ordinary. Solemn, Sunday-in-church-like children are with them, each, with grave intentness, carrying flowers from the home garden. All are moving towards the cemetery spreading over the hillside beyond. This is Memorial Sunday, and several thousand people stand among the grave-stones to hear Memorial Mass said from a temporary altar set high against the sky. After that the graves will be visited and floral offerings laid.

The music of marching bands stirs the afternoon quiet of another Sunday. Orangemen and women—many women— have gathered from all over the Island for their annual conclave, and march in a glory of multi-coloured sashes with all the bands of the town to inspire their measured movement. Even the Salvation Army contributes two, and excellent bands they are. The "foreign" visitor finds great interest in this marching multitude. They come from all quarters of the town, the country, and from fishing villages up and down the coast, an arresting cross-section of people who go far to make up New-foundland. Sunburned and weather-worn, or just sunburned, there is a sense of strength about the faces of these men—keen intelligence here, strength of character there, and no lacking of a sense of humour anywhere. English characteristics show plainly in some, unmistakable Irish in others, and there quite often appears the sensitiveness of the Norman French. They are serious about this parade. The Orange Lodge for them has something worthwhile, and they radiate their belief in its creed and purpose.   The women, all dressed in white, are a bit more grim about it and more logically determined, as women perhaps should be.   Furthermore, despite hills trying to the youngest, they are marching—not riding in cars—though some have reached an age that may be referred to politely in congratulatory terms.   It is good to have seen these people go by. Unknowingly they have revealed much about their lives and this country of theirs.

# 6

*Day of Remembrance—How Newfoundland Went to War—A Brave Old Ship Comes to Her End—Schools and University—Libraries and Theatre—The Newfoundland Dog.*

JULY THE FIRST, Dominion Day for the rest of Canada, is a day of mourning in Newfoundland, or more truly a day of proud and grateful recognition of valour and sacrifice tempered by pain of national and personal loss. On that day in 1918, the Royal Newfoundland Regiment, 753 strong, went into battle at Beaumont-Hamel. At roll call next day sixty-eight answered. St. John's loss was great, but throughout the whole Island there were few who, through relationship, friendship or acquaintance, had not reason for personal sorrow. As vividly as public ceremony can, St. John's marks the Day of Remembrance of those and all who died in the two Great Wars, and observes it with a solemn intensity that strikes a chill into the heart.

Day of Remembrance came this year with cloudy skies and flurries of rain. One by one military, naval units and other organizations headed by their bands and colours took position round the Sergeant's War Memorial Cross in a church-framed square. Medalled veterans, Royal Newfoundland Regiment, Naval Cadets, Church Lads' Brigade, Boy Scouts, Girl Guides, Salvation Army and a company of United States soldiers from Fort Pepperrell stood a few moments while a wreath was laid, then moved in procession through city streets to the fine memorial to the dead of both wars.   Here crowds filling the square and streets joined in the short service—flowered tributes, bands and murmuring voices in a hymn, moments of silence, crash of three volleys from a firing-party, clear call of bugles sounding the Last Post, and then throb of a multitude singing "God Save the King," and once again we have burned the incense of remembrance and honour.

Newfoundland's war effort has been more than worthy of the extent of her population and limited resources.   In the First World War more than eighty-five hundred enlisted in the Royal Newfoundland Regiment and Forestry Corps and the others in the Royal Navy.   The total killed was thirteen hundred from the regiment and one hundred and eighty from the navy.   In the Second World War ten thousand went overseas in various services and six hundred did not return.   Some two thousand men and women also joined up in Canadian services and probably as many, if not more, were to be found in United States fighting units.   Their soldierly qualities compelled admiration from all who met them and justified the lad who, tired of constant inquiry as to meaning of "NFLD." embroidered on his shoulders, replied "Never found lying down."   Over centuries the Royal Navy had learned of Newfoundland seamanship, its efficiency and daring.   *The Cambridge History* of the British Empire says, "The war left them with a greatly enhanced reputation.   They readily undertook almost impossible boarding operations in wild seas which others would not face.   Nothing but praise was accorded by the fleet."   British naval seamanship standards are high and its authorities never were noted for prodigality of praise.

The war memorial, one of hundreds seen and remembered, is notable for dignity and effectiveness.   On a high granite pedestal a bronze Victory lifts both torch and sword.   At the base are figures representing men and women of the war effort. Its place on a hillside with a terraced approach creates a feeling of loftiness and power.   The Island has many memorials recalling heroisms and services given.   There are those who say money so spent is waste—it should build memorial hospitals, schools and such useful things—an attractive thought with reason behind it. But, viewing St. John's monuments, one wonders if any building, however philanthropic its purpose, will bring to life and constant recognition as effectively the human qualities it is intended to honour as will a monument of symbolic beauty set up in market place or city square. That we should have no more of these is not a pleasing thought.

They say sailors are sentimental folk. Well—perhaps they are. A sailor can hate the sea in its ugly moods, but he'll stick to it as an old man sticks to a contrary wife, and he can love ships as a young man loves a proven friend. That is why the good old wooden-walled ship, *Eagle*, having come to the end of happy and useful life, was towed out of St. John's harbour Sunday afternoon, July 23rd, and sent to rest on the ocean's floor in sight of thousands watching from rocky headlands and a fleet of small boats attending her last journey.

For half a century her hundred and seventy-six feet of stout timbered length had fought northern ice on sealing voyages, had faced Antarctic dangers for the British Government, and had plied far-off seas on many a trade mission. She had held high place among Newfoundland's sealing fleets where honour is won only in heroic and victorious battle with Arctic seas and ice in weather almost always hazardous and often frightful in its violence. She had come through these years with profit to her owners and to the seamen who had manned her. In 1916, after twenty days on the ice, she returned to St. John's carrying over thirty-three thousand pelts valued at seventy-five thousand dollars, and over a recorded twenty years had brought home some three hundred thousand pelts worth something like three-quarters of a million dollars. She had served her owners well right up to her last trip of a year ago. But time, ice, and storm had their way, and no longer could her massive frame find zest or strength for adventure as the North Atlantic calls for it.

To be broken up or sold as junk might have been her fate, or perhaps a length of melancholy days as shabby hulk—each an unwelcome thought to men of the sea whose lives and loves she had held. So, they made her brave with flags and streamers, nailed her company's red and white house-flag to the topmast and gave her stately procession full length of the harbour and out through the narrows to the sea. Flags dipped over crowded ships as she passed, and now and then three short deep notes from steam whistles broke the silence.

Five miles out at sea they opened her sides, lit fires on her lower deck and stood by watching until, quietly, she plunged down under. Love for ships and the sea is as much a part of life in Newfoundland as is seamanship with daring and courage to back it up.

In 1726, a clergyman sent out by the British Society for Propagation of the Gospel arrived at Bonavista to give education its organized start. No doubt he found illiteracy general, but probably not relatively more so than in the British Isles of that time. The type of schools he began must have been primitive, and they had to be church schools. Island education has developed from that point, retaining its sectarian character and making Newfoundland the only English-speaking country of any size retaining a school system controlled by churches of its varied religious denominations. The system works and is stoutly defended by a large section of the community. Students from its preparatory schools have taken high place in mainland universities and impressive numbers have won fame in arts, science, medicine and other branches of learning. Those who have gone from secondary or high schools to life and work in other countries seem to have been equipped at least as well as those with whom they had to compete. A somewhat better than casual observation convinces one that children and young people here are bright, adventurous in thinking, well-mannered, speak the language pleasingly and show consideration towards respectable things. For some of this their schooling must be responsible.

The system is not unanimously approved. Objectors to its sectarian character complain of unnecessarily high costs through duplication of teaching staffs and equipment, and say that there are communities where the work could be done better and at less cost by one school rather than by two. The answer given to this is that while it may be true in about twelve per cent of the outport settlements, the inhabitants in others are from seventy-five to ninety per cent of one religious denomination. In St. John's and "company" towns there is a movement towards the amalgamation of Protestant schools.

By an act of the first legislature in 1836, sectarian text-books and teaching were forbidden, but popular feeling and church influence proved too strong and Church of England and Roman Catholic educational authority was re-established to remain complete until the Commission Government in 1934 took the entire system under governmental control, including the United Church and Salvation Army, and so it continues to be.

Since 1942 education has been free and compulsory between the ages of seven and fourteen. Free choice of school is allowed, and scholars may not be compelled to attend schools of faiths other than their own. Attendance at classes of religious instruction is not compulsory. The central department—the Ministry of Education and representatives of the churches—plans a programme of studies, controls teacher training, and supplements local money grants for new buildings for general purposes. Most schools are co-educational. Many combine the elementary grades, one to eight, and the secondary, nine to eleven. Over ten per cent of the children go on to high school, and close co-operation is maintained with the common examining board of the Maritime Provinces which sets and marks all examination papers. Each denomination has its college for advanced students at St. John's where special courses are given in music, physical and manual training and commerce. These serve the whole Island and residences are maintained for out-of-town scholars.

Establishment of a university college was an unrealized dream of people and clergy alike for over half a century, and it was not until 1925 that means were found to allow its undertaking. In that year, with help from the Carnegie Corporation, Memorial University College came into being as a non-denominational institution having representatives of the churches on its board and faculty. It stands a suitable building adequate for the work it then undertook and equipped to give two years of regular degree courses in arts and science, two years pre-medical, three years pre-engineering and three in teacher training, after which students carried on to mainland universities where their years counted.  One of the first acts of the new legislature of 1949 amended the charter and the college became Memorial University of Newfoundland with power to grant degrees.  It now gives full courses in arts and education, but neither buildings nor equipment yet permit extension of the science courses.  That is for the future.  About three hundred students are now in attendance.  But more vigorous economy and new thought may be expected to encourage a greater general interest in higher education and an increased enrolment of students; those, who in the past have gone elsewhere to complete their studies, will now remain at home.  Thus the university faces an urgent need for early and extensive expansion.

The Gosling Memorial Library is another institution that impresses the visitor with the Island's intelligent regard for culture and determination to spread its influence as widely as available means will permit.  The building is large, well lighted and airy, with a most inviting circulating and reference room. Stacks are crowded with books that seem almost to be warm from the printing press, and historic reference sections— particularly those concerning Newfoundland—are rich fields for study.

One of its happy features is its apparent popularity among children whose reading desires, like those of the elders, are attended to by an understanding and friendly staff.  All this is good and highly important, but certainly not more so than the circulation of books among small towns, fishing villages and hamlets around the coast, very likely the most fruitful and valuable part of Gosling Memorial's fine effort.  About two hundred and fifty towns and villages are served by a travelling library at present sending out seventeen to nineteen thousand volumes yearly.  Since this could not adequately serve the outports, a regional library system is in process of organization which already serves about eighty towns and villages, each with its own central library and board, making a total of three hundred and thirty outlying centres in regular receipt of an astonishingly varied supply of good reading matter. The library was founded by bequest of the late William Gilbert Gosling, early and outstanding member of St. John's public-spirited merchant class, the city's first mayor and author of several books of Newfoundland historic interest. The Carnegie Corporation has given the library ten thousand dollars for book purchases for the regional libraries.

Newfoundland has its theatre. It has to be "Little Theatre" so-called, the Island being too remote and the approach too difficult for mainland professional productions to make a profitable visit. But it is little only in a relative way—certainly not in the persistent painstaking effort of those who have brought about its present state of development. Homespun if you like— as it should be—creating something worthwhile out of native material to hand just as did the Abbey Theatre of Dublin, Birmingham Repertory, Hart House at Toronto and the Montreal Repertory along with others that have moved to rescue English-speaking stage from the lingering death of late Victorian days. Little theatre here exists, as it does elsewhere, because of the unselfish hard work put into a project by those who are keenly interested and who possess a clear idea of what they want.

It started out on the right foot with no other purpose than creation of interest in theatre, and development of such talent that might be offered—no thought of collecting money for other than its own needs. A group of people in 1937 dug into their own pockets to organize the St. John's Players for experimental work in play reading, writing, staging and production. More so, perhaps, than in most communities, the fight has been uphill. Public interest, at first meagre, has steadily grown—tribute, no doubt, to effective work accomplished. Courage, or something that proved to be a similar incentive, suggested no less exacting a play than Barrie's *Admirable Crichton* as a starter, and either its success or the experience gained inspired a further bold adventure in carrying on the production of thirty or so plays, giving the community a comprehensive glimpse of fairly late play writing.

This included Noel Coward's *Hands Across the Sea* and *Hay Fever*, Milne's *Mr. Pim Passes By* and *Dover Road*, Anatole France's *Man Who Married a Dumb Wife* and Hsiung's *Lady Precious Stream*. Always present was the promise of a profitable popularity for old-fashioned melodrama, while religious prejudices and political animosities had to be considered in the choice of plays if definite trouble were to be avoided.

Inevitably, St. John's was not for long to monopolize the fascination and cultural value of this work.   Other communities had talent and incentive, all culminating in Newfoundland's first drama festival in 1949 when four outside groups, one each from Harbour Grace and the United States base Fort Pepperrell, and two from Corner Brook, joined St. John's players in presenting an interesting week of theatre.   Encouragement of playwriting by Newfoundlanders is a worthy phase of the organization's effort.   Prizes are offered for plays having Island life, speech and thought as their theme, and it could be that out of this something of broad national value might emerge.   A warm welcome from Memorial University authorities did much to help the project in its early and most difficult days, and it is hoped that when its new buildings come to be erected a fair-sized theatre with a practical and well-designed stage will be included.

Clearly, so discursive a tale as this may not avoid reference to the Newfoundland dog, for long years outstanding contributor to Island fame around the world.   Top-ranking authority on this engaging animal is the Hon. Harold Macpherson, head of one of St. John's oldest and largest mercantile houses and for many years a leading breeder and world-recognized judge of what a Newfoundland dog should be.   Unauthorized visit to his nearby farm is not recommended.   The sudden appearance of five or six of these great creatures, all splendid to look at but each displaying a suspicious curiosity as to your right to be there, is discouraging to unwarranted intrusion.   Properly introduced by their master, one finds them willing to submit to polite admiration, in a dignified, reserved way, of course, but quite friendly.

Their original ancestor, says Mr. Macpherson, was the white

or cream-coloured dog from the Pyrenees. When the Basques came for fish, part of their provisions were flocks of sheep which would live comfortably off the land, and the dogs were dependable shepherds when their owners were at sea. Britishers brought dogs, too, and so, no doubt, did Jerseymen, Spaniards and Portuguese. It is said the Norwegians had dogs not unlike the Newfoundlander, and it may be that a few of these found their way to add their bit to the outstanding physique, courage and intelligence marking the Newfoundlander today. Climate and life by the sea must have contributed to the development, resulting in his cold-defying black, or black and white, hide with its thick woolly undercoat, never wet through, and his large, partially webbed feet helping him swim amazing distances just for the fun of it.

Early Victorian painters and writers established the idea that the ruling passion of this noble fellow, and his chief occupation, was rescuing beautiful children from cruel sea waves. When a job like that comes his way he'll do it and do it well, and it doesn't have to be a pretty child. Many a husky adult, with little claim to beauty, have been hauled from certain death by these stout and fearless swimmers to continue a possibly quite unbeautiful life. But this sort of thing is not his sole occupation. He is a good draft animal. Now and then you see him drawing a cart on the road. In the north he hauls winter mails, and a team of seven will do seventy miles a day with mail and passengers. I am told that the sleigh dog is not the pure-bred show animal, but one in which other strains have lightened his weight and perhaps added something to the enthusiasm with which he will greet the prospect of working for his living day-in, day-out. The same authority suggests that breeding for show has made him too heavy, and has brought him to a point where a highly superior attitude towards his surroundings masks his final decision that hard work is for some other dog—not him. This may be another evidence of well-developed sagacity or, perhaps, a sad instance of what can happen when a fellow gets educated beyond his proper station in life.

Even so, he does his work willingly, and the more so if there be a flavour of sport about it.   None excel him as a retriever, and as a guardian of children his admirers give him many points, almost suggesting him as an answer to all baby-sitting problems.   In Australia he is trained successfully as a sheep-dog.   In Europe he gains fame under another name.   So often, and over so many years, have the dogs of St. Bernard's Alpine hospice surviving disastrous avalanches or distemper epidemics been bred to Newfoundlanders, that the original strain must long since have petered out—but report indicates the work goes on as well as ever and the little brandy-cask continues to perform its humane function.

Tales of the Newfoundland dog's heroism—of lifesaving on sea and shore, of understanding faithfulness to his salt, general intelligence and endurance—fill volumes.   Their truth is not questioned.   At one time you met him the world over, in forms ranging from well-bred down to that closely approaching just plain dog, and always he was somebody's loving and trusted friend.   He is not often seen now, alas, for who today can find food for up to a hundred and fifty living pounds of even the world's most virtuous dog, and who can house him properly.

# 7

*Founding of St. John's—Queen Elizabeth Takes a Hand—1583 to 1832—War, Oppression and Piracy—Home Merchant Control Spells Ruin—Partial Emancipation and Prosperity.*

ALMOST a century passed between Cabot's 1497 landing at Bonavista and the arrival of Sir Humphrey Gilbert in 1583 to establish firmly, with Queen Elizabeth's blessing, England's clear claim to ownership of Newfoundland. Through that century this harbour and others up and down the coast had existed as fishing stations where visiting ships brought their catch each year to be dried and packed for the home journey. Here and there a few settlers had made their homes, and in safe waters of deep bays villages began to form. Gilbert came to St. John's, even then chief port of the Island, and nearest thing to a capital any such unorganized spot on the known world could be. A bronze plaque at the city's war memorial records, "Close to this commanding and historic spot Sir Humphrey Gilbert landed on the fifth day of August, 1583, and in taking possession of this new found land in the name of his sovereign Queen Elizabeth founded Britain's Over-seas Empire."

The scene greeting the voyager sailing up the harbour pool that day must have been unique in history. A frontier town of the sea—more picturesque by far than any western frontier of later centuries. Trees, mostly spruce and pine, covered the hills—axe and erosion had not yet bared the rocks—rugged

77

timber wharves and buildings, fish-barns, dwellings and taverns crowded in confusion to supply the needs of as tough and adventurous, though probably amiable and certainly violent, a mob of sea-going men as might be seen. Englishmen, Spaniards, Basques, Frenchmen, sea-miners all, here for cod and nothing else; but no doubt, getting as much fun as this haven offered; no law, no order, except such as master of each ship might be able to exert on his own deck.

There is no record. Imagination re-creates the scene made alive by dozens of the queer little ships of the time anchored in the bay or at the docks; noise, plenty of it, creaking of blocks as ropes haul through them, rattle of oars and shouts of talk and command in half a dozen languages; and smells—lusty as the talk, vivid as the scene; wood-smoke floating on the air and always that pungency of salted cod drying in the sun, flavouring the breeze as spice flavours a consomme. Something very like this, Elizabeth's messenger saw when his four ships dropped anchor in the harbour.

When Cabot landed back in Bristol to receive the applause from merchants who had sent him, and £10 from the King for having added new lands to his realm, his tales of the inexhaustible supplies of fish really started something. Other countries heard about it and hastened to fill their food-baskets. The legend of England's ownership of Newfoundland by right of discovery persisted, though threatened by Spain then claiming mastery of the seas. Elizabeth, however, farsighted and quick-moving, with a keen eye towards Spanish pretensions, was building a navy. She needed sailors, and fishing fleets offered the best possible supply. Moreover, the fish trade had become of tremendous importance. This matter of Newfoundland fisheries, their wealth, ships and men, called for safeguarding and regulating. That excellent historian, the Rev. Dr. William Pilot, records four hundred vessels then engaged in the trade, of which only fifty were English. So, Sir Humphrey was sent out to do something about it.

Half-brother to Sir Walter Raleigh, and another of those sea-dogs who as much pirates as navy men were making England's name feared over the seas, he apparently did the job in good style. Twenty Spanish and Portuguese and sixteen English ships were in harbour at the time, and the town had become a sizable place. Crews left to cut timber, build fish-drying stages and so on had been the first permanent settlers, and the record says forty or fifty houses stood here thirty years before his arrival. This number must have grown considerably.

Sir Humphrey called all ships' officers together, cere-moniously read his commission from the Queen, and announced Her Majesty's sovereignty over the whole Island. To give it point, he promulgated three laws: (1) that religion should be according to the Church of England, (2) that the Queen's prerogative should be maintained, (3) that any person uttering words to the dishonour of Her Majesty should lose his ears and have his ship and goods confiscated.

Clipping of ears was a favoured punishment in those days, a kindly warning of what would happen to the whole head were naughty ways persisted in. That appears to be the first example of British law to be put into force on the North American continent. Reports carried back to the royal lady intimated that the inhabitants had received her message with loyal enthusi-asm—which may have been true. Elsewhere it is suggested that the first coming of law was viewed in some quarters as not being entirely without humour, and a certain amount of mental nose-thumbing towards the royal edicts is indicated. It is safe to guess, however, that such depravity did not reach the point of "uttering words." To English merchants there present Sir Humphrey gave royal grants for the properties they occupied, and sailed for home, never to arrive. His fleet was scattered by a gale off the Azores and his own ship, the *Squirrel*, went down with all on board. His last words, "Cheer up, lads, we are as near heaven on sea as on land," were very likely a com-forting thought to those who had no forebodings of perhaps a different destination. If all were lost, one wonders who carried home a report of this utterance, but, true or not, it is indicative of the manner of thought among English seamen of those days.

Gilbert's surviving ships carried home information that

brought the Island into public notice as never before. The battle with Spain was proceeding towards Armada climax, only five years away, and when it came, Newfoundland-going ships, skippers and men were there in as great numbers as could be mustered. That vastly important event decided, among other things, that Newfoundland and her fisheries were not Spanish possessions. Raleigh, in the House of Commons, was first to proclaim that "The loss of Newfoundland would be the greatest calamity England could suffer," and that its fisheries were the "mainstay and support of the West of England." Becoming Governor of Jersey, he lost no time in developing a trade connection with Newfoundland which later resulted in an important contribution of permanent inhabitants to the Island.

Life at St. John's must have undergone little change through a hundred succeeding years. Various royal charters granted for the purpose of settlement of the Island, as well as the enrichment of court favourites who received them, almost completely failed. They did, however, scatter a few people here and there among the Island harbours and encouraged development of the codfish trade. Sir Humphrey's laws and the growth of the town brought neither peace nor security. Many of England's sea-captains, no longer employed in what passed for honest war, turned pirates to become wealthy, to die fighting or to meet the fate of their trade on the gallows. St. John's and other Newfoundland settlements, being wide open to profitable rapine, were victims of many disastrous visitations. The usual practice of these gentry was to drop in unexpectedly, seize what ships and arms they coveted—particularly those of other nationalities—reinforce their crews by impressing English sailors and burn the greater part if not all of the town. On several occasions St. John's experienced a raid of this sort, but continued to grow with the expansion of fishing and became the recognized North Atlantic trade headquarters, losing nothing of its lawlessness yet probably increasing in size, turbulence and wealth.

Attempts at formal government were feeble, an arrangement quite satisfactory to the merchants and the West of England generally. They mined the seas for cod and monopolized all

Island trade, no doubt conducted at a highly profitable rate. Interference from government or governors was altogether undesirable. If piratical visits threatened to become monotonous, predatory French ships provided variety. France was succeeding Spain as England's enemy on the high seas. In 1628 a French fleet spread death and destruction up and down the coast and St. John's was not overlooked. This sort of thing was to happen time and again pretty well over two centuries until the Battle of Trafalgar gave the final decision.

The reigns of King James I and Charles I saw great wealth taken from Newfoundland and little returned in the way of protection or assistance beyond establishing admiralty courts to empanel juries and settle fishery disputes—quite an important matter. Cromwell's Commonwealth exerted a firmer hand, strengthened the courts of justice, and even encouraged shipping and boat-building. About this time the idea of taxation began to rear its ugly head. A government emissary sent to St. John's to collect licence fees went home to report a failure and that "He found ye fishermen to be stuberne fellows." They were to prove that through long years of history—"stuberne" fighters for what they held, for honest rights and a way of life they knew. When the course of time brought civic organization and the dignity of a coat of arms, with honourable pride they might well have chosen the motto, "We be Stuberne fellows."

Dr. Pilot throws light on life here under Charles II and James II: "Anarchy, confusion and wickedness reigned for many years." At this time, 1656, there were about three hundred and fifty families settled in different parts of the Island. These petitioned the king for a local governor, but their request was successfully opposed by the merchants of London and Bristol who were interested in the Newfoundland trade, and who considered that all the plantations should be spoiled to satisfy their greed for gain. Half a century onward was a period of oppression to the settlers.

Under Charles II the British navy fell to its lowest ebb. Dutch fleets chased it up and down the seas and even cast anchor in the Thames. They paid a visit to St. John's in 1673, but the "stuberne" fellows there, merchants and fishermen under a John Martin of Devon, put up so hot a defence that the Dutchmen went home, or elsewhere, in search of prey having less of the hornet in its make-up. Defence was one job in which Islanders had plenty of experience. The same year John Martin and his tough assistants drove off an attack by thirty pirate ships ganged up to take over the town and all it contained. Recurrence of such visits grew wearisome, and a petition for a protecting governor and fortifications went to Charles to be refused on advice of his brother James, the king's mistresses and his ministers, all ready to support any cause at a reasonable price; and London and Bristol merchants had the money ready to bestow where it would do them the most good.

They had their way—no permanent colonization of Newfoundland. All settlers were ordered to abandon their property and go elsewhere. This was insufferable. Loud and vigorous protests sent the enforcing messenger back to Charles with a strong recommendation that the order be revoked. It was, with a compromise—settlement was limited to a thousand souls, women were forbidden to land and taverns and houses of entertainment were banned. No settler or planter, as they were then called, might live within six miles of the shore and they were not allowed to cut timber. Just how or to what extent such regulations could be enforced in such a place as this then was is beyond imagination. Records show clearly that America's ancient and ubiquitous order of rumrunners, bootleggers and moonshiners was founded then and there. How could it be otherwise? Every fish-seeking vessel from Europe brought wines and spirits somewhere in its legal load of salt, and sailors living lives of hardship, danger and austerity could not easily be persuaded that these things were unnecessary to happiness and well-being.

Most important of new regulations was the legalizing of government by "Fishing Admirals," a long-recognized arrangement and about as rough and tumble in its workings as could be devised. The master of the first fishing vessel arriving in spring became admiral for the season with all power as governor. The second was vice-admiral and the third rear-admiral. If at a

time any one of them had reasonable qualifications for governor-
ship, such as ability to read or write, the occasion was notable.
In civil law, matters were not much better.   Courts were held
in fish-barns, decisions were swift and punishment savage.
Convicted men were fined, flogged or hanged as occasion seemed
to warrant.   Later, persons accused of murder or theft (of over
forty shillings) went to England for trial, to be hanged, no doubt,
with greater formality but perhaps not much more justice.

Charles II, pensioner of Louis XIV of France, raised no
obstacle to French aggression overseas.   For more than a
century French vessels had been fishing off Newfoundland's
coast and drying their fish on shore, and for the latter part of
that time had been paying five per cent tribute for all fish
caught.   Jacques Cartier had discovered the St. Lawrence River
in 1534, thirty-seven years after Cabot's landing at Bonavista,
and Champlain had founded his settlement at Quebec in 1606,
seventy-two years later.   Development of French enterprise
in Canada with the compliance of England's king and the
wealth of Newfoundland fisheries, encouraged the French to take
over the whole Island and round out their North American
control.   Charles already had given away the best part of it—
acknowledging French rights over the south and west coasts by
a secret treaty to which Newfoundlanders paid no attention
whatsoever.   They continued to fight for what they held
wherever the enemy showed himself.

By 1662 the French had securely established themselves at
Placentia, sixty miles west across the Avalon Peninsula, and
for a century were so to bedevil the colony that survival was a
miracle of most stubborn tenacity.   Ascent of William and
Mary to the throne brought open war.   The first formal attack
on St. John's in 1696 was driven off.   That same year D'Iberville,
with a force of Canadians and Indians from Quebec, marched
over from Placentia in the depth of winter, took the town and
most of the other settlements on the coast.   The defenders of
St. John's were killed or scattered, two hundred and forty
captives were crowded into one small boat and banished and
everything in sight was destroyed.

The Treaty of Ryswick a year later freed St. John's, which again became a town, but left Placentia in French hands, so that eight years later, in 1705, when the War of the Spanish Succession raged in Europe, its governor was able to retake St. John's and generally despoil the coast. A year later a British force and some Newfoundlanders drove the French out. They found not one house standing. St. John's first permanent garrison was then established. The Treaty of Utrecht in 1713 gave the whole Island to the British but allowed French fishing rights on much of the shore, a matter that was to be a nuisance for close to two hundred years.

In all the world was there ever such a forlorn little outpost of civilization so courageously persistent in existing in rigorous climate, on ungenerous soil, and faced with such ever-recurring disaster and discouragement? But continue to exist St. John's did. And even grew a bit, in between troubles. The singular ineptitude which at the time characterized British rule of her people overseas eventually lost the American colonies, and very nearly lost Newfoundland.

Restrictive measures and the French war were having their effect on trade here. By 1700, sixteen to twenty thousand Frenchmen were employed fishing in Newfoundland waters. In a century, English ships here had decreased in number from about sixteen hundred to less than one hundred. Threatened extinction of the fishing trade wealth had brought no easing of strangling regulations. Home authority had stated, "Nothing was more dangerous to the mother country than increase of shipping in her colonies or plantations." The supply of able-bodied seamen was already falling off, and establishment of independent colonial shipping would end it forever. Time brought still more dreadful things. Newfoundland merchants and Newfoundland-going ships began to trade with the fast-growing American colonies and good business was side-stepping old England—a state of affairs not allowable for a moment. For what had God given England colonies, if not to make her rich?

Exasperation and despair moved the Islanders in 1728 to

petition George II for a governor and a more reasonable form of government. It received sympathetic consideration, no doubt to everyone's amazement, and government by high-ranking naval officers was instituted. Fishing trade had to be encouraged, and wartime naval occasions had made St. John's an important North Atlantic naval base. First governor, Captain Henry Osborne, inaugurated a century of naval administration. One can imagine the warmth of welcome greeting his arrival to survey a scene not too different from that which met the eyes of Elizabeth's messenger a century and a half earlier. The town had grown, not much, but was vastly more important. Shapes of ships had changed, and men's clothes—but men were the same—and this time arrival of authority must have been greeted with real enthusiasm. Osborne's advent marked an act of royal grace answering the prayer of petitioners. He promptly set about a measure of law reform, making courts more easily available and their decisions somewhat more in line with justice and equity.

Over the following hundred years thirty-five naval governors succeeded each other to lead St. John's and all inhabited Newfoundland along the slow and painful path toward such freedom and security as British-born peoples the world over were coming to look upon as their birthright—a slow process with many a set back but with spurts of progress here and there. These governors came out with the first fishing boats in the spring and left for home with the last. Threatened authority dies hard. The fishing admirals—representing merchant power at home—resisted naval rule, continued to hold their own rude courts, and for some years did what they could to retard the Island's development and make things generally unpleasant for those living there who were slowly increasing in number despite everything. Of successive naval governors, some took their job seriously for the benefit of the Island, others not so much so, while not a few proved quite ineffectual.

Years passed in such peace as was possible with French fishing rights firmly established on a good part of the Island's shore. Wolfe had extinguished French power in Canada in

1759 at Quebec, but three years later a forlorn-hope force paid a visit and, once more, St. John's suffered French capture. The town was held only so long as was required to bring a hastily organized force from Halifax. For many years a serious threat to British rule in Newfoundland ceased to exist.

Although freedom from war and threat of war helped, naval government brought little comfort to the settlers. Naval administration of justice proved almost as summary and as savage as that which had preceded it. Men were tried for their lives for the smallest thing. The number of courts and their powers were increased, but justices appointed were often unworthy of the trust, unfitted for its execution and over-concerned with fees and court charges. Restrictions on landowning and building remained. The first resident Church of England clergyman arrived in 1704 and sixty years later came the first Wesleyan. He too was a Church of England parson since Wesleyans, later to become Methodists and later still United, had not yet broken from their mother church. Another twenty years were to pass before Roman Catholic clergy might legally set foot on the Island—but they did—as missionaries, and accordingly were hunted and persecuted. Harbouring them was about as serious a crime as murder.

The American Revolution brought more turmoil to an already unhappy colony. They also had grievances in plenty, but apparently no thought of becoming a party to the revolt, whatever temptations to join the rebels might have existed. They went into the war for Britain with a will, net result being a considerable loss through the action of American privateers who throughout the duration pestered shore settlements and fishing vessels at sea. Also, France was again at war with England, and between the three contestants the North Atlantic was a busy fighting area.

The arrival of Vice-Admiral John Campbell in 1782, the first Roman Catholic to hold the office of governor, was preceded by a year's grant of religious toleration to people of his faith— an act having a far-reaching effect on Island life and history. The total population was something over ten thousand; that of

St. John's about two thousand. Troubled Ireland was then staggering through the deepest depths of her morass of sorrows. Oppression, dispossession and oft-recurring famine had brought about mass emigration to the American New World where it coloured politics and manner of living for generations. Newfoundland's emancipation of Roman Catholics opened the way for a flood of Irish refugees, "displaced persons" of the time. They poured into St. John's in dreadful destitution—but they stayed. They settled and lived to set upon both city and Island an indelible stamp of racial characteristics lovable and otherwise. Amongst this army of agricultural workers, and just plain workers, was a scattering of scholars, ex-landholders, tradesmen and others, mostly on the run from hated authority, and forming about as useful an addition to the colony's population as could be desired.

The latest French war called for quick action. Foreseeing an attack, St. John's citizens once again rallied to defence. Merchants, fishermen and roustabouts at the governor's call set about building forts, mounting guns and generally making ready for a first-class fight. It was then the mighty chain was laid across the harbour entrance. Heavy guns set up on Signal Hill completed preparations, and this time the British Navy was on the high seas able and eager to help. The enemy came, viewed the situation with distaste as being too warm for their stomachs, and went where defence was less practicable. The "stuberne" fellows of St. John's had won out again.

The French war had its profitable side. Enemy ships made seagoing dangerous for both French and British fishermen and Island fishing trade prospered. St. John's began to assume the aspects of a town, even starting growth up the hill. Slow amendment to legal machinery came into effect. In 1791 a court of civil and criminal jurisdiction was created and a Chief Justice appointed. Even a post office came into existence in 1805, and shortly afterwards publication of the first newspaper, *The Royal Gazette*, presented an opportunity for discussion of public affairs—no doubt in an extremely guarded way. While ear-clipping had ceased to be the commonplace reward for careless criticism of authority, other punishments provided were almost equally discouraging to anything savouring of dangerous radicalism.

St. John's population was now nearing twenty thousand and up and down the shore where isolated families had settled long ago in lonely harbours, well-established fishing villages were building up a mighty trade in fish. St. John's in 1804 recorded a catch of six hundred thousand quintals of cod—almost seventy million pounds—and thirty-four thousand seals, for seals by now were a source of wealth second only to cod. Most foodstuffs were imported. In one year eight million pounds of bread and flour, over a million pounds of beef and pork, and some quarter million gallons of rum were brought in, which says nothing about quantities run in by Americans and others whose genius for trade had the minimum respect for customs regulations. With growth came business—big business compared with past trading methods. The inevitable was happening. Control by English merchants weakened. Prosperity brought capital for shipbuilding, and to enterprising men opportunity for ownership and operation of deepsea-going ships. Shipowners became employers of labour, traders on their own account, and finally merchants stabilized Island trade and gave it a permanent basis on which to live and build.

The nature of the country and the necessities of its people fostered a system of truck-trading with important advantage to all concerned, until its abuse caused a trend toward the impoverishment of fishermen and the retarding of Island development. Merchants imported the necessities of life and took pay for them in fish. They outfitted the fisherman on credit. He paid off with his catch. A good one gave him credit for the purchase of food, clothing and other needs while a bad one left him in debt. Cash was unnecessary and so seldom appeared that many men lived to old age without ever handling a coin. This was all right in good times and where merchants gave good value for fish taken, but men tended to become completely dependent upon them. Even wages were paid in kind. It was no fault of the men that most of them could neither read nor write, and that keeping of accounts was an unfathomable mystery. Invitation to unscrupulous dealing was tempting, and many merchants set what prices they liked on both the goods they sold and the fish they bought, so that the fisherman had no chance at all and here, there, and everywhere were men who passed their whole lives in debt.

Dissatisfaction swelled to protest and petition for relief to Governor and Admiral Sir Erasmus Gower, a naval administrator with heart and imagination for Island welfare. Then came the summary sort of action that offers the only argument favouring government by a beneficent autocracy. All merchants were to announce annually on August 15th prices they were prepared to pay for fish, and prices of goods offered in exchange. Neglect brought the careless into court, where regulations set prices for their goods at the lowest point reported for the year, and prices for fish bought at the highest. For this and other benefits bestowed, they named the town's new and second most important street after this governor.

However, the other side of this picture must be shown. Trade could hardly have existed without a broad credit system. Months of bad weather or periodical absence of cod did occur, and without credit, fishermen would have gone hungry and even unable to replace losses of boats and gear—an important factor in this highly hazardous occupation. Merchants every year faced the possibility of adverse price fluctuations for fish. The merchants carried the country, founded and fostered its home trade and brought it through to prosperity. Many firms there have been whose unquestioned integrity and fair dealing have established between themselves and fishermen a partnership of confidence that has continued uninterrupted through several generations. St. John's streets and docks today carry signs bearing names of merchant houses founded when home trade first began, and present-day bearers of those names have good reason to reflect with pride upon what they and their forebears have done for their country. Truck-trading continued until comparatively recently. Men are living there today who never handled money until past middle age and whose fathers had only a remote idea of what money was. Not a few of them still voice bitter memories of peonage-like conditions once experienced, and bound to occur when such a system dominates a country's trade. Later on, in the early nineteen hundreds, the organization of consumer and producer co-operative societies and credit unions had important results in trade regulation.

The War of 1812 between England and the victory-flushed nation known as United States of America, brought Newfoundland more fighting when American privateers came pirating along the coast. It also brought prosperity. Prices of fish went to unheard of heights and catches were phenomenally large. The busy navy brought many an American prize-ship to St. John's to be sold there and become an addition to the Island fishing and trading fleet. Money was plentiful, and wages were high. It was Newfoundland's first big party and history would seem to indicate that the usual good time was had by all. For St. John's it was a sort of coming-of-age party. We read of champagne flowing abundantly and imports of luxuries hitherto unknown, while prize cattle and sheep came in as a start towards agricultural development. Island population was now eighty thousand and at least eight hundred vessels were employed in the fishing trade. Laws prohibiting settlement, landholding and building had gradually ceased to operate, and in 1813 the first grants of land were given to those who held it, including in many cases properties that had been in possession of families for two or three generations.

The end of the American and Napoleonic wars brought a sharp finish to the celebration. Wars had to be paid for, and through forty depressed, hungry, and sometimes seemingly hopeless years, Europe paid for past glories of marching armies marshalled for destruction. Natives of countries long consumers of Newfoundland's one export product no longer had money to pay for even the humble cod. Fish became unsaleable and Island trade all but died. Mercantile houses failed; credit dried up; employment ceased for most of the population; and actual hunger became no stranger in the streets where desperate men turned to violence, and citizen vigilance committees fought to maintain the peace.

Depression reached its lowest depths in the winter of 1817-1818, the coldest and bitterest then recorded, and two great fires all but wiped out the town, piling horror on misery. The British government and Halifax swiftly sent relief, while Boston, with enthusiasm equal to that with which she had recently sent privateers to harass Island shores and shipping, rushed forward a shipload of provisions. The third great fire followed a year later—adding another thousand homeless and increasing the destitution just as the promise of improving trade began to glimmer.

A rebuilt city was not the sole evidence of St. John's place as a permanent community or of the Island's importance as a stronghold for trade or war. Summertime governors were succeeded by all-year residents with power to appoint an assisting council. Country roads began to appear, farming was encouraged and facilities for administration of justice were broadened and made more available throughout the Island.

Naval government, by now proven inadequate, came to its end in 1832 when civil governors took over and a new charter granted an elected Legislative Assembly of fifteen members, from which the governor appointed an Executive Council of seven. Then and there came politics to brighten lives of all who had a taste for that sort of thing—and there were many. Folly alone would suppose that a population in which the Irish almost predominated would submit to peaceful living when cause for contention was discoverable. Failing new ones, immigrants had brought from the Old Land ancient quarrels and enough of good fighting nature to keep life interesting. The stout lads from Waterford, for the honour of their county, were ever ready to battle with "yellow-bellies" from Wexford, or anyone else, for that matter. Before politics came, amusements were not too plentiful, and with the end of fishing season life tended to become dull. A half friendly riot offered "diversion" on the occasion when a first-class engagement—accompanied by firing of guns apparently for effect only—was interrupted by sudden appearance of the wife of one of the leaders who, seizing her man by the coat and effectively swinging a big stick, gave direction and speed to his homeward steps. The crowd cheered and laughed. There could be no more fighting—that day anyway.

This sort of thing was different to the rioting that had occurred earlier in the century, about the year 1800, when a serious, though foolish, attempt at rebellion had started on the flimsiest of pretexts and centred around a few disaffected soldiers. Pet hogs then roamed the streets at will—a nuisance to others than their owners. A magistrate's orders for their confinement to backyards was proclaimed a shattering blow to the liberty of the subject and shocking disregard of the rights of hogs to prosper on delights of roadside garbage. Posted bills threatened magistrates' lives and property, and forty or fifty garrison soldiers were persuaded to desert with arms and provide a centre for an armed force arranged to rendezvous outside the town. Seemingly, the soldiers were the only ones willing to face a fight. Embattled hog-owners did not appear but authority's forces and rallied citizens did, and the rebellion was over. After a fortnight's chase, sixteen deserters were captured of whom seven were shot and five hanged following court-martial. Presumably, town hogs retired to less spacious surroundings, while citizen noses took the evening air unoffended by smells that too long had offered competition to St. John's invigorating odour of salted codfish drying in the sun. Documents found show that the rebel plan had originated in Ireland, and that many of those taking part were sworn members of the United Irish Society.

# 8

*Legislative Doings—Fight for Responsible Govern-*
*ment—First Parliament—Religious and Political*
*Troubles—Victorian Propriety and Prosperity—Govern-*
*ment by Commission—Federation with Canada.*

THE NEWLY ELECTED legislature and appointed council set up
for the governor's advice had little enough authority if he
desired advice and chose to accept what was offered. But it
formed a definite nursery for the demand of responsible government. More immediately interesting, it set up districts for which
candidates were to be elected, encouraged parties to form on
this or that platform, and provided matter of passing importance
about which citizens might legally quarrel to their hearts'
content—a pleasing diversion, no doubt, for long winter days
when there was no fishing. When the time for the second
legislative election came round, politics were organized to the
point of enthusiasm where insult and personal violence backed up
arguments that otherwise had failed in their conviction.

There was the time one honourable member of the legislature,
meeting another on the street, shook his fist in the face of his
fellow-statesman and threatened to pull his nose—high insult
in those days, and matter for duelling a few years earlier—and
the offended dignitary appealed to the House with the result
that the offender found himself summoned to the bar charged
with having violated legislative privileges. No soft answer met
the charge—quite the reverse. With the mace on his shoulder

as sign of sovereign authority, the Sergeant-at-arms marched the culprit across town to the city jail. Friends rallied round, and the Chief Justice, a reasonable man who knew his law, ordered his release on writ of habeas corpus. Legislative dignity was affronted. The culprit was re-arrested, the High Sheriff also was incarcerated for having released his prisoner and, just to make plain that the legislature was not fooling, citizenry was given the delectable sight of the Sergeant-at-arms and mace escorting the Chief Justice himself through the streets to join culprit and High Sheriff in melancholy confinement. All blew over in time, but not until England's Privy Council had convinced the legislature that it had exceeded its authority and might better look to the proper exercise of its functions and duties.

One more side light on the turmoil of a government attempting unquestioned rule over a boiling mixture of English, Irish, and Scotch, all possessing an inherent tradition of doing their own ruling and liking it—even if bad. The elected assembly was always at variance with the governor's appointed council—from the one came oppression, from the other incipient rebellion— and no padded gloves were used to soften the impact of freely given blows. The day's newspaper, representing authority, which supported it, scolds what it terms the "arrogant and scoundrelly House of Assembly," and refers to members as "low-life, lawless scoundrels." One gathers that each side had no illusions as to where the other stood. Historian Prowse and the Rev. Lewis Amadeus Anspach who lived in those times have told many such tales, each giving an intimate glimpse into St. John's life of the mid-eighteen hundreds. It is fascinating to walk through these streets among men and women whose immediate forebears took part in, or witnessed, the stirring events that make up the history of this old town.

By 1847 the demand for responsible government superseded all other matters of public consideration. So-called representative government, rendered ineffectual by overriding gubernatorial authority, had failed—just as it had in Upper and Lower Canada where the Rebellion of 1837 had been followed by the Act of Union in 1841 granting complete legislative freedom. Newfoundland's impatience grew and the battle against opposition and indifference was bitter. An attempt at amelioration of injustices and abuses had council and legislature sitting as one body for six years. They accomplished at least one thing of value, the unanimous approval of representative government as a principle, after which they reverted to separate sittings.

The population of city and country was growing quickly. Depression in England and Ireland sent great numbers of emigrants to America of whom Newfoundland received a share. Despite political troubles, the rule of civil governors had brought important progressive measures. Education received something of proper attention, agriculture was encouraged, roads began to stretch between St. John's and nearby outports, and ministrations of clergy and churches exerted a beneficial influence throughout scattered settlements. St. John's was becoming a city. With renewed activity in fishing and sealing, better times were again in sight. While the disaster of its greatest conflagration yet devastated three-quarters of its area in 1846, and more than one gale of terrific ferocity spread death and ruin among the fishing fleets, its people—hardened to adversity and rigorous toil—drove through to solid and permanent betterment.

The fight for representative government had all the animosity and tenacity that had marked the struggle for that same cause wherever peoples of British origin had moved towards the setting up of their own political households. Official authority and its favourites, particularly job-holders, fought hard, but among the politicians were a few leaders of vision and power, and demand became so universal and insistent that the British Government could not but grant what the United States had seized and Canada had won. Queen Victoria was now on the throne and governments everywhere were more or less groping towards political reform. Merchant influence in England, so long the bedeviler of Newfoundland affairs, manned its last ditches in the fight against change. Island prosperity pleased them not at all. "They're building roads in Newfoundland now," shouted horrified scorn, "next thing they'll be riding over them in carriages." But merchant influence waned in the turmoil of fierce insistence on the rights of the governed, and 1855 saw Newfoundland mistress of her own affairs.

Another high spot in Island history is the arrival of a non-dictating governor and the establishment of homemade and fully powered parliament. Crowded that day are the streets, newly rebuilt after the last great fire. Merchants, fishermen, all the wives, and all the children are out to witness this state event marking the triumph of hope and effort through many years. Despite the grimness of life on what was then considered the Arctic's outer edge, St. John's knew something of regal procedure in state doings. Naval governors had been sticklers for ceremonial dignity, with guards of honour and other trappings of official etiquette. One of the last had built Government House to surround himself with such attributes of vice-royalty as impressed and delighted the common people. The legislative building was now five years old, and the spot on which we stood the other day witnessed a scene as similar as possible to the one we were watching, except that crowds were larger, more jubilant and noisier, and far more picturesque. A more brilliantly gilded and feathered guard accompanied the Governor through a sea of tall beaver hats and varied-coloured tail-coats displaying waistcoats as brilliant as crinolines and bonnets gave a final glow to the picture. One difference, of course, was that dwellings now standing across the street and down the hillside were not there to block the view of the little town gathered about the harbour far below.

Government of themselves by themselves brought no political peace. Defeat of those who had united Newfoundlanders in the fight for home rule was followed by an upsurge of religious animosities unavoidable in times so shortly removed from the days of struggle to the death between Protestant and Catholic. The population was about evenly divided, and the unscrupulous on each side sought power and patronage by exploitation of religious prejudices. Rowdies and professional bludgeon-men provoked conflict, and riots became commonplace despite the efforts of control made by authorities and clergy of both sides.

The culmination came in 1861 with a riot to end all riots.

Unprecedented fury shook the town. The riot act was read, then gunfire, with three men killed, many wounded, and the fury subsided into horror. Roman Catholic Bishop Mulock called, even drove a mob of rioters into his cathedral, held the sacramental chalice high before them, and exacted a promise of peaceful home-going. There were no more riots but authority hastened to arrange fair distribution of place and patronage on denominational lines.

An early outstanding historic event had been an appalling outbreak of virulent cholera. The scourge moved freely about the world those days, striking swiftly wherever conditions offered welcome. Suffering and sorrow swept over the community relieved, as far as could be, by the shining evidence of charity's perpetual readiness to answer the call of human need. Historians stress the devotion and sacrifice of St. John's religious leaders of all denominations in fighting this plague and comforting the afflicted.

So, through one trouble and another, and doubtless many joys, St. John's had fought its way towards cityhood, while the Island as a whole was emerging from the state of a sparsely peopled colonial outport on the outer edge of civilization, to take its recognized place as a young and growing country with a character of its own that would not be denied expression.

About here somewhere—in mid-eighteen hundreds—St. John's was assuming something of the appearance it now presents. Fire had destroyed any long-standing buildings, and larger and finer ones were replacing them. Victorian manners and morals flavoured industrial and commercial progress throughout the English-speaking world. Victorian England growing rich and great, set up—among less desirable things—new and different standards of behaviour which, unfashionable as they may be now, gave new purpose and colour to life, and cast a creative influence for good over the whole world.

Prosperity had returned to the Island. Cod crowded the sea in all directions. Increasing European populations now had money to pay for food. Fish-exporting firms multiplied and waxed rich so that outport harbours came to be lined with great warehouses, and Newfoundland ships became a familiar sight in faraway world ports. Cod became a staple of diet for Caribbean Sea peoples and West Indian trade flourished profitably. St. John's must have been one of world's busiest ports. Records do not tell how many ships bore the name as home-port, but seemingly no harbour many times its size could shelter them all at one time. One firm alone had a hundred seagoing vessels fishing and trading, and the port homed at least eighty others, busy rendering good red gold out of the sealing industry.

Such a flood of wealth could not but bring far-reaching social changes, and Victorian graciousness of living became the standard striven for and attained. Returning ships brought back new tastes, fashions and commodities to gratify them, and homes reflected a flavour of culture and knowledge up to now infrequently discernible. Fine houses were rising for a better measure of enjoyment, and country homes, ever a hallmark of Englishmen's stabilized prosperity, began to spot the nearby countryside. Even the horrid fears of old-time English merchants were realized. Newfoundlanders were driving over their new roads— and in carriages. Naturally enough, the inbred English and Irish love of horses brought racing, continuously enjoyed through the years, until today's well-attended annual trotting meets in the park down near Quidi-Vidi Lake.

Government House set the standard of social etiquette to which garrison officers and visiting naval dignitaries frequently added grace, and gave delight to St. John's ladies who, report says, and present evidence would suggest, were as lovely and charming as they were numerous. Government House always had been a stickler for propriety. There was the occasion of the ball at which His Excellency had graciously consented to appear. Three o'clock in the morning came but no Governor, and the welcoming committee, giving up its long wait, went about its business of enjoying the party. His Excellency, arriving later and unmet by official salutations, turned about and drove home in what then was termed high dudgeon. He had to be sent for, handsomely apologized to, and otherwise mollified before returning. The ball, no doubt, was resumed and joy was unconfined.

Propriety seeped down the line of officialdom. There was the Chief Justice who had the royal coat of arms set up over his door and insisted that every passing hat should be lifted in respect. The penalty for not doing so was a fine or perhaps a day or two in jail—about the same meted out to citizens over-imbibing to a point of public nuisance. It is clearly recorded that more than one of His Majesty's chief officers of the law had been stout-hearted, forthright sort of fellows, given to direct action and, under provocation, to language considered violent even in a seaport, and if the man with the coat of arms was of that kidney, it might be that passers-by, neglectful of hat-raising, suddenly found the Chief Justice bouncing out of his front door armed with cudgel for effective belabouring of impolite, rebellious so-and-so's. Many times in the past had public offenders met such swift rebuke at the hands of the chief guardian of law and order. But softening influences of Victorian moderation must have toned down such brilliant spots of colour in the life of the old city. One hopes that not too soon did police constable uniforms fade into modern dullness. Their tailed blue coats, red waistcoats and cocked hats of early days must have contributed greatly to law's majesty and the cheery appearance of city streets. Requirement of full dress always for judges and magistrates would be even slower dying out.

The inauguration of responsible government was followed shortly after by a visitation that set the stamp of royal approval and good wishes on Newfoundland's job of setting up housekeeping for itself. H.R.H. the Prince of Wales, much later to be King Edward VII, dropped in on his way to Canada and the United States to receive a welcome from three-quarters of the Island's entire population that, for enthusiastic expression, outdid anything St. John's had ever seen, and was only to be equalled, or perhaps exceeded, upon occasions of later royal visits. Not that Newfoundland was entirely unused to the august presence of royalty on its shores. Long years before, the sailor son of George III, later William IV, appeared several times in St. John's when on West Indian naval duty.

By now Newfoundland had its "society," and a very pleasant form of society it was, as much given to balls and other polite forms of amusement as any vigorous young community could be, all of course conducted with punctilious regard for Victorian niceties, some now considered more amusing to read about than to observe. Long winters must have been gay times for young and old in those days—parties, sleigh rides and music filled the nights. And, of course, there was skating, but for young women that came a little later on for it was somewhat too boisterous, and perhaps a little unladylike. Daring spirits who tried it, and there were a few among the many who wished to, are reported to have been persuaded to confine themselves to less immodest activities through threat of distinct social disapproval.

Prosperity again was general. Ships from all Europe filled the harbour for outfitting and trade, and brought varied products to a ready market. Their crews gave life and colour to sailor's haunts. Songs of Spain, Portugal, Italy, and rousing roars of English chanties and Irish melodies, twanging of guitars and wailings of concertinas were heard from every harbour-side tavern where port was a shilling a bottle and rum from the Jamaicas hardly more costly—good old days for merchants, gentry and workers, days such as old men sigh for and young men never believe to have existed. And on the other side of the towering wall of rock forming the harbour lay the rude, challenging North Atlantic, inviting adventure in calm or in storm, but ever offering bountiful harvest to those having courage and stamina to go out fighting for it. Such qualities had Newfoundland set deep in the makeup of her sons and daughters, and without them existence in this land could know neither pleasure nor profit.

So life here moved on to take on the colour of our own times. Awakened civic pride brought fine buildings and churches, bearing witness to the excellent standard of taste then current. Better still, liberal expenditures carried improved educational facilities into outports where hunger for knowledge was keen among communities whose opportunity for even rudimentary schooling had been meagre, if existing at all.  Illiteracy had been widespread back home, when and from where the immigrants had come in earlier days, and for many of the older generation education had little or no significance.  Communication between shore-hamlets was by sea only, often difficult and sometimes impossible for lengthy periods, and the cost of schooling for tiny, isolated villages had been far beyond the colony's resources.

Except in a few local instances, established churches provided the sole means of instigating and carrying on this work.  They did it as well as means and opportunities permitted, so that religion and elementary teaching went forward hand in hand. English contributions for missionary endeavour, and the sending out of workers from the homeland, had greatly broadened church work and influence throughout the Island.  With representative and later responsible government came recognition of educational needs, and as generous a contribution to their fulfilment as was then possible.  Scholarship of high standard was far from unknown.  Learned men were among the clergy of all denominations, and in professional and other walks of life were many from universities of the Old Land whose public spirit and intelligent knowledge of the country's need made them leaders in the educational effort.

The history of the latter half of the nineteenth century and early twentieth is the story of economic struggle and growth, slow but definitely forward against many and grievous setbacks.  Early eighteen-sixties saw the opening up of interior areas, awakening interest in farmable lands of the far west coast, while discoveries of copper ore started mining operations.  But thereabouts came three years of poor fishing, and since fishing totalled over ninety per cent of entire industry, trade stagnation was inevitable.  Later business improvement brought into political consideration possibilities of establishing a sounder economic base for future development through union with Canada then moving towards Confederation.  The government in power fathered the project and carried negotiations far.  To many, the prospect of relinquishing the freedom to do their own governing, long and hardly fought for, was far from pleasant. The opposition party opened a vigorous campaign in which feeling ran high, and the following election saw the government defeated and Federation definitely shelved, while Canada went on her own way towards Dominionhood.

Well before the nineteenth century's end a fair measure of prosperity returned with an abundance of fisheries and some development of home industries. Always daringly adventurous, Newfoundlanders now set out upon that period of railway construction that before it was finished pretty well ruined the country's credit. Meanwhile, however, road-building and opening of farming areas and other costly projects went forward while the population increased to somewhere about two hundred thousand.

In the year 1892 disaster struck hard. Gales, even violent tempests, with consequent damage and loss of life were commonplace happenings on that Northern Atlantic coast, but in all memory nothing had been recorded to equal the fury of storms experienced that year. Fleets of fishing vessels were broken up and mostly destroyed and many a shore village came to be inhabited largely by widows and orphans. The same year saw St. John's greatest conflagration yet. Three-quarters of the city was destroyed and eleven thousand people made homeless. In such times as these rich and poor suffered alike, and the demands of common humanity brought each closer to the other in an effort of mutual aid.

Two years later, ere the fire-swept ruins had been cleared away or the fishing industry had half recovered, came an economic crisis compared with which all others seemed trivial. Government spending on railroads and other public services, together with other requirements, had exhausted resources and piled up debt to a point where credit ceased to exist. Banks closed; business practically stopped; employment dwindled; and want manifested itself in bread-riots. They were grim days, with no promise of escaping complete ruin visible in any direction. A swift and generous grant of British money for relief purposes ameliorated distress, but proposals for the Imperial

Government's taking over Newfoundland's affairs came to nothing since they involved the Island's possible loss of financial control. Union with Canada again emerged, this time as a possible lifesaving opportunity. Exploratory negotiation proceeded very well, with Canada proposing terms somewhat more liberal than previously offered, but the railway debt was too great for the Dominion Government to assume in fairness to the other Provinces and Federation went back to its place on the shelf.

Nothing was to be done but grit the teeth, square the shoulders, and carry on with what native stubbornness they had and whatever good chance Providence might send them. They did just that. Stubbornness paid, and Providence proved kindly. Canadian banks took over their monetary troubles and, as time went on, fishing improved, new ships and gear slowly came into production and overseas markets for fish were more than ever receptive. Most encouraging sign of betterment was a widening diversification of Island industry. Though greater in volume than ever before, fish had decreased from ninety to seventy-five per cent of total exports, while those of mineral and forest products had tripled. Development of rich iron deposits on Bell Island in Conception Bay opened the vision of a new source of basic wealth, and the completion of a trans-island railway to Port aux Basques, with the establishment of regular passenger and freight shipping services, helped to broaden production and trade. Meanwhile, the long-continued argument with United States on fishing rights in Newfoundland waters was satisfactorily settled. More important still, French claims to exclusive rights on much of the shore were relinquished in return for British government concessions in North Africa. Thus a bitter controversy spiked with frequent and always annoying incidents came to an end, and largely, says Rev. W. Pilot, through the personal intervention of Edward VII, the peacemaker king who had fond recollections of his long-past visit and the opportunity to become acquainted with Newfoundland's troubles.

The First Great War in 1914 found the country comfortably

recovered from earlier depression and left it in a short-lived condition of prosperity. Happy days those, in most parts of the world. The war to end all wars had finished in a manner satisfactory to most of those involved, and who could be so mad as ever to start another. But the early nineteen-twenties saw the bills coming in demanding payment, and Newfoundland escaped none of the world's reaction to the business booms which followed the war. Those were difficult times, particularly for the debt-laden, and of such Newfoundland was an outstanding example.

Newfoundland's contribution to the British war effort in men and treasure was, for so small a population of limited wealth, too great for her economic resources, even though wartime inflation carried fish prices to unheard-of heights, and every young industrial activity brought unprecedented returns into the country. Terrific war expenditures had piled up a national debt of serious proportions. All might have been well had not railway operating costs so far exceeded revenues that private ownership failed. The company went bankrupt and operation stopped dead in 1923. Only government credit could lift such a load, so the government took over and carried on with borrowed money, borrowing being not too difficult in those flush days. How different a little later on in the thirties. The unrelenting, uncontrollable fish-trade barometer fell lower and lower, business touched new points of depression and government revenues dwindled. Debts called for payment when the interest charges were almost more than could be raised. Again credit was suspended and borrowing impossible.

Final and only source of help was appeal to the British Government for a royal commission of experts to explore the whole desperate situation and find a way out. The result was that in February, 1934, responsible government passed out of existence as a luxury no longer possible, and politics, patronage and party prejudices virtually ceased to exist as an influence in the control of public affairs. This was Commission Government—three men from Great Britain and three Newfoundlanders, all to sit under chairmanship of a British-appointed Governor, and to rule the Island under general supervision of the British Dominions Office experts. It worked. Britain, having control of the spending, advanced money to carry on, and the Commission sat down to its job of dealing with the general depression, widespread unemployment, and a heritage of sadly involved finances.

Commission Government lasted fifteen years, and when time brought its finish, it was because the work had been well done. Newfoundland economy once more had been placed upon a sound basis. Not without criticism was this accomplished. There were those who did not like its original set-up, disapproved some Commission acts or charged it with autocratic disregard of Newfoundland advice—all perhaps inevitable. But the fact stands that, aided by steady if slow improvement in world affairs, Commission Government led the way to a considerably developed fish-trade on more modern lines; opened up wider agricultural possibilities; instigated new mining, pulp and paper and lumbering operations; effected important educational and social measures; improved railway and coastal ship-carrier services; and finally left in the country's coffers a matter of some thirty million dollars. The Second World War found Newfoundland no less swift and eager to take her place in fighting lines on sea and land, and in the air, she made generous contributions as wartime trade expansion hastened a return to economic wealth.

Having their affairs in order and every prospect of continued solvency, her people now turned definite thought towards the re-establishment of responsible government. The original agreement gave life to Commission Government only until the country should again be self-supporting. The British Government, having decided such situation had been arrived at, called for the general election of a national convention to formulate a "free and informed decision" regarding the future form of government.

Forty-five elected convention members gave long and careful debate to varied solutions offered, discussed terms under which Commission Government might be perpetuated, sought from Canada and United States suggestions of what might be hoped for from federation with either, and finally recommended a referendum to voters giving a choice of either responsible government or continuation of commission, the proposed inclusion of confederation with Canada having been defeated in convention by twenty-nine votes to sixteen. The British Government, in light of strong protests from the federationists, decided that voters favouring union with Canada should have an opportunity of saying so, and in a national referendum of June, 1948, sixty-four thousand said so. But sixty-nine thousand odd stood for representative government and twenty-two thousand called for continued government by Commission—clearly no absolute majority in any direction and reason enough for seeking decisive answer from another vote. In July of the same year, the voters again went to the polls to record seventy-eight thousand for confederation and seventy-one thousand for responsible government. A seven thousand majority in a total vote of one hundred and fifty thousand was not great, but the Canadian Prime Minister, Mackenzie King, a week later heralded it as "clear beyond all possibility of misunderstanding, an expression of Newfoundland's will to federate," and at midnight, March 31, 1949, Newfoundland became the tenth Canadian Province.

Campaigns preceding the voting were vigorous, exhaustive and stubbornly fought, and public interest keen enough to take eighty-eight per cent of the electorate to the polls on the first referendum and eighty-five on the second—an Island-wide display of individual concern in national affairs such as seldom is witnessed among the workings of democratic government at its best. Naturally enough, intense feeling, even bitterness, had a place. Every side of opinion was subjected to sharp examination and, not infrequently, to outspoken suspicion, and frequently to a direct charge of being inspired by motives less patriotic than profitable to its supporters. As in no previous election here, radio carried argument for and against into every isolated seagirt hamlet, and no voter could be ignorant of what it was all about, or how the decision might ultimately effect the future manner of life. In short, it was exactly the kind of election it should have been—an entire people spoke their will, and that from the heart.

If the final decision left regret or even bitterness in the minds of anti-federationists, it hardly could have been otherwise. But already time and experience dull the sharp edges of controversy, and most likely the coming generation will have time or patience for none of it. The truth is that throughout the Island few Newfoundlanders had much liking for what seemed to be a surrender of their supreme governing powers to "foreign" authority, no matter how close the kinship with future partners in nationhood, nor how bright future horizons might promise to be. Past history had made them home-rulers at heart, and a proposed change for all time could not be viewed without misgivings, distrust or even dread. Comparatively few knew Canada except as a rich western country that had turned them down twice before when they had approached federation in time of dire necessity. Not as impoverished, bankrupt and creditless distant relative did Newfoundland now offer herself in partnership. Her debts controlled, a comfortable surplus in the bank, prospects of modernized ways of fishing and marketing, broad development of forests and mines, all these created visions of stabilized well-being, but the wiser among them knew them as visions only to be realized by force of great capital expenditures under industrial leadership that had to come from the outside.

World wars had clearly demonstrated that the Island defence was a matter far beyond Newfoundland's strength and resources, and protection could come only from some powerful allied state. But such protection would offer far from one-sided benefits. The North Atlantic has no finer naval bases than those which make the Island a mighty bastion standing in the sea-gateway to North America's heart. Almost any of them could be another Gibraltar. Without Newfoundland Canada could be only incomplete, both geographically and in matter of defence—pre-eminently important in a world which seems to be stumbling back into the savagery of continual international violence.

Of the other contributions to Canada's enlargement, outstanding were the huge mineral resources already discovered with the likelihood of greater yet to be revealed on both the Island and in Labrador.   Cubic miles of high-grade iron ore are only an instance, important as they are.   More than one Islander, not liking Confederation, complains that Great Britain had thrown his country into Canada's eagerly welcoming lap to preserve for both this lifeblood stream of industrial effort and wartime power.   True or not, that and the St. Lawrence defence could be weighty factors in any balance of negotiation.   Free entry of Canadian products into Newfoundland's comparatively small market might be no tremendous boon, but worth considering.

Had Newfoundland brought into Confederation no contribution other than the thousands of opportunity-seeking young men and women which present-day home economic conditions thrust into other countries, that was a consideration to out-weigh many an objection to the proposal.   The most urgent need of Canada is more people of her own kind, and nowhere than here are better to be found—with the same racial origins, the same language and religions, a similar political background and aspirations, and completely inured to Canadian climatic vagaries.   Through past years a great number have gone to the United States. From now on, probably more will move west to another part of what is now their own country and shall inherit their proper share of it since, in the matter of inheriting, courage and industry would seem to be a very good second to simple meekness.

# 9

*Now Let's Go On to See the Country—Train Journey
North along Conception Bay—Carbonear the Codfishing
Town—The Irish Princess Who Became Newfound-
land's First Mrs. Pike—Carbonear Island's Gallant
Stand.*

YOU MUST SEE Carbonear, they told me—and, while Harbour
Grace was beautiful and Bay Roberts lovely, Brigus was a place
where wealth of history and charm compelled a visit from any
inquiring soul seeking knowledge of Newfoundland and its
people. So, since these notable outports and others equally
promising in interest lay along the shore of Conception Bay,
obviously there ran the path of one journey into the Newfoundland we came to see. A branch-line of the railway, and an easily
navigable hard-surfaced road extends northward over most of
the peninsula's length. It is a peninsula with Conception Bay
on the east side and Trinity Bay on the west, and between the two
lie most of the history and population now to be found outside
the ancient capital city.

The railway journey promised added interest—travelling
people, station-platform groups, and wide views of country not
otherwise to be seen, so the first happy sojourn in St. John's ended
when our busy little train boastfully snorted its way up-grade
from the town's innermost and busiest harbour-side corner into
open country far behind the protecting barrier of a grim rock
coast. Doubtless the country hereabouts is seen at its best on a

sunny midsummer morning, and very lovely it then is. Again vividly colourful landscape assaults the eye. Groups of tree-sheltered multi-coloured houses give place to suburban areas where modern homes stand in blossom-embroidered gardens. Flowers do well in this country, a bit late in coming, perhaps—compared with those back on the mainland—but very glorious in their profusion. Lilac and wisteria run late into June when long days of sunlight bring every growing thing forward with a rush. Then comes farming country, and there seems to be quite a lot of it in this part of the Island. The land looks good and growing crops show promise, while groups of well-fed, contented Jersey cattle speak well for the food value of the soil. Soon we are in sight of Conception Bay and run some fifteen or so pleasant miles along its shore.

No hurry about this train—it just meanders. True, it puts on a burst of speed now and then as grades permit, and goes ever forward as though determined to get somewhere some time. But when we come to a station—that's where we have a rest, and enjoy in placid quietude the long minutes to spare allowed by those little bursts of speed back along the line. There's much to be done at every station, too. Country folk have many parcels to collect before they alight, and almost always a few children; passengers coming aboard have much to say to friends seeing them off. Then there's express matter to be delivered, train despatches to be read and discussed, and important things like that. So, happily, we have plenty of time to view the station, the community it serves and the surrounding country with the ocean spread out far behind. But best of all, we meet good-natured groups of people brought together by the train's tri-weekly arrival.

Conception Bay is a twenty-mile-wide arm of the Atlantic thrust thirty miles deep into mostly mountainous rock. All along its shore are bays and river mouths around which farms, summer homes and villages vary the oppressive monotony of wild and rugged scenery. Pretty homes they are, along this south shore of the bay, with Holyrood offering perhaps the greatest delight in its charming setting and picturesque spotting of modern styled houses along the shore and highway that passes through here on its way up the peninsula. Holyrood is one of those places approachable on the land side only from the clouds. Long before the station stop it appears far below, spread about the southernmost corner of the great bay, and just here one longs for a camera charged with some highly efficient colour-film, and resolves never to travel without it again.

The pleasantest part of this trip is the run from St. John's to this spot, for much of the way lies at the ocean's edge, with here and there a stony beach for track-bed. In every bay are fishermen's homes with prosperous-looking potato patches alongside. Here's a picture for memory's book—a young woman saunters between fat green rows of plants leisurely swinging a hoe as though in time to a tune, and maybe she is singing—she looks as though she would on slightest provocation. Her breeze-fluttered frock reveals a strong lithe form standing out against sea and sky, as a wave of the hand and a grave slow smile sends her cheery benediction on our train-borne travelling.

At most of these villages a dock stands out into the sea where sturdy-looking youngsters dangle a hook from rod and line and watch caplin playing around it. The clarity of the water here astonishes the newcomer and so do shoals of little fish teeming landwise in green sunlit depths. Caplin time is at its height and children's pails and baskets quickly fill. Along the shore groups of wading men slowly drag fish-swollen seine nets to land and the wriggling contents are shovelled into rude sleds until stout ponies can drag no more over the stony beach, and away they go—some to the frying-pan, more to be sun-dried for winter meals, but most to straw and refuse piles, rich food for next season's vegetable garden.

At Holyrood we leave the sea and climb a toilsome grade for a dash over the hills to Brigus Junction, where the northern branch leaves the winding main line. A barren sort of country this, rock, clumps of scrub bush, wide patches of peaty soil, many of the little lakes that account for one-third of the Island's surface, and generally an air of melancholy solitude to which the summer sun imparts little geniality or friendship. Two or three tiny lumber-built hamlets house forest workers, cutters of timber and pulpwood, and here again a few sheep wander over the lonesome village areas and seem to scrape an adequate living from amazingly unpromising hillsides of rock.

Brigus Junction is just that, a place where the only industry is the shunting of freight cars from one track to another for passing trains to pick up—and that takes time as the Newfoundlander does it. Something has been written about trains always being on time—true enough for main-line travel in summertime, but branch-line business is different. Travel here is mostly a social affair, and well enough done in leisurely fashion. The train's main business is freight and mail, and neither in vast quantities. For those in a hurry there's the road and bus services of one kind and another, and, to tell the truth, most people travel that way except in winter when railway business picks up. Fellow-passengers by now are reduced to a small number of comfortable-looking country people, and all know each other, or know somebody who knows somebody more or less related, and conversation fills the air in a chorus of births, deaths, marriages, domestic misdoings and important things of that nature.

Seated at the end of the car are a man and his wife whose appearance commands study. No blight of frustration or lack of dignity mars his face stamped with eighty or ninety years of rugged living. Plenty of iron-grey hair and a bristling moustache give character to his round ruddy face from which intelligent inquiring eyes modestly scan the chattering groups nearby. His rough costume is that of the woodsman with heavy half-knee-high boots. Strong hands clasp a "turkey" filled, no doubt, with a change of clothing as fresh from the tub as the tieless shirt emerging from his home-knit guernsey. He is not mentally at rest—unaccustomed, perhaps, to sitting idle amongst strangers. His wife is not so disturbed—maybe the stronger character of the two. Hers is a placid unruffled face to which a smile comes easily, as we learn when he directs a gruff remark in her direction. The long nose and broad brow suggest Norman-French origin, and the comfortable girth many years well carried—altogether a capable personality imposed upon what must have been striking beauty in youth. The jar of a sudden train-stop and falling baggage brings a welcome opening into a conversation that could hardly be intruded otherwise. Talk is friendly but politely reticent and the picture emerges bit by bit. There's many a taste of old Devon in their speech. Eighty-six years lie behind him, most of them spent in fishing. Hard times sent him back into the woods where he stayed. He is going now to visit a son and see salt water for the first time in twenty years. To that he eagerly has looked forward despite the long journey of almost a hundred miles. But he knows it will not be like old days.

"Fishin's nowt like to wot it were in moi toime. When oi were a young-un a boat full of cod were nowt to make a man fish-proud. Boats came in loaded to the gunnels and for every fish there'd be salt and a barrel waitin'."

But life hasn't been too bad. A decent living came from the woods with a fair enough share of pleasures. Twelve children this couple have given the world—a son at Carbonear, two girls married back home, a boy lost at sea and boys and girls away off in Canada—all married and doing well, too, he supposes, for it's seldom they hear from any of them. Eleven grandchildren make up the latest count, but that was some while back and surely there's more now.

On the platform the couple are met by a young man and woman and two children—all as modern in appearance as St. Catherines Street, Montreal. Greetings are quiet, even reserved, as they crowd into an ancient motor car and roll on down the road, a typical family of one basic way of life in this country. Astonishment will agitate no Island eyebrow because of the twelve children. Here again I learn of one pair still running their own home in stout and hearty fashion, whose offspring number twenty, of whom nineteen are alive and well. One would like to know the number of grandchildren, but that seems to be beyond counting or memory. St. John's newspaper this month records the passing of a citizen entitled to much honour by reason of a grand total of ten children, thirty-two grand-children and thirty great-grandchildren—may his tribe increase.

Our train turns seaward for frequent and leisurely stops

serving villages scattered along the shore.   In time, a couple of
hours behind schedule and who cares, we arrive at Carbonear,
end of the line and one of the larger outports of the Island.
You'd hardly think so to look at it now, or guess its history
crowded past.   A kindly station-agent directs us to a preferable
hotel—the only one—with meals hearty and good and rooms
clean enough.   Further comment is uncalled for since patrons
seem mostly business travellers intent on laying in sustenance before rolling on their way.   Courteous friendliness greets the visitor throughout this pleasant town.   Over three thousand people
inhabit the frame houses standing in gardens—more or less cared-
for—around the harbour and up the hillside beyond.   A lively,
quietly busy, self-respecting people they appear to be, with a
liking for salty humour, more given to hearty inward chuckles
than to boisterous laughter.

English origins predominate.   The 1945 census for the town
and district reports that of the 13,000 total, 10,500 are English,
2,200 Irish, 35 Scottish, 30 French and a dozen or so from lands
of little importance to the record.   Religion is somewhat more
important, for here it has a strong impact on life.   Two-thirds
of the people are Protestant, the United Church handsomely
leading with 1,600.   The Church of England has 600, Salvationists about 300, Pentecostals fourteen, and Presbyterians one,
the latter, no doubt, firm against church union but having no
kirk in the neighbourhood.   The Roman Catholics number
about eleven hundred.

The main street, beside the water, has an old-world look,
not so old that it reeks of history, but old enough to have a long-
settled look and an atmosphere hinting at times of bustling
prosperity.   A hundred years might cover the life of the oldest
of these stout frame buildings and cheery, busy shops, and since a
respectable age already had graced the town when they were
built, they have but replaced others swept away by recurring
fires.   Between street and harbour are wharves and business
places, and many a tidy ship lies alongside or anchored out in
the bay.   Time was when warehouses and stores were stone-
built, but fire destroyed them too, and sawmills and lumbering in

the district made timber plentiful. Oldtimers quote their grandparents that rocks now bare were forest covered to the sea a hundred years ago when men were doing too well on the sea to be tempted from home and families by arduous toil in the woods. Besides—Providence had clearly designed trees and timber for the building of ships, and where many ships took the sea, many men were needed to work them.

Those truly were days of many ships here—hundreds of them, bringing in wet, silvery cod and carrying salt-dried cargoes across the world to bring back gold and merchandise. An ancient townsman blueing the air with tobacco, leaning on a convenient rail and casting a critical eye on men repairing the dock below, enlarges on this:

"No, sir, fishing's no good just now." He points seaward. "Lots of fish out there, but what's the good of bringing 'em in? Nobody overseas got any money to buy 'em, and their money's no good anyhow. But it'll come back some day. Fifty years ago it was different. Man, I've seen this harbour so full of ships tied up you could walk dry-foot across it over the decks."

You look at the mile-wide bay, wind-tossed and sun-glinted, murmur polite amazement and set it down for a good story, but a couple of days in town and hearing it often enough sometimes from undoubtable authority compels acceptance. What a joyous sight it must have been on a day such as this—a never-ending maze of masts and rigging; the crowded busy decks; sea-going sounds of creaking blocks and rattling capstans; all the mad call of faraway seaports; and the challenge of a rolling sea and a favouring wind to urge a tight little ship over it. Who could expect youngsters with this before them to discover a desire for working in the woods or on the land.

Midafternoon sees the street at its busiest. Shoppers throng the sidewalks, motor cars buzz about, and busses from the highway stop to exchange old passengers for new. The ever-present ponies haul two-wheeled carts up and down. And here it is we have our first meeting with the Newfoundland goat for which, apparently, no Newfoundlander has a good word, but few towns or villages lack their presence, giving a touch of colour to the streets, and perhaps an added diversion for the children at least.  Sheep are there, of course, but they keep to the side-roads where grass is more plentiful and people less so.  The goat finds human company of some interest and strolls through busy areas with mild unconcern.  There's fun in the sight of a deep-bellied, street-crossing nannie with a pair of frolicsome kids at an age when even a goat can have charm holding up traffic and pausing midway to enjoy a discarded banana peel, while the brakes of an on-coming bus squeal in agony and gears grind in noisy rage.

In early evening after tea, for in most Island homes the evening meal is tea, throngs of young people liven the scene going movie-wards, or to meet friends when work of school or home is done.  The number of girls and young women is astonishing since here, and throughout the Island, men are in the majority, and keen smart-looking young people they are, both male and female.  Generally it is a scene that might be witnessed in any mainland town, more colourful perhaps, and somehow gayer.  It may be that the girls' costumes and their kerchiefs are brighter.  Slim, slack-clad figures dash about on bicycles numerous enough to recall long past years, and useful here where automobiles are few.  They say the number of bicycles has more than doubled on the Island since Federation's tariff changes cut the cost almost in half—a source of much youthful satisfaction.

Obviously, not all young people have turned their feet towards foreign lands of promise, and one wonders how their time is occupied and what the future holds for them.  Industrial opportunity is limited.  A fish-packing plant at nearby Harbour Grace employs some of the girls, small town industries, local shops and domestic activities a few others, but there must be many of both sexes for whom youthful visions of broader fields for living and working are brighter, and more insistent than ties of home—a sad thing for those left behind, sad too for those who go, and good only for the far-off country receiving them.  All this seems inevitable under present economic conditions, and a situation to be corrected only by industrial development.  Competent

authorities see possibilities in this direction and the present
government is making strenuous effort to interest foreign capital
and leadership. Therein lies the hope of economic salvation.

A hundred, even fifty years ago, it was all so different.
Homes were more self-sustained and there was more to be done in
sustaining them. Fast freighting of mass-manufactured commodities at low rates had not yet seized the home markets rendering
unprofitable the home production of foodstuffs, clothing, home
furnishings and even desirable luxuries. Gardens and farms
made an all-important contribution to daily living. The home
spinning wheels and looms, and small local industries retained for
home circulation and employment much of the wealth now going
abroad. Here is one instance. Modern mass production and
low shipping costs have flooded Newfoundland with Prince
Edward Island potatoes despite the suitability of its soil and
climate to their production. Here they say it's not worth while
growing them—surely defeatist reasoning. Modern methods
and machinery are not the exclusive property of any one area
or community. A relatively small capital surely could supply
both, and train young men for successful operation, not as a
small part-time occupation but on as broad a scale as has elsewhere been proved possible. Good land is being farmed in this
neighbourhood and much more awaits clearing, draining and
plowing.

Carbonearians are a kindly and genial people, and notably
so among them is the friendly man who left his shop to an
assistant while showing me the huge timber United Church
standing in a well-cared-for graveyard well up on the hill. Here
lies an ancient cannon half buried in the sod about which no
date, record or legend whispers of its history or how it came
here. The oldest gravestone discoverable bears the date of 1717.
Queen Anne ruled then, and forty-two years later Wolfe took
Quebec. One builds visions of what the churchyard, town and
harbour looked like almost two hundred and fifty years ago.
There is no evidence of any church having stood here then, or
for long after that time. All other inscription on this stone is
undecipherable and others of a similar date are equally unread-

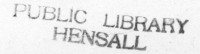

able. But in 1785, four years after finish of the American Revolution, and at age of twenty-three was laid to rest:

> The prudent Mary dere & only wife
> of Jemmy Gary now of Carbonear
> Who wholly the laws of God did fear
> For whose good works let each who passes pray
> Her soul to rest full blessed forever.

Certainly neither United, Wesleyan nor Methodist Church was here in those days. It was years later the Roman Catholics were first allowed to practise their religion, and there is that about the inscription suggesting that Mary was one of the first of that faith to be allowed public burial according to its rites.

They were long-lived in those days, too, as indicated by the line, "Here lies Elizabeth Penny, died June 16, 1815, aged 102." But for a time at least the most recent arrival at this final gathering of local worthies promises to be Fanny Soper, whose tombstone, bearing her name in golden letters and no other word, stands waiting for her arrival—for the lady still lives—or, according to my guide, did so at time of this visit. A sound idea, greet the inevitable with graceful resignation and be prepared.

The Roman Catholic Church is a building of Gothic-like dignity and goodly size. The soft-coloured bricks of its walls came from England, welcome ballast, no doubt, for a cod-carrier's homeward journey. Trees shade its well-kept graveyard, all the more pleasing to the eye since town streets and immediate neighbourhood are bare for lack of them. On a side street stands the efficient-looking little library open three busy days every week, and on the way there, or anywhere else, there's always someone ready to spend a few minutes in chat with the passing stranger. One such is the retired man who welcomes a pause in restrained potato-hoeing effort, and seemingly is pretty well informed on national and even foreign affairs, for which he is becomingly grateful to radio. But the joining up with Canada pleases him little; he thinks Commission Government was good enough and probably less expensive than the new government will prove, and that to him is of first importance

since retiring pensions here are tiny and living costs move up
with those of all the world.

William Pike is philosopher and town historian, the latter
by reason of a long life here with many generations of his family
harking back to the earliest days—sea-going people all of them,
and of the stout kind. His grandfather, born in 1798, lived
eighty-six years, was master of his own ship at eighteen and as
daring and successful a sealing skipper as any in this town, where
sealing, or "swoiling," as oldtimers still call it, made many
wealthy and not a few famous throughout the Island and around
the North Atlantic. Small ships they had in those past days,
going north every March to brave spring gales and treacherous
fields of floating ice—ships so small that in early winter they
were hauled up on the beach for safety. But they brought home
pelts "in galore," six hundred thousand one good season, and
that meant wealth for shipowners and townsmen who perilously
had gone ahunting.

The staple product and mainstay of the entire community
life was salted sun-dried cod. There may have been other finny
creatures in the sea such as haddock, herring and mackerel, but
with them people along this shore were not greatly concerned.
It was cod they took, turned into food and sent abroad, and
when they said fish, they meant cod, and nothing else. Men
spent their days on the sea, bringing laden boats home at nightfall. Men and women cleaned and packed the catch into salt
barrels, and six weeks or so later laid them to dry on the flakes—
bough-built platforms standing well off the ground so that cool
breezes might hasten drying through many sunny days. At
evening women and children piled them into beehive-like
mounds, canvas covered against heavy dews or possible showers,
and the next fine morning spread them out again. St. John's
Gosling Library has a copy of a rude drawing of the year 1600 or
so showing exactly the same process followed then and still
employed this 1951—surely rare example of a trade having
changed so little in methods and tools over three centuries.
Steam power and gas engines in smaller boats are about the only
important innovations that have eased the toil for fishermen, and

it is only within the past fifty years or so that they have been a factor in daily work of this part of the world.

Through those three centuries, too, there can have been but little change in diet of southern Europeans for whom salt dried fish has been about as important as bread or wine. Usually inexpensive, and high in food value, it took the place of meat almost always unobtainable for some millions of people. Necessity, inspiring intelligent ingenuity, has led them to devise methods of cooking to bring to the table dishes that are as appetizing as they are satisfying. A Portuguese fish merchant tells me his government has published a booklet giving one hundred ways of cooking dried cod, and that some of them make delectable dishes indeed. It might be good business for Newfoundland's government to copy such an idea and spread them through inland North America, keeping, one would hope, a few for distribution at home for special attention of those who cater to visitors from foreign parts where salt is considered a flavouring rather than an item of food by itself. Newfoundlanders seem greatly inured to salt. In one or two places stopped at it was served with a slight fish flavour as a main course. It also makes a generous contribution to some meat meals. At one place boiled beef was of excellent colour, tender and, possibly, pleasant to the taste—if one could have tasted it. I asked how long it had been soaked in fresh water after coming from the barrel. "Overnight," replied the amiable lady of the house, indicating no approval of a suggestion that it be put back again for another week, or two. It was at this table that the American traveller pushed away his plate and said, "If I'm going to be pickled I'll choose my own pickle—and it won't be salt," a remark that at the time seemed to have much merit. There's a legend that excessive salt in diet hardens the arteries and so shortens life. Maybe so, but the upstanding physique and vigour of elderly Newfoundlanders met has awakened in my mind some doubt on the truth of this theory.

Time was—and long enough ago to warrant drawing a veil of modesty across the numbering of years—when childish eyes were brightened in most town groceries back home by dried cod

piled like kindling wood, with a proper sense of suggestion, somewhere between the cracker-barrel and bulk-oyster bucket.
Alas, all three no longer are there to awaken visions of far-off
seas tossing stout ships skywards, in a pleasant and not dis-
comforting way, of course, and pretty fisher maids with nice
bare arms and feet carrying baskets of gleaming silver fish—
perhaps even singing as they went by.   They are gone, all three,
or at best are replaced by something dreadfully more expensive
and sadly less inspiring to the imagination.

Perhaps they will come back, who knows?   Sun-dried cod
might.   Every evidence of present days and the intervening
past years seems to support the century-old theory of the
philosopher Robert Malthus that human population increases
faster than the world ability to produce food.   And he said that,
mark you, long before medical science had got far in its business
of keeping in this world large numbers of people whose age, or
perhaps their manners and habits, would, in the judgment of
friends, justify an early promotion to a better—or somewhere.
The time may yet come when the humble dried cod will be
welcomed with enthusiasm on tables where now it is scorned.
That is, if present-day steam efficiency in fishing has not, as seems
quite possible, depleted the North Atlantic of this interesting and
useful creature.

The gallantry of its people through the early fighting days and
its fame as settling place of the first Pike, whose descendants have
spread over the Island as ivy spreads over stone walls, will ever
assure Carbonear a high place in Newfoundland history.

Here we run down the most authoritative Irish Princess story
told in half a dozen varying forms, in as many widely separated
parts of the country.   Somewhere near the year 1600, a young
and charming lady in the family of a tribal chieftain set sail
from Ireland for France to have her education convent-polished
under the direction of an abbess aunt.   But education for her
took another and possibly less studious form.   A Dutch warship
intervened, and since it was one of those times when Elizabeth
of England and the Holland States General were at war, Sheila
and all with her became prisoners, only to be swiftly rescued by

a small British fleet under command of a Captain Peter Easton on his way to Newfoundland where he later became widely and most unfavourably known.  Sheila found interest in the enforced westward voyage, being wooed, won and married by Lieutenant Gilbert Pike, one of the rescuing officers whose gallantry and charm must have been too much for that warm Irish heart.  At any rate, the ship's chaplain married them, and for some reason now unknown they elected to make their home in this wild austere land.  It is said that Sheila was first white woman to do so hereabouts and that the pair presented to the country its first white, native-born citizen.  Tradition makes her an Irish princess from Connaught.  And as one teller of the tale said, "Mebbe so, as many kings in Ireland there was them days as a dog has fleas."  Throughout her life great deference was paid her, particularly by the Irish, and legend credits the garden of a Pike home on Pike Lane here as being the burial place of Sheila and her husband, while a more definite authority places it in a wagon-yard off the main street—a question that surely might profitably be explored.  The spot, when finally decided upon, would seem to call for a suitable memorial cairn.

Standing up from the ocean well outside Carbonear Bay, and plainly discernible from land, is the island of that same name, and of it a Newfoundlander never speaks without your discerning in his voice a glow of pride in the history of his land and the stout deeds of his forebears.  It is the only piece of Newfoundland soil never to have been in possession of an enemy.  When, in the winter of 1696, d'Iberville with a swiftly moving force of French-Canadians and Indians swept up the coast, destroying every settlement including St. John's, he found Carbonear Island fortified as well as could be and stoutly garrisoned by about two hundred fishermen, most of whom had escaped from other villages down the coast.

The island was no easy nut to crack.  High cliffs at the sea-edge offered one possible landing with a steep, narrow pathway up to a plateau on top, half a mile wide and a mile long.  Boats the Frenchman had in plenty, left but not burned when the town went up in flames, and for a week he laid siege, meeting stiff resistance at every point. The defenders had four or five small cannon and whatever small arms could hastily be found. But they used them with excellent effect. The last desperate assault took place on the night of January 31, 1697, and early morning found the enemy appetite less keen for unprofitable fighting, so they completed the destruction of the town and went on their way, leaving one bit of Newfoundland unconquered.

The leader of this band of fighting fishermen was a Captain Pynne, a settler from nearby Bristol's Hope who, and again quoting legend, never to be relied upon completely, had apparently hustled out of the Isle of Wight a leap or so ahead of law's avenging arm, or had been persuaded to leave as one whose politics or religion were distasteful to authority—just the sort of person likely to be most useful out on the fighting fringes of an Empire. His memory gained further distinction as a direct ancestor of Newfoundland's General Sir Henry Pinn who alongside Wellington struck mighty blows for England in the Napoleonic Peninsular War. He is also credited with having some relationship with William Penn, founder of Pennsylvania.

This was but one of several times in which Carbonear Island was scene of bitter fighting in a last stand against invasion. More than once surrounding rocks have re-echoed gun-blasts marking French-English naval battles in the neighbourhood. A Captain Littleton commanding a small English frigate slipped into the bay one day to discover five loot-laden French ships at anchor. He went to work with a will, drove one ashore and scattered the rest considerably damaged—Regrettable it is that further details of this event, like those of many other bright spots in the history of this island, are no longer easily found. Carbonear Island is a lonesome waste today. The merest vestige remains of earthworks or rude fortifications that not many years ago must have been preservable, and a few ancient guns lie embedded in the ground, presenting a pathetic appeal for attention from authorities concerned with sites of national historic interest. In all North America few spots are more worthy than this of restoration or, at least, some measure of preservation.

# 10

*North-going Road and Round by Trinity Bay—Villages of Thankful Hearts—Harbour Grace—Ear-clipping Comes Back—Where Cod-liver Oil Comes from—Federation and Shoes.*

BOTH THE northbound, hard-surfaced road and the railway from St. John's end here at Trinity Bay, and in any but favourable weather gravel and clay roads are likely to prove troublesome to motorists. This is unfortunate since the shore abounds in scenery that to become world famous needs only to be opened to comfortable and safe driving made pleasant by a reasonable standard of accommodation at a few places along the way. Towering cliffs, long beaches and tremendously broad views exulting in rich colour extend on all sides wherever the road reaches the sea. Majestic in sunshine, mysterious and lovely in mist and awesome in storm, it is a land where nature speaks in moods, where dwellers cannot help but be poets and a belief in fairies must ever be present.

Around the end of the peninsula the road passes several places of historic interest including hard-to-get-at Grate's Cove, the most northerly spot hereabouts. Here is a rock bearing a time-obliterated inscription supposedly recording a visit of John Cabot. Elsewhere no relic of the past remains. Climate is not kind to man's handiwork, and building always was for the immediate present, the needs of the day being too urgent to allow much contemplation of past troubles—for history here is mostly a record of war, trouble and grief, and little thought there must have been of building for future years. Tiny hamlets tucked away in rocky coves reveal nothing of relic and little of memory.

Across to the west, and now on eastern shore of Trinity Bay's fifteen or twenty-mile sweep of tossing water, both road and accommodation improve. Here again are settlements of past importance and delightful setting. What else could be expected where the first views of the earliest settlers inspired such place-names as Heart's Content, Heart's Desire, Heart's Delight and Heart's Ease. Purely English names these, setting on record for all time the joy of seaweary, homeless wanderers who saw before them promise of peace, plenty and happiness. How much of each these newcomers were to experience in this new land is a question. French raiders and pirate ravishers brought war, murder and rapine time after time vaguely memorialized in local legend by such names as Bloody Point, Bloody Bay and so on. Those things needed for life's sustaining may have been more readily obtainable here than back home. Of happiness, one imagines, they enjoyed a fair share in between troubles, no doubt being much like their present-day descendants, quite capable of making the best of things as they were, and without too much complaint when adversity came.

Villages along this shore are tiny places and unimportant in the matter of industry compared to what once they were. Heart's Content, a well-built and pleasant town, acquired fame in 1866 when the first transatlantic cable was landed there—an event as arresting then as Marconi's receipt of the first radio signal from Europe on Signal Hill at St. John's thirty-five years later. A busy place this was then with fifty to sixty cable-station workers and active fishing and lumbering industries.

Here we turn south-east, leaving the Cabot Highway for a twenty-five-mile run back across the peninsula. Not that the journey down the shore to Trinity Bay's southern end lacks either interest or charm, but time passes and southern Conception Bay calls. They speak of crossing the peninsula as "going over the barrens," and perhaps they are right. It looks like that, but there's a lonesome beauty about the land that has appeal, and here and there one sees small areas that seem to call for husbandry of some kind, be it only sheep-grazing. The end of the run brings us back into Carbonear, and after the quietude of places visited, the little town looks busier and more populous than ever.

By road and bus obviously is the way to go on to Harbour Grace four or five miles down the coast. The bus proves to be an ancient but energetic station-wagon with room for eight and usually carrying up to twelve. But it tackles hills and curves with cheery abandon, and in no time at all we are looking down on as pleasantly situated a seaside townlet as you would wish to behold. Reasonable comfort prevails in either of the two hotels. Long hours of July sunshine happily keeps one out of doors, and if temperatures are a bit on the low side at night, early to bed is an excellent practice for the traveller whose meanderings are hampered by neither time schedules nor business interferences.

Like all outports up and down this coast, Harbour Grace scatters itself around the deeply inland end of one of those innumerable arms of the sea marking the Island's entire coastline. Here again the water side of its one long street has but few standing buildings where once busy fish-trade warehouses and factories lined the shore. Here and there remains of stone foundations offer evidence of a past flourishing industry now making no demand for rebuilding. August 17, 1944, was the day of the most recent disaster when a six-hour blaze entirely devastated the business area and many residences and stores across the road. Standing walls of what once was an impressive red brick post office and town hall are a melancholy memorial of that event, and an indication of the activity and dignity in earlier days when Harbour Grace laid fair claim to second place in population and wealth among Newfoundland communities.

Glimpses of the past are caught here and there where houses of respectable age stand half-veiled from the street by garden shrubbery; or an ancient shop or two with walls and roof-lines settled into comfortable angles and curves as though long since too tired to worry about rules of architectural perspective. There's one little old shop leaning this way and that all round a street corner so that surely it might fall apart at any moment, except that craftsmen who dove-tailed and dowelled it together did so good a job that you feel it never will fall, but some day, hundreds of years hence when its now solid timbers finally disintegrate, it will blow away in a cloud of dust.   Inside and out it looks a little dejected and sorry for itself, doubtless because a century or so ago it was outstanding among the town's twenty or thirty taverns, a place where deep-chested, broad-shouldered men told tales of heroic seamanship, adventure and profit, and sang their songs until its walls rang like the singing belly of a bass-fiddle — and now it offers women's stockings and baby clothes to an apparently very indifferent clientele.   Could it have been at this pub—or was it at St. John's—that one aldermanic civic dignitary invariably spent his evenings until the family Newfoundland dog came scratching at the door bearing a candle-lanthorne for lighting the civic father's homeward steps?  It could have been either—a good story anyway, particularly as illustrating another endearing characteristic of that noble canine.

One building stands here for which time has not altered nor custom changed its original air of superior but not ungenial dignity—the courthouse.   A century and a quarter ago it was well and truly put together in honest blocks of limestone, and its opening was an event warranting the presence of the Governor and whatever military fuss and feathers could be staged by a small but probably efficient garrison resident in this then important outpost of sea power.   There it stands, a bit of nicely proportioned Georgian architecture, and to go through the wide door is to step back into past days as one is seldom privileged to do. The courtroom is a perfect setting for some famous trial out of history when bewigged justice and litigants droned through the process of law by the dim light of tallow candles.   Here it could have been that Mr. Sergeant Buzfuz thundered about chops and tomato sauce in that merriest of trials Bardell vs. Pickwick, and here over the century must have been recorded many a grim legal battle, and dispensation of much summary justice with, one hopes, a reasonable amount of mercy thrown in.

Twenty-five years earlier, in 1807, a timber predecessor to

this courthouse had been erected near by. By that time Harbour Grace had been a place of varying importance for about two centuries. Stocks, pillory and whipping-posts contributed to both town adornment and effective law enforcement. They had three whipping-posts in those days, and for particularly outrageous offences the culprit was marched to each in turn for part of his punishment so that all the town had a fair chance to observe how bitter was the way of transgression. On record is the case of one man, having been convicted of stealing cod, making the unhappy journey with a large and very dead fish tied round his neck. Of the original courthouse no small splinter remains nor a single stone of the garrison barracks, though one or two old houses date back a hundred and fifty years or so. One comfortable-looking timber structure stands as a legendary army commissariat, straight and sound as though not a quarter its age.

A short stroll along the shore is Bristol's Hope, mostly a ghostly relic of a place overlooking Mosquito Cove, and here, perhaps, stood the original settlement of all Conception Bay. A few scattered stones mark spots where tiny dwellings stood, homes of adventurous Jerseymen, first to settle around these shores. Portuguese fishermen may have visited here at that time, or even earlier, as witnessed by Portugal Cove, named in 1501 by the world navigator, Gasper de Cotreal, but Channel Islanders from Jersey it was whose annual visits opened up the fishing and led to settlement. The village grew and spread around the bay to more commodious anchorage where the soil and lay of the land were more inviting, and so Harve de Grace came into being, a name all right for Jerseymen but soon to become plain Harbour Grace when men from Devon, and Ireland crowded in to turn the rich stream of fish wealth Bristolwards—or in any direction so that finally it arrived somewhere in the west of England.

For many years Mosquito Cove held power over the neighbourhood. Here in earliest days shipdecks, fishbarns or harbourside docks were the scene of fish-admiral's courts and fierce punishments for infringement of such laws and regulations as then seemed necessary for public, or perhaps private, security. Somewhere here it was that gallant Lieutenant Pike and his Irish princess built their first home, and Newfoundland's first white child was born. From here, as at Harbour Grace, when the French came burning and looting, townsmen drove their cattle back into the woods, and making tracks with snowshoes reversed, hurried off to Carbonear led by Captain Pynne. Town burning was no novelty those days. It seems to have happened every now and then, mostly by accident, and quite often from forest fires sweeping out to the shore, thus offering evidence that this bare rocky shore and most of the country behind it once was as forest-clad as the hills of the Island interior.

John Guy, who was sent out by Bristol merchants and did as much exploration and settlement in Newfoundland as any man, visited this spot in 1610 and two years later returned with fifty-four men, six women and two children as colonists. In 1620 Captain Richard Whitbourne published a book of travel in which he says of Harbour Grace:

Divers worshipful citizens of the city of Bristol have undertaken to plant a large circuit of this country and they have maintained a colony of His Majesty's subjects these past five years who have built there fair houses and done many good services; who have lived there very pleasantly, and there they are pleased to entertain upon fit conditions such as will be adventurers with them. At the Bristol plantation there is as goodly rye growing as can be found in any part of England. They are also furnished with swine and a large breed of goats fairer by far than those that were sent out at the first time.

All this, of course, was long before home-government policy changed and colonization of the new land was considered a threat to Britain's fish-trade supremacy, and it became an offence to hold land or erect a habitation on the shore.

Families now exist on this coast whose traditions carry back through all these years. Records are scarce and meagre, but enough remains to put together fascinating glimpses of a way of life heroic in effort and indomitable in unfaltering persistency.

Pleasant it is to hear an old man sing—singing because

there's a song in his heart and the morning calls it forth.   In early sunshine I sat gazing across the bay to where one or two villages clustered each around its big white church and tried to recreate such busy harbour scenes that must have been common-place as late as fifty or sixty years ago when fishing enjoyed one of its prosperous periods.   The first agreeable interruption was the sudden appearance of five or six mildly astonished goats coming around the road's bend accompanied by gambolling kids each as freshly new and clean as a youngster off to Sunday School.   Footsteps of the elders slowed as awakening suspicion greeted the wayside stranger and one stealthy reach for the camera sent them scampering off.   Then came the song, a hymn it was, "Jerusalem the Golden," judging from the tune, sung not lustily, but quietly, as a man sings to mark musical beat of his feet along a pleasant road.   The wind-borne voice from around the corner had suggested youngish middle age, but he came into view bearing seventy years with virility of fifty and friendly smile of twenty-five, and his "Good marnin' zir," was promisingly amiable as he leaned on his stout staff and set about discovering from where the foreigner came, and what quest had brought him to this part of the world.   Easily satisfied on both points, he welcomed the opportunity to gossip of old days as we strolled townwards.

Let's call him John—there's something terse and confidence inspiring about the name that seems to fit him.   His speaking voice was Devon English, soft-vowelled with a rising and falling cadence and having no place for anything like the letter "H." One of his forebears had been in the fight for Carbonear and since then they had come down through the years fishing, trading and sailing as occasion advantaged, except that one or two— more adventurous or wayward—had perhaps gone in for piracy when that was a recognized profession not too hazardous in relation to promise of swiftly acquired wealth.   All this took time to discover.

"This were a gran' place when oi were a young 'un," he said. "Busy all through the year except in midwinter when everybody was glad of a rest and could afford it.   Most toime there'd be fifty to a hundred and fifty ships in this 'arbour, and that meant a lot of work 'andlin' fish and outfittin' an' one thing and another. Oi've seen time so many ships was tied up 'ere you could walk across the 'arbour over the decks." I remembered Carbonear and made no comment.

In days of Harbour Grace prosperity it was mostly Labrador fishing that kept the town busy. In early spring away would go the ships, large and small, carrying anywhere from five to fifty men with perhaps a woman to cook, mend clothes and anything else a woman could do—and not seldom a goat went along to keep the dairy supplied. On the Labrador coast men were landed for the season, cod-drying stages were built, and thousands of tons of cured and dried fish were moved back to harbour warehouses for packing and marketing. Whalers went out of this port, too, and sealers; and along towards wintertime when sea harvest had proved plentiful and markets promised to be generous, times were very good. Winter had few terrors—time for social gatherings in homes, churches and taverns. Elders gossiped around blazing fireplaces and young people danced, courted and sang songs of the country (of which there are many) through Christmas and New Year and on until softer winds and the ice break-up gave an urgent call back to sea.

Walking with John set the town alive with colourful ghosts of his youth, and those of his father and grandfather when big square-riggers rode the harbour taking on loads of fish to replace tons of salt brought as ballast from foreign ports where fish had been sold. Salt went into the warehouses and when they could take no more it was piled in huge heaps on the rocks and burned over with a covering of tree branches. The resulting heat created a hard crust over the salt impervious to the worst weather that might come. Few fishermen handled money. They took their wages in trade, and, said John, "Oi wouldn't say but what we were just as well off. We wanted for nothing and there was no waste. Merchants did well, and if one was unfair we all knew it and sheered off 'im. There was money enough.

in the town.   Spaniards and Portuguese paid for fish in gold, and in good times there was plenty of it around."

Political strife between Protestant and Catholic was no less bitter here than back in the capital.   The unfortunate editor of St. John's *Ledger*, a newspaper represented as an assailant of the Irish people and the Roman Church, rode horseback this way one night returning from a Carbonear visit.   A committee of angry politicians met him at the town border, cut off both his ears and sent him on his way—an incident that somehow harks back almost four hundred years to the Elizabethan promise of ear-slicing as a corrective for careless speech.   This illuminating story stands corroborated by that excellent historian, Rev. Lewis Amadeus Anspach, who goes on to remark that no one came to punishment for this outrage, and suggests that little effort was made to discover the perpetrators thereof.   Other authorities state that a government reward of £1,500, increased by the editor's friends to £3,000, together with promise of free pardon and safe removal to a healthier clime, failed to bring forward any information.   Five years later in St. John's, a homeward-bound printing foreman of same newspaper was seized, questioned, and released after being warned to silence.   Unwisely he told of his adventure and three months later, at the same spot, masked men rushed him and before he could use the sword-stick he carried, he also was earless.   Offer of rewards again brought no information and nothing further appears to have been done about it.

Long years before this, when the practice of Roman Catholicism was drastically punishable, a priest now and then slipped through to carry spiritual comfort to a sparse and widely scattered flock in peril of his life.   The least he could expect was a sojourn in the town stocks as the target for Protestant scorn and very likely the odd handful of filth tossed in his face as expression of religious zeal or just barbarous cruelty of the times.   An informed whisper of the forbidden mass celebration in a fish warehouse here reached the Governor's ears in far-off St. John's and swiftly came orders for the stamping out of this abomination and punishment of all concerned.   That warehouse went up in flames, men were imprisoned and flogged while the priest escaped through some sort of underground arrangement certain to be established where such conditions prevailed.

When Irish immigration was heavy, many of the newcomers settled around Conception Bay. Says John, "The Irish went back on the land farmin' and growing potatoes. The English settled on the shore and 'eld on to the fishin'. They were seamen, not farmers." Official tolerance of Roman Church services did not bring peace in religious matters, and newly arrived Irishmen included Orangemen to whom old feuds were precious. Dissension here culminated on one religious holiday when opposing marchers clashed in a struggle which included the firing of one or two muzzle-loaders stuffed with odds and ends of scrap-iron. Panicky scatteration followed, and though fast-flying rumour up and down the land told of dozens dead and dying, it finally simmered down to one not definitely authenticated death, and a small number of rioters more or less peppered. "But," says John, "that ended it. A warship lay in 'arbour all winter to keep the peace. But it needn't 'ave. The foight was all gone out uv 'em."

Harbour Grace churches are dignified buildings of a size perhaps more in keeping with population figures of earlier days— ten thousand in the most prosperous times and now about twenty-five hundred, two-thirds Protestant, of which Anglicans outnumber the others almost two to one. The Roman cathedral is a graceful Gothic building of stone and the fourth to be erected on the site since 1830 when a Franciscan missionary from Ireland built a wooden chapel having a hundred-foot tower.

St. Paul's Church of England is a solid-looking square-towered building that would appear comfortably at home in any English village. It dates back to 1835, following a succession of wooden buildings, the earliest having been erected in 1764. A royal coat of arms on the gallery wall would imply that its predecessors had been garrison churches. A gallery around three sides gives a Georgian tone to the well-kept interior made bright by flower-decked altar and polished brasses. Churchyard memorials go back to the early eighteen-hundreds. One commemorates Johnathon, son of Henry and Elizabeth Webber, as follows:

This stone was erected by his sorrowing parents. He was a dutiful child, a loving brother, his parent's chief hope of children—was drowned by the stroke of a whale, was found July, 1872, aged 18 yrs., 9 months, and was buried here.

Imposing in size, and frankly new, is the present United Church, successor to several built and burnt since 1780 when the first Wesleyan chapel was opened. Preachers of power have occupied their pulpits, and when church organs were unknown here congregational singing was led by violins, bass viols, flutes, and a choir of famed excellence all, no doubt, obeying the psalmist's injunction, "Let us make a glad noise unto the Lord." Unfortunately the church doors today are closed to week-day visitation. Among its gravestone epitaphs voicing pointed sermons on life's vanity and death's certainty, is that of Charlotte Stevenson, buried June, 1838, aged five years, who, inspired by some local poet, speaks from the tomb to say:

> When the Archangel's trump shall sound
> And souls to bodies join—
> What crowds shall wish their lives below
> Had been as short as mine.

Could suggested pessimism go farther—or is it optimism?

Cod-liver oil—gallons of it, steel drums full of it, great vats holding tons of it—what could be more revolting to one whose tender sense of taste in childhood was periodically insulted, outraged and violated by frequent doses. Well—here's a place where it's made, perhaps the world's largest and most productive plant of the kind, the place a survivor of the days before the dreadful stuff was slyly administered in capsules, or cunningly robbed of some of its flavoured horror, could approach with fierce joy as having traced his enemy to its lair and being able to bring about a reckoning. The natural impulse to set the place afire and sit watching those tons of cod-liver oil roll heavenwards in fat black smoke as a burnt-offering was restrained.

AT MANY ROCK-CRADLED OUTPORTS HOUSEHOLD SUPPLIES
GO ASHORE BY LIGHTER   (*C.N.R. Photo*)

THE PAPER MILL AT THE TOWN OF CORNER BROOK  (*Marshall Studio Photo*)

RICH FIELDS LIE ALONG THE LITTLE CODROY

St. John's Outlet to the Sea and Signal Hill   *(C.N.R. Photo)*

Entrance to St. John's Harbour   *(C.N.R. Photo)*

No Shore Too Grim to Harbour Fishermen's Homes and Fish-drying Flakes
One of the Hills in St. John's

PORT DE GRAVE

THE LEGISLATIVE BUILDING AT ST. JOHN'S

LOOKING DOWN LONG HILL, WITH THE CABOT TOWER SEEN IN THE DISTANCE
(*Marshall Studio Photo*)

A RESIDENTIAL STREET IN ST. JOHN'S

A Typical Newfoundland Outport

There's a Ship at the Bottom of Every Street in St. John's

Along Water Street, St. John's

Ancient Cannon Made into Churchyard Gate-posts at Bay Bulls

HILLSIDE PLOWING NEAR BAY ROBERTS

FISH-DRYING FLAKES AT POUCH COVE

A Pleasant Country Road along Conception Bay    (*C.N.R. Photo*)

Salmon Cove, Conception Bay    (*C.N.R. Photo*)

Harbour Grace

Picket Fences Keep Wandering Goats and Ponies out of the Potato Patches

Frogmarsh, near Brigus—a Bit of Good Farm Land by the Sea

Deepsea-going Fishing Boats at Brigus

Fish-houses and Cod-drying Stages at Petty Harbour
Newfoundland's Humber River is Famous for Salmon Fishing

A South-shore Village in Placentia Bay

The Freight Schooner Calls at Harbour Buffet, Placentia Bay

Grand Bank, the Busy Home of the Grand Bank Fishermen

Cod Ready for Salting and Drying at Grand Bank

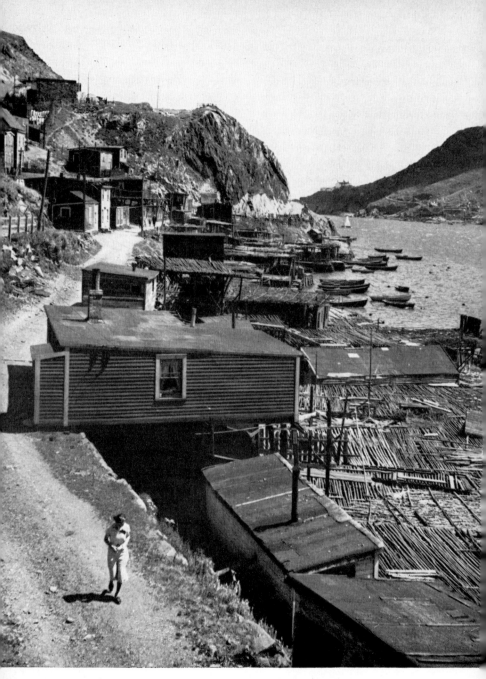

COD-FISHING IS THE STAPLE INDUSTRY AND FISH-DRYING FLAKES CROWD
THE SHORE WHEREVER FISHERMEN DWELL    (*Wallenberg Photo*)

Over generations the name Munn has stood high among Newfoundland shipowners and merchants, and for sixty years their fish-oil plant has contributed to the Island's economic development. Fighting down an inclination to shudder, one enters to discover that a fish-oil factory can be as clean and as inoffensive to the nostrils as any food plant need be. A friendly greeting from chemist-manager disarms any prejudice as he recites interesting details of this important industry. In outports all round the Island cod-livers are thrown into pails as fish are cleaned. In some cases sun is allowed to free the oil from coarse fibrous matter. At other ports small factories buy the livers from fishermen, and by steaming and straining produce a crude oil which is shipped to this refinery where it goes through several processes to ultimate purity varying in vitamin content and other qualities. The top-grade product is a scientifically selected blend exactly fulfilling the requirements of British or American pharmacopoeia and so is qualified to make the utmost contribution to human well-being.

About one-third of all oil processed reaches this perfection, and since yearly output here runs from two hundred and fifty thousand to three hundred thousand gallons, one comes to view the whole enterprise with that respect due an undoubted benefactor of humanity at large. Lower grades are used in tanning high-class leathers and the finer chamois skins, and in forming a highly nutritive addition to cattle and poultry food. During earliest infancy, one is told, pigs are subject to anaemia against which cod-liver oil is the surest guardian, so every year thousands of gallons are consumed in assuring health and happiness to little pigs—all of which is very good indeed for the breakfast rasher of bacon in its earlier stages.

I left the place entirely reconciled to cod-liver oil and grateful to the manager for his courtesy and much information; grateful, too, that he did not offer a generous bumper of his fine product which politeness would have compelled me to accept as a parting toast. They did so once at a brewery that called for inspection— but that, of course, was very different.

It seems that almost any time, day or night, you may hear

singing in this land, and pretty good singing it usually is.   Five o'clock in the morning is no exception, and it's not at all unpleasant to be called from sleep about then by a group of girls merrily caroling their way down the street.   They had come off the night-shift at the fish-packing plant and, far from being work-weary and listless, they were as songful as a flock of cock-robins in springtime.   Certainly, this made a visit to the fish-plant that same morning a "must."

Three or four fishing boats lay alongside and from their well-filled holds men were pitchforking cod onto the dock.   The fish were swiftly cleaned and hurried on a travelling conveyor into an upper storey of the factory.   Refuse from the cleaning went into tubs, later into trucks to be hauled away for drying and grinding into fishmeal, another valuable cattle-food, though much of it becomes fertilizer, adding beauty to the rose, flavour to the onion, or increased productivity to the potato.

The first impression on entering the factory is one of excessive cleanliness everywhere and ever-flowing streams of water to keep it so.   The fish arrive cleaned and washed at one end of long tables where men swiftly remove bones and skin and pass them on to girls who cut them into gleaming white fillets, while others pack them in neat containers and rush them on to refrigerators, ready to move in trucks, car-lots or ship-loads to a final place of marketing.   That is just about how long it takes. From a fisherman's boat to cold-storage is a matter of very few minutes.

Establishment of more fish-packing plants of this kind is judged to be one answer to economic problems.   Thirteen such plants are now operating in various parts of the Island and the building of others is contemplated.   Many millions of pounds of Newfoundland fresh-frozen fish go annually to the United States and Canada and it is desirable that these quantities be increased. Present-day meat prices would seem to assure a greatly increased consumption of fresh refrigeratored fish if it quickly could be laid down at far inland points in perfect condition at not too great a cost.   Newfoundland is not too advantageously placed in the matter of transportation, but it is difficult to believe that freight-carrying aeroplanes will not soon be more generally used. Even now they carry high-priced lobsters from the west coast to American cities. Flying "box-cars" are dropping tanks, artillery and what-not on far-off battlefields. Perhaps, when peace raises its timid head, engineering ingenuity will make them economically usable in carrying perishable foodstuffs from production points to tables of far-away hungry consumers. In the bewildering unknown world into which we are moving, that well may be aviation's outstanding service to humanity.

Here in Harbour Grace is Newfoundland's only boot and shoe factory, and an interesting sidelight it throws on one phase of the economic results of Federation. Under complete home rule this small industry had a thirty-five per cent tariff protection. Today, Canada's three hundred or so factories, large and small, have free entry while the local manufacturer has to pay federal taxes of one kind and another. He is not in the happiest of positions.

A bright, cheerful place in which to work is this factory, with windows looking out over the sea. In times past, says the manager-proprietor, seventy-five people had employment but at the time of our visit twenty-eight are moderately busy and have less certainty of continued employment than ever before. Small as it is, there have been days when six hundred pairs of shoes came from busy machines and skilful hands of its men and girls. Now it faces competition with factories turning out five and six thousand pairs daily. As to prices and quality of its output, the fact stands that when in full production it was able to compete in eastern mainland markets. With Federation came invading hosts of salesmen representing every form of manufacture. Their welcome was mixed—they were invaders—but persistence has carried their campaign far and the mail-order catalogue has swept it farther still so that home-industries languish and some Newfoundlanders go far abroad to find employment in boot and shoe factories or anywhere they can get it. This is a perplexing question—which is best for a community, wage-paying employment for seventy-five or any number of its people, or somewhat lower price commodities that might be made at home but are not because of distant mass production and possibly lower freight rates often government subsidized? This we leave for economists to discuss and politicians to make capital with.

"Thar she blows"—a shout that in every northern language has been heard the world round ever since whale-oil first fed lamps and whale-bone began to define desirable curves in female forms. Through all these years it has rung out from crowsnests of Newfoundland ships all over the North Atlantic and whaling ships and men have brought back golden contribution to the Island's wealth. Not so much in recent days since lamps turned to paraffin or passed away altogether, and fashion scorned whale-bone helps. From sixteen to twenty whaling stations, the Island industry has dwindled to two, and a whaling trip means travelling hundreds of miles to sea where once they could be taken ten miles from this coast. But the inoffensive whale still has his uses and men are here whose life business it is to hunt them.

Mr. Hanrahan lives in a pleasant house overlooking the cathedral when he is not whale chasing or back country "trouting," which is the kind of busman's holiday he favours, and what he does not know about whaling has not yet been discovered. The season runs from June to November and ships nowadays go out equipped with every necessity for the crew's welfare including a qualified surgeon often the most urgently needed man on the ship.

"It's a rough and dangerous job at times," says Mr. Hanrahan. "But nothing like it was in old days when you went for the whale in small boats and threw a harpoon into him by hand, and had before you a hard fighting battle for maybe some hours. A small explosive shell fired from a gun now brings the whale alongside in no time at all. It's merciful and has saved many a whalerman's life.

"Whaling's an easy enough way of seagoing these days," he says. "Men have comfortable quarters and are well fed, not like what it was in days of sailing ships and first steamers. But sure that's true of all seagoing—more like a gentleman's life it is—less work and more money, though the money doesn't buy as much."

In the head of the sperm whale is a reservoir carrying about twenty-five barrels of heavy oil used in tanning and for making soaps and candles. Oil from other whales makes excellent margarine, being quite tasteless. The meat is good human food, particularly from around the tail. The fin-back whale has a pleasant venison-like flavour and much of it now goes to England frozen. Less desirable portions are consumed on fox farms and as dog food. Oil is extracted from the blubber, and most of the meat after steaming in pressure kettles, is dried and ground with the bones into meal for use as fertilizer. Over recent years the two whaling stations where all rendering and packing is done have produced about fifteen to twenty thousand barrels of oil, considered a fair catch for four hunting ships and two tow boats. Whaling ships that come to these waters from Europe are equipped to do all this work while at sea.

# 11

*Bay Roberts and Its Goats—Crossroad of Inter-*
*continental Conversations—"We Don't Love England"—*
*More about Pirates.*

FROM Harbour Grace south this branch of the Cabot Trail mostly
skirts Conception Bay's west shore, and we take the road in
weather offering not an unwelcome change to almost uninterrupted weeks of sunshine.   A sweep of wind-borne rain comes
off a sullen whitecapped sea.   Clouds massive as the rocky cliffs
below move overhead.   But early in the short overland journey
a burst of sun lights the lonesome heath, imparting splashes of
vivid yellow and green to verdured hills and jewelled brilliance
to scattered lakes and ponds.   We reach the sea again with
summer all benign at Spaniard's Bay, a name from the earliest
history and a hamlet presenting as typical and pleasing a sight
as any to be found along this shore.

Another little dash over the hills brings us into Bay Roberts,
where polite inquiry at a townsman's house, doing business as a
local hotel or boarding-house, brings seemingly reluctant
admission as guest.   Commercial travellers passing up and down
this way or truck-drivers enter as a matter of course and are
welcome enough, but the foreigner—he's different—and the
better he explains himself and his reason for being in these parts
the less chilly will be his reception.   Once accepted in such
places—the only accommodation available in most outports—the
visitor is greeted by every assurance of comfort.   Meals are

generally wholesome and hearty, and there's no doubt about it, housekeeping here is serious business indeed, and cleanliness a virtue persisted in with religious zeal.   Dust does not appear and universally linoleumed floors shine like polished dinner plates. But these are a hardy people for whom cool houses and almost heatless bathing and shaving-water have no terrors.   Visiting foreigners may admire such virtues in other people, but June temperatures hereabouts have an early morning chilliness that imparts a dim view to the prospect of cold-water tubs.   Hereafter, meeting people with such strength of character as to have a liking for this sort of thing, one will suspect them to be Newfoundlanders—if not, of course, from England.   A Canadian met here declares he has not suffered so from cold indoors since one glorious June spent in England—and that was before wartime difficulties rationed fuel.

Happily other and more welcome features of Bay Roberts remind us of England.   As you walk along its main and harbourside street, past its few shops, the bank and post office with war memorial standing before it—a busy place by midmorning—and pass on to where a few ancient houses stand that have escaped succeeding conflagrations, you can almost imagine yourself in some Devon village by the sea.   Creeper-covered and lilac-shaded stone walls hold back old gardens that threaten to spill over into the roadway, and about the whole place there is an air of having been lived in a long, long time and something of an atmosphere of stubborn determination to stay there unchanged so long as its rocky shore holds back the sea.

Here again we see ghosts of past glories, times when fishing was big business and this four-mile-long sheltered harbour was home to large fleets of fishing boats and to oceangoing ships. The inevitable ancient enjoying his afternoon pipe on the dock could tell about that.

"Must have been a busy place here years ago," I suggested. The old boy did not fail me and picked up his cue like a well-rehearsed actor.

"Aye, zur, that's a fact.   Oi've seen the time that many boats lay in this 'arbour you could—"

"Yes," I said, "I know—you could walk across it on ships' decks and never wet your feet." But I was too smart.

"Well, no—I wouldn't say that," he said. "But you could walk a mile or a mile and a half up and down shore that way, and I've done it." The rebuke was unanswerable.

Seaward the harbour is protected by several rocky islets that must surely make entry difficult in bad weather, and in far blue distance Bell Island, long a source of iron ore, breaks the misty line between sky and sea. Across the harbour here and there a white church gathers a few tiny dwellings around like chicks around a hen. One is the hamlet of Bareneed, known to have been referred to as Bare Knees and, like so many others in this land, demanding explanation of its apparently whimsical name. It's very simple, really, and you must not believe the jocund local citizen who will answer your question by closing one eye, shaking his head gravely and disapprovingly assure you it is no story to be told when ladies are present. Since he will not tell it even among men, one is left with suspicion either that it is a very shocking story indeed or that he has not been able to think up one fully justifying possibilities. The latter suggestion is most likely true. Best authorities give Barren Head as the original name. Turn that into Devon English and you have Bar'n 'eed, a short jump to Bareneed and Bare Knees, a colloquialism hinting at a touch of rollicking humour in the make-up of early inhabitants from whom that sort of thing might have been expected. Another such island name is Blow-me-down, clearly what now stands for Blomidon.

The name Barren Head given to this spot would imply that the shore-line elsewhere once was quite otherwise than barren, corroborating an ancient loiterer's assurance.

"Trees, aye, plenty of 'em. Oi've 'eerd me gran'feyther tell it was a good land in them days with trees all over the 'ills. People came from far away to get masts for their ships, and got big uns, too."

Not many trees here now—but there's good workable soil with patches of tall hay and healthy looking potato plants lying between winding picket-fenced pathways. Visible landscape hereabouts is a crazy patchwork of small plots or sizable fields each protected by weathered silver-grey picket fences effectively forbidding to wandering ponies, goats and sheep. At the northern end of the town is Jones' Head, a high, rocky cliff overlooking the sea. Spiked boots carry one to the top readily enough and give a comforting non-slip feeling when gazing two or three hundred feet straight down to the white-surfed shore-line. Far below, to the north, is a toy village, its white houses, crooked paths and potato patches against a background of rock and deep blue sea forming a scene which leaves one with hope of returning to enjoy it again some future day.

Northward along the road is a huge frame church shining in white paint and of a type that might be found in any western prairie town. Bay Roberts' population is about fourteen hundred, and six-sevenths Protestant. A hilltop and well-kept cemetery contains few if any reminders of past history. One feature is a neat garage-like housing for the parish hearse that every sizable settlement seems to keep under the protection of one of its churches—a simple railed platform on four wheels and all decently painted black. This shed door bears a sign, "Persons using this hearse are requested not to tie anything white (or other) material to the sides. Such things have no meaning and are of no use.—The Rector." No funeral practices of possible pagan origin are allowable here.

For all its being a small place on the outer edge of world happenings, Bay Roberts is a crossroad where news of every important event in current history passes through and is recorded almost while happening. Five Atlantic ocean-bedded cables having their other ends three thousand miles away in Europe land here, and back and forward through them flow unceasing streams of words as one continent speaks to another. The building is a modern stone structure having the appearance of a large residence built when homes could be of generous proportions with spacious interiors. To enter is a little like visiting a church—everywhere is evidence of meticulous care and the visitor has a feeling that if one atom of dust slipped through the doorway, loud alarums would sound off calling swift dust abolishers into action. Around and about a maze of tabled instruments a few attendants silently move somehow suggesting priests in a sanctuary, and you speak only in whispers. But the room is not silent. Here and there an instrument is tapping off a message. From one come signals loud and insistent on the importance of their message—report of a speech at this moment being made in London's House of Commons by Prime Minister Attlee. Vividly the scene presents itself—Attlee persuasively talking to crowded benches raptly attentive, the operator in the House telegraph room sending the utterance paragraph by paragraph as reporters bring it in—and here, its instantaneous arrival flashing on its way over plugged-in wires to newspaper offices in every North American city. A few moments after the Prime Minister has finished, editors are pondering his statements and preparing to tell their readers what to think about them, while readers are forming their own opinions—in the main, most likely to be fairly sound.

These cables cross the Atlantic straight enough east and west, but curve wonderfully up and down over an ocean-bed of mountains, valleys, plains and precipices. At one place they lie two miles below water surface, but in this building are instruments that swiftly locate a break or interference so that trouble-shooting ships may hasten to the spot, fish the cable up, make necessary repairs, and lower it again to ocean floor—difficult enough task in fair weather but surely a challenge to masterly seamanship when waves run high in storm.

When Marconi on Signal Hill received the first trans-ocean radio signal there must have been many who thought the usefulness of the telegraph cable was drawing to a close. After fifty years of wireless telegraphic development, cables are busier than ever and there seems no reason why they should not continue so. "Weather conditions or atmospheric disturbances never bother cables," says the station manager, "and their messages cannot be intercepted or picked up." Important factors always, and imperative necessities in war.

Bay Roberts goats are remarkable for size, agility and comeliness and, according to Alf Wood, a town citizen of high standing and undoubted veracity, they are noted for perversity of nature, original sin and calculated wilful wickedness. "Devil's children," he calls 'em, and declares they haunt the roads gleefully intent on maintaining a high rate of heart-failure among motorists, although far too fleet of foot to ever get themselves hit.  For years he has been trying to run one down, half-heartedly, one imagines, and with no success at all—but he has hopes.

Corroborating the perversity charge, here's an incident to the truth of which I bear witness.  Two little girls, say, ten and seven of age, appear at a crossroads, the elder, apparently named Sarah, frantically trying to persuade a matronly nanny and unco-operative kid homewards.  Persuasion is utterly without effect; nanny will go any way but the right one.  The switch in Sarah's hand is useless but a stout stick lying in a road-side puddle may help, and Sarah reaches down for it, presenting the plumpest and roundest of targets for a touch-down.  Nanny makes it with swift and perfect timing, like the blow of a perfect boxer—unbelievable but beautiful.  Reluctantly the puddle relinquishes Sarah's face and frock.  Wells of wrath rising within her, she says nothing, for a moment.  Then it comes, a flood of right royal rage voiced in terms undoubtedly inspired by a long line of fishing, sailing and fighting ancestry, and before which one stands in respectful admiration hardly restraining the impulse to lift the hat.  I doubt if nanny or offspring heard a word of it.  By that time they had galloped over the hill—on the way home.

Out of Bay Roberts run several pleasant roads over the countryside.  Winding they are, and hilly and well gravelled, altogether inviting to motorists in good weather, but most of all a delight to those fond of country walking with little road traffic to worry one, and with interesting views on every hand.  Up through a little valley towards Shearston is one of the best. There's farming here, some of it good farming on soil that has been intelligently and vigorously cultivated so that it produces cabbages and other delectable vegetables of a size and quality promising to hearty and discriminating appetites.  Hereabouts they still talk with pride, as well they might, of a twenty-seven-pound cabbage that last year burgeoned its glory on one of these fields.

At one time, they tell me, and that not more than a generation ago, soil here was not good and farming a dreary and penurious business so that young people scattered to foreign parts and the whole district languished. But some of the wanderers kept alive their love of the homeland, as Newfoundlanders have a way of doing, and having done fairly well abroad, came back, bringing something of better farming experience and some capital with happy results for the whole area, which now has a comfortable air of wellbeing.

Shearston is home to six or seven hundred farming people almost entirely English in origin. Time was when the Pentecostal Church was dominant here and they speak of camp meetings with baptisms in a nearby pond with as many as a thousand present. The total number here now might be fifteen or twenty, United and Anglican churches having taken over the whole area. Back farther in the hills, says one local authority, lies more land as good as any here and quite as capable of supporting family homes were it broken to the plow and properly prepared. The somewhat casual but not unobservant wanderer through this country cannot repress the conviction that in some such development as this lies best promise of future permanent welfare for a large number of the Island's people.

Journeying by motor under the guidance of friend Wood carries us away from Bay Roberts with pleasant long-lasting memories. We leave the Cabot Highway and turn out along another narrow peninsula, over another winding road with hills and grades more astonishing than any yet, but now and then offering over land and sea broad views demanding more time than any one summer's day can give. Through many villages we pass, including Bareneed where we marvel at the size of its white frame church and go on to descend the steepest and narrowest of hillside roads at bottom of which is Port de Grave—probably the most artist-infested spot in all Newfoundland, and no wonder.

Closely gathered around a cliff-framed cove, thirty or forty frame dwellings seem to occupy every level ledge in the rock hillsides, and wherever it is possible to hang them, fish-drying flakes are propped out on forests of slim poles. A crowd of small boats fills the harbour, each a lively spot of colour like the houses. Paint is used to good advantage here, and a naturally sombre scene becomes vibrant with living interest. Somehow the feeling comes that here is a glimpse of the small Newfoundland outport as it used to be in years gone by. No occupation other than fishing exists and there are no happenings other than those of normal family life and its labours, the recurring seasons and varying moods of the sea with its uncertain generosity of harvests. This is Sunday. Docks, fish-houses and boats are deserted. The population is away visiting or enjoying Sabbath rest. A few sedately dressed children stroll chattering along the hill paths. No fish are drying on the flakes—even on weekdays just now there'd be few for there's little demand and prices are low. Cod crowd the sea. "They're eatin' rock," as the saying goes, "but what's the use of takin' 'em times like these?"

Port de Grave's little cove is rich in history if one could find the records or even faint relics of its past. The earliest west of England fishing adventurers made it a summer station, and a busy place it must have been when the fleet was in. That would be somewhere about year 1600. Ten years later John Guy, arriving off shore to establish his colony from Bristol, met with a friendly enough reception from those already in possession who, having no desire to see others crowd in on their fishing grounds and settlement, persuaded him that better land and more commodious harbourage was to be found elsewhere. So away he went to set up his flag and settle his people where now stands the village called Cupids.

The road lures us on to the end of the peninsula with every mile as interesting and every wide-open view as arresting as any passed this day. Each village has its own charm and not soon to be forgotten is one that rambles up and down two hills sheltering a small cove and presenting the puzzling problem as to what would happen if two motors found it necessary to pass on either of the roads.

Skirting the fiord-like arm of Conception Bay, we come to Cupids, once a seat of government and a fortress, later a busy fishing station and village, and now little more than a place where these things had been.  The sole visible reminders of those days are remains of a shattered flagpole standing up from the rock on which John Guy is supposed to have erected the standard of King James I, and a cairn of field-stone erected in 1910 bearing a bronze plate:

To commemorate the landing near site of this memorial of John Guy—First Governor of Newfoundland—Master of Bristol Society of Merchant Adventurers.

The plantation which he founded in this place then known as Cuper's Cove was the first chartered or authorized settlement in Newfoundland.  In this settlement the founder lived for a season and returned to his native city of Bristol to receive the honours, rewards and esteem of his fellow citizens, A.D. MCMX.

Mayor, Member of Parliament and Master.

Gift of citizens of Bristol and Society of Merchant Adventurers of Bristol.

How the place came to be called Cuper's Cove is long forgotten.  The suggestion that it was the name of the lieutenant left as Governor when Guy went home is reasonable enough, and here again easy-going pronunciation or an irrepressible twist of humour gives the name an otherwise unexplainable change into Cupid's.  Legend reports that another first white child to be born on the Island here met its parents—could there be an interesting love story hidden somewhere in long-forgotten folk-lore?

Guy came armed with a royal charter detailing exactly what was to be done about the fishing trade, farming and lumbering and very carefully guarded the king's interest throughout. The colony lasted less than twenty years.  War, piracy and most of all later active hostility of the west of England merchants would have discouraged a far more vigorous attempt to people a new land.  Other settlements established about the same time failed for similar reasons and, a recorded credit of bronze tablet notwithstanding, Bristol's Merchant Adventurers were among those persecuting the settlements in a determined effort to abolish them. During the reigns of Charles I and II this culminated in laws forbidding English ships to carry settlers to Newfoundland, or to leave any of their crews behind when they returned. Settlers here were deprived of their cleared land and homes and were forbidden to take fish until the spring arrival of the merchants' ships. But the "stuberne fellows" carried on one way or another for almost two hundred years, many building homes in hidden coves scattered along the rock shores and quite unapproachable by land.

These things are remembered today by descendants of those who suffered, and it was along this coast I first heard the remark, "You know, we don't love England—ain't 'ad much reason to." Several times again I was to hear it, and more than once in St. John's from people whose education and culture evidenced fact that such an attitude had not unreasoning prejudice for its foundation. Through almost its entire history, Island government has been under domination from England, in earlier days complete and repressive when not downright antagonistic, and even in recent times under Commission Government not always following a line which Newfoundlanders, rightly or wrongly, desired or would have advised. Government from overseas in no way responsible to the governed could never be more popular here than it could in Canada, United States or, for that matter, anywhere else.

I remembered Newfoundland's magnificent effort in two World Wars and brought that up.

"Ah, yes," came answer, "We don't love England, but we love the English way of life, and we'll fight for that." Which surely they did.

"I notice you gave England's king and queen a right royal, all-out welcome when they came here," I said.

"Certainly, and we meant all of it. He didn't come here as King of England. When we had our own government he was King of Newfoundland—and now he's King of Canada—so why not?" and shrewdly he added, "British form of government is best yet devised—so long as we can run it ourselves." And that seemed a fairly sound piece of political philosophy.

Back calls the Cabot Highway and the journey south, regretfully leaving for a time views of the sea and fascinating tales of the past abounding throughout this area. There's not a village along the coast but out of its stormy story has preserved faint wisps of legends of pirates and piracy as dramatic as any ever put down on paper. Believe all you hear and you'll suspect there's pirate treasure buried in almost every cove visited. Along the shore out of Bay Roberts is a small natural cave accessible only when the tide is favourable. On its wall is carved what might be a rough map leading to buried wealth which so far has evaded searchers. Tales are told of actual finding of treasure, all highly legendary and difficult, if not impossible, to verify. There's the story of the fisherman on Bell Island who acquired a certain piece of land, was seen to be digging it over most assiduously, and who later suddenly left for the States where he was reported to be living in affluence. Treasure or not, there's no doubt that over a long period of history, pirates were an ever threatening menace to life and property and their disastrous visits were frequent.

In the latter years of Elizabeth's reign piracy stood high among the more gainful and popular occupations. Sea warfare authorized by national need and royal approval fell upon dull days. Captains and fighting men who had driven Spain's Armada off the seas could find little to do as profitable as plundering Spanish or even French ships. Fighting seamen of other nations found themselves in the same fix. The English Channel and North Sea, pathway of much world commerce, was a fruitful field for this line of effort and was haunted by Dutch, Flemish, French and Spanish seagoing highwaymen, to say nothing of adventurous spirits from England with a natural liking for the trade and nothing much else in sight upon which to expend their abundant energies. As ocean trade with the west developed, the pirates followed as foxes would follow a flock of fowls, and among most notoriously daring was Captain

Peter Easton or Eastman, whom first we met as naval officer rescuing the Irish Princess Neigra from her Dutch captors.

"Arch-pyrate," he was called in chronicles of those days, and with some reason. Phillip Goss, in his *History of Piracy*, records that in 1610 Easton appeared in the Bristol Channel commanding an armada of his own numbering forty ships, doubtless to the great annoyance and loss of many honest west of England merchantmen. Later on he appeared off Newfoundland with ten ships and proceeded to ravage up and down this coast. Off Harbour Grace an islet of rock today bears his name and, of course, a legend of buried treasure. Somewhere along here he set up a fort as a sort of permanent headquarters. His first visit to Harbour Grace was by no means to be forgotten.

Somewhat misty records state he robbed the settlers, burned the forests, took five ships with one hundred pieces of ordnance, stole loot valued at £10,400 and impressed into his services from here and there along the coast some five hundred English sailors before proceeding on his notable career of murder, rapine and spoilation. This troublesome person seems to have been very much of a character and one wonders why he is not more celebrated in sea-history. At any rate he did not come to well-merited hanging on Wapping Stairs. The man must have had good judgment. He retired from professional life when retiring was good, settled on the Riviera, built himself a palace, and opened up negotiations with England's government for a treaty of peace which should include pardon for himself allowing him to go home where, no doubt, he would have lived as a public-spirited and exemplary citizen. Home authority did not see it that way. His was not quite the kind of buccaneering that might be condoned even in those days, and most likely too many rich and influential British merchants had so suffered through his activities as to justify in their minds a lively longing for his hanging. He continued to enjoy life in the Riviera palace where it is suggested his death was both pious and peaceful.

It could be that Lieutenant Pike, husband to the Princess, had carried on as one of Easton's officers, and that their home-making in what sometimes must have seemed an uncongenial climate was born of desire to live where the eyes of avenging law would be least likely to search. If so, the lieutenant probably would not be lonely for kindred company. I am told that through early years few communities in these parts could not boast of one or two bold-spirited and useful members willing to let bygones be bygones, and anxious to intrude the fact of their continued existence as little as possible on the attention of authorities back home. Surely, these men must have made their contribution to the daring and fine seamanship that marks the Newfoundland sailor wherever he may be.

For the sake of villages to be glimpsed as we pass through and for sea-views not to be missed, we follow a side-road good enough for midsummer travel and come to Clark's Beach in a hill-surrounded setting worthy of a more romantic name, one such as many found in this land of romantic and whimsical nomenclature. We pass a church notable for its separate belfry, standing nearer to the priest's house than to the church. Quite often the priest is bell-ringer, too, and one can understand that on a cold winter's morning, or when storms are at their worst, distance from bed to belfry should be as short as possible. From here the main highway goes overland, crossing the valley of South River where salmon still run in early summer. More good farming is being done up and down this valley and more unbroken farming land lies back among the hills. Our road now is towards Brigus, a town of many honourable years and great renown among sailors all round the Atlantic Ocean.

# 12

*Brigus, Sea-salt Town if Ever One There Was— Rockwell Kent House—The Parson Turned Experimental Agriculturist—Bob Bartlett, Master Mariner— Seals and Sealing—The Wool Industry.*

LEAVING Cabot Trail, we run down to the sea through a rocky once-wooded ravine at the bottom of which lies a small area of flat land covered with comfortable-looking houses scattered along winding paths that are the streets of this interesting place. An air of settled age pervades its busiest way where half a dozen or so shops cater to town needs and social gossipings. After rounding a corner or two and making inquiry we stop before the hotel. From a century to half a century ago Brigus was home to many retired sea-captains, merchants, sealers, whalers and what not—men of achievement and considerable substance. They built themselves stout and pleasant homes for retiring days and the hotel is one of the few of those now standing for useful purposes.

A tree-shaded, square house, it looks every day its age whatever that may be. Entry is a slow process this Sunday evening. Much bell-ringing and knocking brings no response, but a passing townsman explains. The hotel includes a tavern and on Sunday evenings the lads of the village, having little else to do, would like to drop in to discuss this and that over a bottle of beer. But no, laws here are as restrictive and citizens as docile as in most other North American communities—and there's no Sunday beer.  The landlord is a kindly sort of chap hating to say no, so he locks the door and retires to some place where he will not be bothered by customers he may not serve.  The friendly townsman goes home, telephones the landlord, and eventually the door opens and entry is permitted.

The retired seaman who built this house did himself rather well.  A wide central hall and stairway, and generously proportioned rooms on either side each with black marble fireplaces and high ceilings, suggest spacious living and when graced by furnishings of the then current fashion brought from overseas it must have spoken of liberal hospitality for welcome friends.  Bedrooms, too, are large and airy.  Here again meals are ample, homely and good, and rates altogether reasonable.

Going from one place to another in Brigus is a short walk. Small wharves, fish houses and many boats line the little cove that opens out into the broad, deep, hill-sheltered arm of the sea. The peaceful quiet of Sunday afternoon extends pretty well through the week, except that men and women move about with brisker walk, greetings seem cheerier, and children noisier.  A carpenter's hammer beats out a snappy tune and gas engines shatter dawn's stillness as boats hurry seaward to fade out in blue mists of morning.

As pleasant a walk as any is through the village, past ruined foundations no longer supporting factory or mill, and up a steep hill topped by two large well-kept frame churches and their rambling churchyards.  The one painted a soft yellow is the Church of England, its "United" colleague is of a dazzling whiteness and together they dominate the view from every side. Tombstone dates go back only a hundred years or so, and one wonders what has become of the graveyards of earlier days. First Wesleyan chapel was built here in 1801 when the first minister arrived.  Anglicans were served by a visiting parson from St. John's, when weather and convenience permitted, until 1830 when a church was built and a rector appointed.  Roman Catholics first built in 1826 and now have a dignified church down below at the town's other side.

Our path winds past cemeteries and down to the sea again,

and here two or three flower-gardened houses modestly give life to a placid scene once as crowded and busy as any along the coast. Five hundred paces from here a knoll of rock divides land from deep harbour water, and through its twenty or thirty feet width a tunnel has been chiselled out large enough to allow the passage of men drawing wheelbarrows bearing burdens from ships, or salt cod from fish-house to holds. For that purpose it was hewn out of the rock, eloquent witness of activity and prosperity long departed. So crowded with warehouses, fish-drying flakes and wharves was this shore that a late-coming merchant could find no place for his buildings other than this fenced off from the water's edge. So he cut his tunnel through rock wall and erected his dock and buildings on the waterside. Now, all up and down this part of the harbour neither stick nor stone exists to record the work of those who laboured here and whose ships went out over many seas. Nothing but the hole remains—but that seems to be as good as ever.

Ten minutes farther on the road crosses a stony beach at Frogmarsh where a tiny and vividly green valley runs back into spruce-clad hills. A pungent odour of drying caplin fills the air. Here and there a cottage looks out on a narrow path wandering off between small fields where a pony or two, the odd cow and a few sheep graze in lush tall grass. Boats on the beach and drying flakes indicate that a living hereabouts comes as much from sea as land, and at the moment nobody seems very busy about gathering either. A village stood here when d'Iberville burned Brigus on his way to Carbonear. Mostly hidden by forest and quite deserted by inhabitants, the French would have passed it by unnoticed except for the untimely crowing of a rooster, and Frogmarsh went skyward in flames.

Descendants of those who witnessed this event live here now. Over the years a small host of children has entered life to be drawn swiftly away to scenes where labour was more profitable, employment more continuous and a natural desire for better-ment of social conditions had a fair chance of fulfilment. Such places as these are home to aged people, a few middle-aged and some children. Youths and young women have gone afar and the old people are lonely. On the way back the lady of a gardened house tells about this. A grandmother she is, with children unseen for years and grandchildren never seen. There's a quiet smile deep down in her dark eyes, a smile of loving and longing, perhaps even of hope—but it's a sad smile and you wonder if ever it breaks into the dreams of grown-up children far away to give their hearts a homeward tug. You hope so— but you feel that here you glimpse Newfoundland's major tragedy that will not pass until some power vitalizes and organizes its industry so that her children may stay home to aid in stabilizing economic self-sufficiency.

Out along the harbour's north shore a road passes through the town's older part with a street or two on which houses stand close together as though once part of a closely built-up community. Up hill it goes past a large and seemingly modern fish-house where stocks of last year's unsold cod are being taken from barrels for another drying and refreshing sun-bake on the flakes. A government inspector has looked them over and condemned any showing signs of less than standard curing— another of those chances of loss the fish merchant has to take in his stride.

This walk seems to end a mile or two along the shore at what town gossip calls the Kent House. It is not much talked about and getting to it takes a bit of inquiry. Rockwell Kent, whose moody and powerful sea paintings are known to most art-conscious Americans, lived two years here the more or less solitary life of the man who wants to be left alone with nature and has no interest other than the study of her tempers and the toils of those who faced them in the strife of daily living.

They say the house was different in his time—just a small fisherman's cottage perched on a rocky ledge high above the sea and looking up and down the fiord that ends in Brigus Harbour— a sombre view on brightest of days and on others at times a spectacle of brooding immensity with awesome possibilities. Somebody has taken the place over and with quite nice architectural sense has given it a new outside, happily leaving the interior just as it was—tiny rooms and low ceilings. Furnishings suit admirably—small period pieces mostly. Kent's studio would be about ten by twelve feet, just about room enough to swing a brush and no more. The rock ledge has been gardened into a delightful spot for midsummer sun baths.

Legend says Kent's Brigus sojourn had little social significance. He seems to have kept to himself, an attitude which the neighbourhood came to approve as concerning a foreigner whose business here was not well understood, and gossip wondered. First World War then being fought brought the enemy submarine menace into every island harbour and permitted no fooling about blackouts. Too many Newfoundland ships and lives had been lost that way and when nighttime flashes of light were observed in the vicinity of the Kent domicile, suspicion and anger were aroused. Without doubt Kent was innocently flashlighting his footsteps from house to gate or to some other spot on a rock ledge where light surely was needed— in several directions one step too far might have meant a broken body at the sea-edge below. Or perhaps he was careless about window blinds. Anyway, his public relations standing went to a new and unpleasant low and, one gathers, departure to his own land was accepted as a satisfactory event by both Rockwell Kent and a sizable part of the community.

On the town's outer edge is a garden offering living proof that Newfoundland soil and climate, under intelligent encouragement, can grow most things with which kitchen gardens enrich and diversify mainland diets. I stood gazing over a five-foot board fence admiring bright flower borders leading up to a neat white cottage offering every evidence of having been home to several generations of men, women and children, every one of whom had loved it. Some houses get to look like that. This one had an air of having settled down into its surroundings such as could not possibly be acquired in less than a century.

A pleasant voice extended an invitation to enter and meet Rev. Ezra Broughton, a retired United Church minister, five feet six inches of geniality and an enthusiastic and successful gardener. The garden was small, but the variety of things it produced was amazing. There seemed to be a healthy and prosperous patch of every vegetable a well-ordered garden should grow, and some I never have met outside the covers of seed catalogues. A small glass-covered lean-to covered fruit-laden tomato plants set in after other seedlings had moved outside to face cold realities of outdoor life. Fruits grew in the garden, too—berry bushes, strawberries and a few apple trees promising well. It was, in short, that kind of a garden making a highly profitable adjunct to any home, and bringing a sharp reminder that nowhere in my village wanderings so far had I seen anything like it. Potato patches, yes—nothing much else.

"Why don't other people do this sort of thing?" I asked.

"Ah, they don't think it can be done and they never try," and Mr. Broughton chuckled happily as though enjoying one of the world's best jokes at the expense of his fellow-countrymen. That's the kind of man he was. His enthusiasm for gardening flowered in humour to bubble over in merry little laughs.

"That's why I do it," he said. "They all ought to have gardens. They'd be much better in health if they had and I'm showing 'em it can be done."

"Are you having much success in getting them to try it?"

Now his laugh had a tinge of regret as though inspired by the vagaries of a well-loved child. "It's very slow," he said, "very slow. They're fishermen. They work on the sea and they have no love for handling a spade or working on the land. But some of them are beginning to think about it, here and there."

Good to look upon, and as pleasant to linger in as the garden was, inside the house was more so. No exact record of its building existed but a good hundred years and more lay behind it. The cheery sitting-room had a fireplace that once had spread over all one wall. It recessed back with settles on either side and between them the whole ceiling opened into the chimney. What roaring log blazes must have heated its stone hearth in days gone by. The ceiling is closed now and a small fireplace piped into it offers a warm glow for cool evenings, but the old settles are still inviting as snug spots for leisured ease.

The story of Mr. Broughton's career has more of interest than that of any house could, and its telling in full would throw vivid light on two generations of Newfoundland outport living. He came from England in 1900, a young man and a Wesleyan missionary and had for his first charge a tiny hamlet on Trinity Bay. His sparse flock spread out some twenty-five miles in every direction except seawards and pastoral visitations meant much walking. For "relief" came a period of missionary work "down on the Labrador," outermost wan edge of human habitation, where urgent need of priest and doctor and every humanizing influence was commonplace. All is changed now, he says, by the Grenfell Medical Missions and other agencies, but at its worst in those early days was a terrible thing to have seen.

"But why," I asked, "should people live like that when all they had to do was to move in their own boats to more companionable surroundings?"

"A free life," he said, "answerable to nobody, not even God, and very likely many of them fugitives from law—or their fathers were. They were trappers, too, wanting their trap-lines where none would trespass."

That was the worst side of the picture—but even so rigorous a ministry had its joys. In isolated hamlets there was always a welcome for the ministering visitor, and in far-off lonely coves were families innocent of knowledge of communal life in villages and warmly grateful when priestly comfort and companionship dropped in from outer worlds. It was hard to depart sometimes without accepting a present of some fine pelt specially reserved from a stock that at best brought meagre return in cash or supplies. Furs were fairly plentiful, beaver, fox, otter, marten and others, but prices paid by the Hudson's Bay Company those days were low. No lack of food was apparent for fresh meat and fish were available for the taking on every hand. However, prices for flour, tea and such necessities were high, cutting deeply into trap-line earnings.

All this looks like life gone backwards towards the days of Adam and Eve or worse, and the happiest thought about it is that social effort, mechanics, and science, are successfully employing themselves in abolishing its horrors. The thought also comes that Reverend Ezra Broughton was of ideal temperament and

metal for a mission such as this.  He could not be other than
of friendly approach, and it is good guessing that genial insistence
would carry far whatever message he had to deliver into the
hearts of those he came to serve, no matter how estranged from
the way of life he sought to teach.  No influence is more humanizing than kindly laughter; no lesson, however spiritual, but may
gain penetration therefrom.

Much revealing talk we had in front of that sitting-room fire.
Forty years of ministry had left no scars, only a deep and broad
understanding of his people and, one gathered, it had changed
him but little.  His speech was that you'd hear in any Devon
market-town now, or a hundred years ago, broad vowels, deep-
toned with pleasing rise and fall—the speech most often heard
among those with whom he had lived and worked.

The room we sat in was not less English, and in its way of
quiet comfort probably like thousands of others scattered around
the Island.  Willow-patterned plates spotted the walls and other
touches here and there reminded of the land that had once
been home.  Suddenly the picture and personality brought
realization that in some respects parts of Newfoundland are more
truly transplanted pieces of England as it once was than perhaps
any others on the North American continent.

We said good-bye in the front garden where he pointed to
successes in producing blooms not supposed to prosper in these
parts.  He pointed with pride to a couple of experimental sugar
maples doing very well down by the gate and prophesied a
maple-sugar industry for the Island, if Islanders could be
persuaded to develop it.  One wish he had, and he was a bit
wistful about this—he wanted a holly bush or two.  They grew
about his English home and would make home here complete.
Besides, he wanted to know if they would live here.  "I'll get 'em
some day," he chuckled.  "I don't know how, but they'll come."
We left that garden with a far clearer view of Newfoundland
and its people than we had carried in with us an hour earlier.

Every Island town and village seems to have its local historian—one whose family history reaches far back—having a
love for the scenes about him and respect for valorous men and

women who have made his neighbourhood a place to live in. Brigus has John Hearn. His great-grandfather came here in 1798, built a house of square logs the next year and John now lives in it. Repair work forty years ago uncovered interior sheeting of birchbark laid on in two to three-foot squares, and there it still is, apparently as sound as ever. John talks of early days almost as though he had lived through them and, amongst other things, has records of the first property-holding registrations issued after the ban against permanent settlement finally was lifted. Among the more interesting is that of Widow King and sons who arrived in 1763 and in 1784 were granted registry for ownership of two hundred and ten yards east on west on waterfront by ninety yards back, one stage (wharf), one flake, one house, one garden and one meadow upon which they had lived twenty-one years. The Goushons, from Jersey, registered their holdings from 1785 and now live on it with their names somehow changed into Gushue. William Percy in 1770 registered a property which his family had somehow contrived to use, if not to live on, for one hundred and twenty years previously. His descendants are still there fishing. In earliest days a Stephen Percy had established an "accompting house" doing general banking business, most likely the Island's first, or very nearly so, and an important institution when Brigus docks were as prosperously busy as any on the Island. These are a few of a long list recording the tenacity with which these people have held on to their birthrights and emphasizing the fact that they are no recent migrants from foreign lands, but descendants of original settlers whose speech and customs they have retained and made outstanding characteristics of this newer land—a matter to be borne in mind by those who would pass judgment upon their manner of life and thought.

Shipbuilding yards flourished here in year 1800 and respectable farms were being chopped out of back forest so that later a water-powered gristmill ground native-grown wheat and oats, and one Charles Cousins from his farm about five miles away won a prize in Scotland for oats grown here. The theory that Newfoundland offered little or no opportunity for farming had not then become popular—nor has it yet on this particular farm which is still being worked.

Brigus prosperity through the best of days was but part of that prevailing all up and down Conception Bay. Outer world contact was almost entirely with England and Ireland. Newfoundland ships carried fish to Spanish, Portuguese and Mediterranean ports but brought back no influence on life here other than foreign commodities and gold. About 1800 came the heaviest inflow of English and Irish immigration, predominately poverty stricken perhaps, but having a lively yeast of scholarly men and others trained to trade and industry. Education came with them, says John Hearn, and apart from St. John's, Conception Bay ports had the best on the Island. Men from English universities and Dublin, here for reasons best known to themselves, set sound standards in their work teaching mostly first essentials, reading, writing and mathematics—the latter in branches most useful, and most thoroughly it was taught. That was before state education came. Private grammar schools or individual teachers did the job with what pupils they could get and did it very well. Gone were the days of sea-captains taking ships round the globe but unable to read, write or figure and finding in their trade little need for such accomplishments. A new and scholared generation came along to help bring to Newfoundland its most prosperous era.

Seamanship was and is Newfoundland's breath of life, and her heroes were seamen—gallant men who dared the worst of storm and danger and came off victorious—sea-captains who brought ships and men safely home through terrific perils, who by skill, courage and cunning made fast voyages or sailed off to fishing or sealing grounds to return first of the fleet laden to the "gunnels" with record gold-paying loads. Of these men and their deeds Newfoundland's best ballads and come-all-yees are made, and their number is untold. You'll hear them sung with a hearty will wherever a few Newfoundlanders get together, and always they are good to listen to.

Outstanding among sea heroes and always to live in memory here is Captain "Bob" Bartlett, world-famous navigator of

Admiral Peary's ship on his second and successful trip to the North Pole in 1909. Bartlett was an Island hero before that—a typical example of the Newfoundland sea-captain at his best. Bartletts have a place in John Hearn's list of the earliest Brigus settlers. They came from Dorset and received title to their shore-holdings in 1769. Bob—you never hear the name Robert in Brigus—was born in 1875, inheriting and absorbing sea traditions with every drawn breath—a sea urchin, no doubt, if ever there was one on land. At seventeen he commanded one of his father's schooners and not much later received his master mariner's certificate. Here they talk of him as the kind of captain good seamen love to sail under—as successful in his voyages as daring and dependable. "Sailing with Bob, you never saw the lee rail," was told me more than once. He flew his canvas to the last safe ounce of groaning strain, and record voyages were his regular performance. He knew his ships, knew his rigging and knew his men, and from each he exacted all they had to give. By no means patient with neglect or shiftlessness, he was a hard man to cross and spoke his mind with sailorly freedom. Fishing and sealing filled his early days and hazardous trips to northern icefields equipped him for the world-prize of taking Peary north. Experience of more than one disaster made him a better sailor. Three times was his own ship sunk or ice-crushed—the sharpest of training for that historic dash to the pole.

One story throws a flash of light on sealing days and hunting methods before aeroplanes sought out and marked the prey for easier approach. The fleet lay in some convenient northern harbour, among them one captained by Bob's father and another by his brother. Wide search had discovered no seals. They were late or they were elsewhere. Bob was roaming afar on his own independent hunt following a "hunch" or, more likely, hints from wind and weather that experience had taught him to be useful. Radio they had, and out of the air came a bewildering message from Bob to his father making reference to a "lame schoolmaster" of early days and not at all clear. Long they pondered. Why call up the ghost of the old schoolmaster

Lawrence at this time.   Then they saw it.   "Bob's at Cape
St. Lawrence and he's found seals."   At dark of night with lights
all out two ships stole out to sea.   They found him at the cape
where he had spent hours in the crow's nest watching seaward
for the first sign of their coming.   There were plenty of seals for
all three ships.   And they arrived home first, heaviest laden
of the fleet.

Behind a neat whitewashed picket fence and a pleasant
garden stands the Bartlett paternal home presided over by
Bob's two charming sisters.   Unmarried, he always lived here
and the house has become a shrine to his memory.   A friendly
house this, built and furnished for comfortable living with one
room devoted to Bob and the record of his achievement.   Its
walls are covered with pictures of his ships and signed portraits
of great men in tribute to his eminence as sea-captain, and his
power of inspiring friendship.   The central figure is Peary and
another is President Theodore Roosevelt.   Both of these men of
strong character seem to have found in Bob a kindred spirit.
There are letters from each evidencing friendship that had
crossed the line into affection.   A mahogany casket is filled with
decorations and medals, among them the United States Con-
gressional Medal and many from geographical societies and
various European governments—altogether a brave show and
splendid recognition of a useful life.

The tale of the two voyages that ended in Peary's reaching
the Pole, with all their troubles, disappointments and joys, is to
be read in Peary's books.   His own story is modestly and briefly
told in *Bob Bartlett's Log*.   It was a bitter disappointment to him
that he was not permitted to accompany Peary on the last
dash over the ice to the Pole.   His duty lay with the ship
standing by awaiting the return of the polar party.   Death came
to him on one of his New York visits.   His grave is here on the
hill close to the two churches, beside that of his brother Captain
Wilfred Rupert Bartlett, Military Cross and Bar, Cavalier
Crown of Italy, killed in action at Cambrai, November 30, 1917,
aged twenty-eight years.   Down at the harbour's edge stands a
granite shaft facing the sea and bearing a bronze portrait plaque

and inscription, "Robert Abram Bartlett, Master Mariner, Born Brigus, August 15, 1875.   Died New York, April 28, 1946."

Somewhere about the end of the seventeen-hundreds the useful and valuable qualities of seal-oil and seal leather came to be recognized.  The result was start of an industry making an important contribution to Newfoundland's wealth and at one time threatening to place the North Atlantic hair seal on the list of creatures once having inhabited this world but now extinct. An engaging creature on many counts is the seal, and perhaps most intelligent of all ocean dwellers.  They come in two kinds, Hoods and Harps—Hoods named from a rubber-like protuberance growing over male heads, and Harps from supposedly harp-like markings on the hides.  Most of their time is spent north of the Arctic Circle—Hoods east of Greenland, and Harps on the east side of Baffin Bay.  Along about September's end, some say on September 20th, for they are peculiarly punctual, they start south in two long lines down Labrador's coast and into Newfoundland waters—Hoods to the east and Harps between them and the coast.  Perhaps northern food supplies have given out by this time, or they just want a change of diet and think longingly of the vast swarms of cod moving northward off the Banks when winter brings freezing temperatures south.

By early February the southern diet satiates.   Fat and hearty they turn north in search of Arctic icefields drifting south to meet them and convenient for climbing out upon.   Here the snow-white babies first open their big brown eyes on a world that at first glance must seem little worth coming for and may explain the look of astonishment and curiosity reportedly habitual to a seal's countenance through life.  But mother is there and she does her job splendidly.  If she be a Harp she has bored through the ice from underneath and the surface surrounding it is her home and nursery.  Away fishing all day, she bobs up with the groceries about nightfall, by which time the little fellow probably is developing his lungs with hearty bawls like those of a two-year-old child.  Kittenishly playful when they take to water a few weeks later, these youngsters must be fun to watch, and they can grow up into amazingly amiable pets with a pronounced sentimental side. Music of any kind seems to affect them deeply, particularly when played on instruments having a flute-like tone. They are known as "bedlamers," another French word turned into something more easily pronounced. Early Jersey settlers named them "bete de la mere," animals of the sea, but how could Devon Englishmen be bothered with any such outlandish term!

As a household pet, the seal would seem to have his inconveniences, a bit cumbersome perhaps, and taking up a lot of floor room. But there have been instances. One "pup" brought home in infancy and reared with loving care became the children's play-fellow and the subject of adult affection. Growing up, he developed traits less endearing and the day had to come when he was taken out to sea, dumped overboard, and told to go fish for himself. The return journey was a sad affair, even tearful for the youngsters who were there to see him off. But the home arrival was considerably brightened by the sight of the seal waiting at the garden gate registering loving welcome and, no doubt, some glee at having beaten the family home. The relater of this tale could not say if, when, or how, the seal finally was persuaded to take up life in his native ocean.

Also, there's the story of the man living on the shore whose pet seal shoved off to sea every morning, returning at eventide to lay a fat cod at his master's feet. You do not have to believe that one. I'm not sure I do—anyway, who wants to eat cod every day?

In late March or early April, when the babies are six to seven weeks old and have been taught to swim and look after themselves a bit, away go the herds to their Arctic summer homes, leaving the youngsters pretty well to themselves. But not all go. It is when they are on the ice that sealing ships steal in through the mists and many thousands of them find their destiny in barrels of seal oil, ladies' fine leather purses, and what not.

Scottish seal hunters were early visitors to these waters and gave a lead in the trade, swiftly and intelligently followed by Newfoundland sailormen. In the early days seals were taken in stout nets strung from shore to outlying rocks. Later on they were hunted from small boats and shot—a most hazardous business and wasteful of seal life and quite often human. Most seals sank when shot, and bad weather, contrary winds or swiftly rising fog, accounted for loss of many men. Boats used were small shallops, mostly deckless or partly decked sailing craft and dreadfully unsuited for long trips over wintry seas. In 1804, a year of exceptional gales, thirty-five shallops went sailing from Conception Bay and twenty-five were lost. The first decked schooner for the trade was built near Carbonear in 1794 and by 1806 shallops no longer were used.

Sealing started the building of large ships, making it an important industry, and Newfoundland ships had to be as rugged and well-found as craftsmanship, ingenuity and honest work could make them. Hardly a harbour up and down Conception Bay cannot show shipyard remains where once stout and tall ships of forty to seventy-five tons took shape from timbers cut in surrounding forests, and glided down to the sea for a long or perhaps short life of viking-like adventure under strain and stress as severe as ocean anywhere could offer. The *Sealing Book* of L. G. Chafe, published through forty of those years as an annual record, is authority for the statement that round bows of schooners soon gave place to sharp stems cut away underneath so that the ship might run up on ice-pans to crush them with its own weight. In time this type of ship became general all up and down the North American coast and, no doubt, was the forerunner of smart sailing schooners typified by the sweet-lined Nova Scotia built *Bluenose* happily immortalized on every Canadian ten-cent piece. Newfoundland shipyards did more than bring wealth to the Island—they made notable contribution to shipbuilding and sea mastery in waters far beyond their own.

Trade flourished. Makers of rigging, sailmakers, ironworkers and men of other trades found steady employment. English craftsmen, previously only summertime visitors, stayed through the year and brought their families, and Conception Bay outports began to be home towns with active social life. The historian, Anspach, says the whole plan of sealing was altered by the enterprise and industry of these people who developed strongly built ice-resisting schooners profitably usable for cod fishing. When the short sealing season was over such ships went far afield and down on the Labrador where cod harvest ever was plentiful. Brigus early took a lead among Bay ports, rivalling St. John's where merchant wealth soon built up an imposing fleet. Brigus Harbour was fortunate, easier than most to get out of in early spring. Much rivalry existed up and down the Bay, and for Brigus even jealousy—but wealth made up for that and everybody in Brigus was well off. They tell of one sea-captain who had to have the help of two men to carry his casket of golden sovereigns to a new and finer house he had built.

The matter of getting to sea early in March was of first importance—an annual race to the icefields and back home with the spoil. It was tough work getting the ships land-clear sometimes when ice covered the harbour. Lanes of open water were cut and, favouring wind or no wind, they were towed to open water. The last issue of Chafe's *Sealing Book*, edited by H. M. Mosdell, M.B., and long since out of print, reproduces an old-time engraving of this event in St. John's Harbour. With the city rising as dim background, great square-riggers move slowly through the ice as crowds of men hauling on tow-lines give them motion. This happened in every port. John Hearn tells of one hard and late winter when ships were hauled out of Brigus almost to the Labrador—fifteen days or so of ice cutting and towing, night and day.

Interesting it was to talk to Otto Grimm, rotund, bright-eyed and cheery sealing-captain of many years' experience, and spoken of in his home town, Harbour Grace, as having as much as anyone on the Bay to tell about sealing and the most likely to tell it. We sat in his friendly, comfortable kitchen for sake of welcome warmth from the stove. In early days, says the captain, ships of fifty to sixty tons went out with twelve to twenty men aboard, crowded more or less spoon-fashion into sparse sleeping space, but fed in a hearty style if captain and crew were to get along together and work was to be attacked with right good will.

An important person the cook, dishing out tough sea-biscuits and making palatable barrelled salt beef and pork, and dried peas and beans—stout food for rugged stomachs, and they had 'em. Parsimony or carelessness in providing food caused many a row between shipowners and crews, and later on—many years later—legislature passed a "Bill of Fare" regulations against which owners raised woeful wails of ruin. Items called for included fresh vegetables, soft bread now and again, "fig duff" three times weekly, and for Sunday morning brewis, that special treat—to a Newfoundlander. You pronounce that brews or brouse, and here it is as porridge to a Scotsman. Its base is a biscuit a couple of inches square, fat and rounded, as soft and easy to bite as a beach pebble. Much soaking makes it cookable and dried cod is added after, one hopes, lengthy immersion in water. Nourishing food this. I met it more than once—at its best quite likeable. At its worst or saltiest, one sizable unexpected spoonful could inspire saucy back-talk to a mother-in-law.

The search for seals could be long or short as seasons varied, and it was not calm, clear weather hunters hoped for. Mosdell quotes Anspach presenting a picture of "Rock-bursting frost, gales whistling and howling in huge uproar, masses of snow or sleet or thick fogs freezing as they fall to cover with ice decks, rigging and clothes of the mariners. This on a sea covered with mountains and islands of ice in perpetual motion—a situation Newfoundland seal hunters court with as much ardour as vessels in other cases study to avoid it." That is worth quoting, and from what I can learn, is fact not too greatly embellished from imagination.

When seals were sighted ships moved alongside the ice. Men spread over its surface, made and skinned their kill and gathered it into piles marked with a flag for later hauling aboard. Changes of wind, movement of ice or other causes frequently made it necessary for ships to move away to return later for men and seals. But too often storms or fog arose, ships failed to return and men were lost. Here is a typical yarn of that sort of thing. The brig *Atlantic* sent thirty men over the ice, promising to pick them up about dark. A sudden blizzard brought darkness but no ship, and the men thoroughly alarmed, wanted to go and find her. Their leader had trouble holding them, but in black night when hope was all but gone, sound of rattling ship's blocks came through the dark and the skipper's hail rode the storm, "All right, b'ys, we're nearly there." As often happened, men's lives were saved by the extraordinary Newfoundland sense of sea direction and power of smelling out the right path to follow.

This was in later days when bigger ships and steam power made seal hunting less rigorous, but hardly less hazardous. The first steamers, still wooden-built and sail-rigged, appeared about 1860 and carried the trade forward to its highest point of development. About then, too, captains schooled in navigation had taken over from those who had no such good fortune but could usually find their way about the ocean with little trouble. They had to if they would hold their men's respect. There's the tale of the skipper who groped his way through fog and storm into what he thought was his own harbour to find himself several hundred miles away, and soon after was very lonesome for all his men had walked out on him in disgust. And there was the one who sailed for Conception Bay home port to arrive at St. Pierre well up the St. Lawrence Gulf and thought he was in France so that all Newfoundland rocked with ribald laughter of a stomach-shaking heartiness. That sort of thing did happen once in a while—but amazingly seldom.

Men were paid in shares of the ship's catch and they had little use for the captain whose voyages too often were unprosperous. At best, rewards of a hard life were far from high. In sailing days men paid up to forty shillings, called berth money, for the privilege of going on the adventure, but travelled free if they owned their own guns. The first recorded protest against this arrangement was a strike of three thousand men in Brigus in the year 1860 which was settled on some sort of compromise, but berth money remained until 1902 when a strike in the St. John's fleet won its abolition and increased pay for the men. A big to-do this, but settled in short order. All the crews in harbour, some three thousand men, got flags and banners, marched in orderly fashion to Government House and told the Governor what they wanted. In two days they had arrived at a satisfactory compromise with shipowners and bustled out to sea to arrive home shortly afterwards with something like a record catch of 274,000 seals. That was for St. John's fleet alone; add Conception Bay's kill, that of ships from Scotland, from Norway and other countries, and the wonder is that a single seal has survived over the years. In 1851 ninety-two sealers sailed out of St. John's with 2,480 men aboard, from Conception Bay 160 ships and 5,835 men, while other eastern Newfoundland ports swelled the total to 323 ships with 10,682 men, and that was before steam gave impetus to the hunt. For 1848 the total Island catch is stated to have been 631,004 seals.

By 1900 large steamships entirely had taken over the trade. That year St. John's fleet of nineteen ships brought home a record catch of 353,276 seals, having a total value to ships and their 3,760 men of $483,601. March 10th was sailing day that year and the first ship home arrived sixteen days later. She carried 139 men, brought in 13,318 seals valued at $18,385, of which each man's share was $44.08. Highest individual pay that year was $58.48 for 117 men on a seventeen-day trip and lowest was $3.16 for ninety-nine men on a forty-four-day trip. Returns to the men frequently ran up to one hundred dollars—no great reward for the effort expended and danger faced. Record says one ship paid off two hundred dollars per man, which must have been occasion for tumultuous celebration even to the point of inspiring more than one lusty ballad. The number of men carried by the larger ships was astonishing. The five-hundred-ton *Arctic* out of St. John's in 1882 carried 313, and that season each received $64.57 for a month at sea.

Possible extermination of seals appears to have received little consideration prior to steam days and probably was then forced on government attention by apparently diminishing herds. A sealer member of the legislature in 1870 put forward a bill setting March 1st for departure of sailing vessels and March 10th for steamers. This was a help for slower sailing ships and may have given young seals a slightly better chance if any there could be. In 1892 came a law prohibiting Sunday killing—a matter close to the heart of a great many church-going men and some captains with decided views thereon. In 1898 a highly beneficial law regulated the number of men per ship according to its tonnage and thus greatly improved living conditions at sea. Many regulatory laws were passed later. Limits were set to catches, second trips in any one year were forbidden, and adult seals were protected, but nothing seems to have been done to protect the youngsters—surely, short-sighted policy.

A list of the losses of ships and men over recorded years makes shocking reading and highlights the fact that for often meagre returns, hardships and dangers were appalling to any but those born to them. Out of seventy-three ships recorded out of St. John's by Chafe through fifty-four years up to 1918, forty-eight were lost and too often all their men with them. Judging from tales told of earlier times, a season seldom passed without at least one major disaster. Besides storm and ice, strange and unexpected things could happen. The first decked schooner built, the *Sarah Kemp*, a thirty-tonner from Carbonear, returning from her first voyage with a heavy load of seals, ran into moderate breeze. As she lay over her cargo slipped to one side. She capsized and sank. Her captain promptly built another and instituted the practice of subdividing the hold with plank partitions, effectively preventing similar accidents.

Seasons there were when seals were scarce, or continuous bad weather took unusual toll of ships and men. The year 1811 was one. Though the number of schooners and boats lost is not remembered, legend says it was disastrously large and many men perished, carried away on fast-moving ice in sight of shipmates unable to effect any rescue. The year 1844 is remembered as "The Spring of the Growlers," small icebergs moving fast and crushing swiftly, and many ships and men were lost. In 1845 three large ships met disaster. In one case all her crew but six were out in small boats when a storm struck and all were lost. Gales of 1864 sank twenty-six craft and left one hundred and forty others jammed in the ice. Many men were lost and fifteen hundred were marooned on the ice without food or shelter for several days before relief came. In 1852 in a sudden northeast gale forty vessels were "smashed to match-wood" and several set afire by overturned hot stoves. Again many men were lost and more left defenceless on the ice. In 1914 the *Southern Cross* went down in fair weather with all hands lost. The story goes that somebody was careless with fire near a barrel of gunpowder, and that is a good enough guess. That same year is remembered as one of storms. The steamer *Newfoundland* lost seventy-seven men overtaken by a blizzard on the ice. They had walked far out of sight of their ship and perished trying to find a way back, as many hundreds of others had done over the years. A few recorded instances these, out of a list that would make a huge book of grisly reading, par-ticularly if regularly recurring tragedies of the fishing were included. It should be told, too, that three if not four large ships and their men went down as wartime victims of enemy torpedoes.

One more tale of sealing. Seasons came now and then when strong winds drove seal-carrying ice shorewards even into larger bays—which was bad luck for seals. On such occasions most of the population deserted land jobs and went sealing. In 1843 they blew into Bonavista Bay. Some even went ashore, "looking for cabbage patches," says the old story. One wonders why, since they are fish-eaters—and yet a little cabbage on the plate with cod sounds rather attractive to one whose food-taste tends towards the homely. In the year 1862 Green Bay similarly was favoured, and men, women, children and dogs went to work for a reputed profit of £10 each. St. John's had its chance in 1890. Seals were sighted from Signal Hill and about thirty-three thousand were brought to the city by ponies, dogs and just plain hand-hauling. Even this comparatively easy method of sealing had its dangers. In 1867 a sudden change of wind off Catalina broke up the ice, drowning ten women and two men, and in the following two years fierce gales in Trinity Bay blew many small boats to sea and thirty to forty lives were lost. Sealing may have brought great wealth to Newfoundland, but generously has it been paid for in human lives and sorrow, to say nothing of the exacting toil and hardship.

The trouble with a place like Brigus is you drop into the town and for a day or so wonder in leisurely fashion what there is on display or hidden worth telling about.   Then, bit by bit, appears a wealth of fascinating things, each part of the tapestry of this country's life.   Finally you come away knowing very well that lack of time or failure of vision has left half undiscovered.   There are threads of the tapestry, too, seemingly of no importance whatsoever, but each adding its touch of colour to the story. There's Brigus cats, for instance—more numerous than dogs or even sheep.   Eight of them I counted—eight, in the moonlit backyard of the hotel.  Among them was a tenor magnificently voiced with bravura and tour de force and everything else more expensive tenors boast—and one soprano had a vibrato to bring tears to the dullest of sleep-laden eyes.   Most certainly it was opera they were putting on—and very good, too, if you like opera.   Drama was there and passion such as no stage could hope to instil in the hearts of human listeners. But the show had another admirable feature lacking in the human variety—it could be shut off like a radio.   The bomb-like impact of an empty beer bottle on stage centre was completely effective.   There are those for whom enough opera is too much.   It was instructive to have seen the cats.   Fat, sleek and of happy appearance, they advertized the good people of Brigus as of kindly habits, good to children, provident and comfortable home-keepers.   If ever you enter a town where the cats have lean and hungry looks, sly suspicious eyes and slink to shelter from your view, pass on, friend, pass through.   That is no place in which to seek friendly fellowship or warm Christian hospitality—at any price.

Then too, there's the early evening activity of lads and maidens busy laying out a workman-like tennis court—and should you make the mistake of thinking young people of this Island have no inclination for keeping up with the rest of the world in sport as in other things, this tennis court and others like it in many a village show you to be quite wrong.

One bedtime walk countrywards under the brilliance of stars in a blue-black velvet sky brought an astonishing vision. High on the hills a ship stood bow on, port, starboard and masthead lights blazing brazenly with even the reflection of lights on upper deck-housings—unbelievable, but there it was. Night's darkness showed no way of approach through or around fenced-in fields, and no telling how near or far away the phantom rested—clearly a matter for daylight investigation.

Next morning discovered no ship or suggestion of a ship anywhere in the neighbourhood. But high on the hills stood a small bungalow and a large flagstaff flying a Union Jack, while anywhere up to forty children gambolled over the bare surrounding field. Behind the cottage the hill dipped to where one of those fresh-water ponds often found on Newfoundland hilltops had been made into a splendid bathing pool, transparently clear as the sea far below, with a shallow beach, diving boards and dressing cabins—delightful spot for hot August days, and August here can be hot enough for any reasonable taste.

With evening came John Hearn with an invitation to visit the ship, for ship it was when once you had stepped inside the door, and a museum filled with countless pictures and relics of the sea and seafaring days long past. The sitting-room looking out over the town was a lounging room with a comforting fireplace, the sole landlubber note. Ship's lanterns gave light, a ship's clock rang four bells of the night watch and every inward door had proper designation lettered above—Galley, Captain's Cabin, Mate's Cabin, Cabin de Luxe—all shipshape and Bristol fashion. A little staircase—or should it be companionway—led up to the bridge or wheel-house complete with big-ship-sized oak wheel, binnacle, chart table and stout arm chairs from which to view the ship's course over the town and out to sea on a voyage it never will take. The perfect setting for yarning old "salts" talking of heroic days and dangers gone by. The house and all it contains is the interesting and useful hobby of Job Roberts, a member of St. John's merchant family with history going back to earliest times.  Partly weekend cottage, it is mostly a museum for gathering together records of the past and domestic and seafaring tools long since discarded and in danger of being lost and forgotten.  No doubt it finds greater appreciation locally as a gathering place for children when Job Roberts welcomes them to playground and swimming pool, as often he does.

Not far from Brigus and almost on our way south lies Mackinsons, hardly a discernible village but an important centre of the Island wool industry.  A sunlit gravel road runs into the hills through more farming land, the last several hundred yards being a steep forest-shaded pathway down into the valley of a pretty river that once turned the water-wheel of the mill standing alongside.  A noisy gas-engine now activates spinning and weaving machines.  This is Newfoundland's only mill manufacturing woollen goods, and before Confederation it was more important to Island economy than it is today.  The protective tariff that prospered its earlier years has gone, but it still is a busy place and the young manager brought from Huddersfield, where they know all that is to be known about turning sheep fleeces into usable materials, breaks into his crowded day to show the visitor over the plant.  Here wool is sorted and separated as to quality; dyed, carded, spun and woven; and when clattering machines are finished with it, bales of blankets, tweeds, motor rugs, plaids and other materials are the result.  The quality and appearance of the tweeds examined suggest suitings good enough for any taste, and there'd be a lot of snug sleeping under any of the blankets turned out.

Operators are mostly girls and not too many are available. The girls who stay in the country, says the manager, are bright and nimble-fingered, so that reasonable training makes them skilful workers.  It is hard to believe after seeing sheep in every village lane and country road, but the Island produces not nearly enough wool for this small mill's requirements.  All wool offered is bought but much more has to be imported from New Zealand.  True, much locally grown wool goes into home spinning and weaving.  There are no large flocks—perhaps not even small ones. Families have a few animals picking up a living as they find it, just as they would keep a few hens for table use. But sheep seem to thrive with the least possible attention, except that years of happy-chance in-breeding has resulted in deterioration of the wool's quality. Rigorous climate conditions may have developed unusual hardiness. Wherever asked about, annual dipping or any treatment against ticks or other sheep worries seems unthought of. In any case, the suggestion is inevitable that this could be a sheep country with prosperous flocks contributing to labour employment and economic welfare generally. Newfoundland now has no monopoly of cod and there is no evidence that the supply is increasing. Products of mines and forests are almost the sole dependable commodities, other than fish, the Island has to offer in trade. The future of these industries may be great—time will tell. Meanwhile, no wealth is to be gained by the importation of foodstuffs and other commodities that could be produced at home.

The suggestion of the possibilities in the sheep-industry offered back in St. John's brought a characteristic reply from one patriotic and thoughtful citizen:

"Yes, an outsider coming in and glancing over the country might think so. But he wouldn't know our climate's winter cold, dampness and heavy snow. Losses would be too great."

Perhaps he's right—but conversation since then with men who have been there, plus some reading on the subject, would indicate that climatic conditions in the Scottish Isles differ little from those of Newfoundland, and from there comes some of the world's best wool—quite a lot of it. Importation of a flock or two from those same islands, together with a few men trained in handling and shepherding, might have astonishing results.

The journey back to St. John's by road is an interesting and delightful trip. We touch the sea at many points and continually have in view harbours, hamlets and people, presenting new interest round every curve of the road. It is an easy fifty miles or so, ideal for a day's loitering run. Hills going down to shore and climbing back up rock cliffs lend varied charm to every view. Beautiful, restful Holyrood makes a wistful appeal for a stopover if time would allow. Here summer cottages give colour to the scene, and garden flowers in profusion gloriously celebrate long days of northern sunlight.

Far across the bay rise the blue heights of Bell Island from where one of the world's largest deposits of red hematite iron ore runs many miles out under the sea to employ up to two thousand men, according to the rise and fall in the steel industries of other countries. It is good ore but has certain constituents making its smelting difficult, and affecting a continuous marketing, with the result that employment fluctuates. Modern machinery and mining methods are here in use and the men are paid up to mining standards elsewhere when work is available. When it is not, many of them move off to mining centres in other parts of Canada. Doubtless vastly important iron ore deposits now being opened in Labrador will give employment to large numbers.

Around the southern end of Conception Bay and along its eastern shore runs our road to Topsail where it leaves the sea for a dash across the peninsula. Archbishop Howley of St. John's made an exhaustive study of the matter of place-names, thereby greatly illuminating Island history. He says Topsail is a corruption of "Top's Hill" from Devon-English "Tapor Thorp." Perhaps the original meaning was top o' the hill. The hill fades out behind us, and very soon we are concentrating on navigating the busy St. John's streets and bringing to an end a journey through what is said to be as typical a part of Newfoundland as may be found.

# 13

*A Glance at the North Country—Pirates Again, and Ghosts—Bonaventure Bay and Notre Dame—The Grenfell Mission.*

THE NORTH SHORE of the Island may not be ignored in a tale such as this. The coastwise journey north from St. John's, west to Straits of Belle Isle and south down the western shore presents mostly another series of heart-gripping north-sea pictures with living conditions a bit more rugged, climate and weather running somewhat more to extremes and settlement more widely scattered as the journey progresses. With the exception of a spur railway running up to Cape Bonavista, communications between the hundreds of villages and hamlets is entirely by sea, and the coast depends for regular service upon the excellent summertime steamship service operated in connection with the Island railways. Passenger ships rounding the coast do seven hundred miles between St. John's and Port aux Basques and drop in on thirty or forty of the larger outports along the way.

Northward they go from St. John's past a high wall of rock cliffs into Conception Bay, and then fifteen miles across Trinity Bay, leaving its fifty-mile land sheltered depth on the left, to arrive at Trinity, one of the Island's older towns rich in sea-lore and having a harbour that for three centuries has been a calling-place for ships from most of the world's ocean-going countries. A small town now, its great land-locked harbour is one of the

179

finest on the coast. It was first visited and named by the Portuguese Gasper de Cortreal in 1501. Near by is Port Union, headquarters of the Fishermen's Protective Union, earliest co-operative organization designed to assist the fisherman in orderly marketing of his catch. For many years this has been an important and successful institution. Under Commission Government a Fisheries Board was set up to regulate the industry both as to production and marketing and to provide bait depots and other facilities helpful to the industry. Its work has been highly effective and it now acts as an agent of the Canadian Department of Fisheries.

Nova Scotians stoutly may claim that it was Cape Breton rocks that greeted John Cabot's first land-sighting of this western world, but Newfoundlanders will not believe a word of it. For them it was their own Cape Bonavista he saw. He so named it and so it is today and, viewing its grim aspect from sea, one suspects that when he so named it he either must have been very sick and tired of his westward journey, or that it then must have appeared somewhat different from what it now does. Beyond the cape lies the tremendous expanse of Bonavista Bay, island-crowded and with shore-line greatly broken by innumerable deep fiords, each one offering comfortable anchorage for almost any kind of ship that rides the seas, and having on both island and inlet shores small communities that are homes to the men who fish these waters and spend their summers on the Labrador.

Northward and westward around Cape Freels are more islands without number. Away to the north is Fogo, large as many a mainland county and having several townlets and villages, each on its own good harbour—a green island with a comfortable growth of hemlock, spruce and jack-pine and the town of Fogo with a history behind it going back almost into talking distance with Cabot himself. Joe Bats Arm is near here, too, known world over for its curious name but otherwise a quiet little place greatly like to hundreds of others all along this coast. Most important of all is Twillingate with town of that name, metropolis of the island-studded sea, and claiming for itself and nearby settlements a population of about four thousand.

It was a fishing station before year 1700 and by 1893 had grown to be home port to over one hundred and fifty fishing and trading schooners. In 1880 it had a weekly newspaper, *The Sun*, still sending a glow of enlightening rays over a wide sea-scattered area. Almost entirely Protestant, Twillingate has the usual assortment of churches and an impressive Salvation Army citadel and an outstanding feature here is a fine modern hospital excellently equipped and operated.

The matter of maintaining round-the-year medical and nursing services in this part of Newfoundland is no light thing. The doctor has to be a sailor up to Newfoundland standards. I liked the story modestly told by a young medico from these parts back in Brigus where he was enjoying a holiday. One wild autumn night shortly after he took up his work, a small boat brought two men three or four miles across a violent sea. The wife of one was in desperate need of help. By the time the doctor was ready to go the storm had worsened. From the dock the three viewed the unpromising prospect and the men put it up to him. Did he think they could make it? He knew they would go anyway, and had a feeling they were searching to find what kind of stuff he was made of. Scared stiff to go and not daring to refuse, he looked over the boiling sea and stepped into the boat mentally bidding good-bye to life and all its joys. Three hours later he arrived at the other side, safe, but scarcely less a physical wreck than was the almost dying patient he came to visit. Cheering it was to learn that both made a satisfactory recovery, and one has no doubt that in due time word went around the shores that here was a young man up to his job.

Old inhabitants say that Twillingate once had the appearance of a tree-covered natural park. Never would one guess it now. The trees are gone except in a few odd places, and there seems to be no prospect of there ever coming back again. Bare rocks surround the town and its groups of fish-houses and cod-drying flakes.

But the scenery on this western journey is far from monotonous. From Cape Freels, through Sir Charles Hamilton Sound to the end of Bay of Exploits the countless rocky or tree-clad islands have their brightly coloured fishing villages nestling in quiet coves, and every open vista has its trim fishing schooner or two moving against the sky or small boats busily puttering about on their earnest daily vocations.

Along here, too, comes a change in the character of the coast. Over much of it forbidding rock cliffs have given place to low-lying lands. The northern side of the peninsula is known as "The Straight Shore." Low wooded hills run down to the sea, and there are places where excellent fertile soil allows a respectable measure of farming, and kitchen gardens promising pleasantly varied diet for their owners. At the lower end of Bay of Exploits—gallant name that, setting light to imagination—is Lewisport, as busy a place as any on the coast.

Here a branch from the mainline railway every summer hauls vast numbers of tons of paper from the mills at Grand Falls so that it may go on ships to England to find ultimate usefulness as an informative adjunct to British breakfast tables. At the base of another nearby arm of the bay, waters of the important Exploits River reach the sea after running through a valley from which flows a constant stream of pulpwood to swell wide acres of booms floating in the bay until they are whisked off by rail to the paper-making machines at Grand Falls. In wintertime when these northern waters are frozen over such rail traffic as this moves otherways, and along most of the shore the few people who may have either need or desire to travel do so by pony or dog sleigh. Nearby is Botwood, airport for seaplanes serving this wide north-shore area when open water permits.

Notre Dame Bay is another maze of islands and arms of the sea running far back into the hills with tiny outports here and there like a meagre scattering of currants in a shopful of buns, and each has its church or two as centres of social life. Nearly all have English names, though here and there is reminder of early French visitation. The people are overwhelmingly of English origin, descendants of those who sought these shores a hundred, two hundred or more years ago. In and around this area live some thirty to forty thousand people of whom less than one-tenth stem from other races, and most of these are Irish. As far as generations of living in this land will allow, they are English in thought, speech and faith and have lost none of the sterling qualities of their origins.

Confidently these people look towards the future of their land, and sure they are that a wealth of natural resources awaits exploration. Their rivers are rich in water-power possibilities and there are indications of mineral deposits that may in time give employment to armies of workers. Meanwhile, as deep-sea and off-shore fishermen they are excelled by none, and they are sure that, if and when the world settles down to something like that once known as normal condition of trade and commerce, the fishing industry, employing modern methods of catching, packing and marketing, again will experience a measure of reasonable prosperity. Fur trapping is a moderately profitable occupation with fishers and woodsmen. The island's total annual catch runs in value well up to the half-million-dollar mark. Principal furs taken are beaver, otter, fox, marten and lynx, and some fur farming has been carried on with profit.

In this area has been discovered most of such scanty relics as exist of the aboriginal Beothuck Indians found here when white men first came. An exceedingly primitive race, the impact of the white man was too much for them and their extermination followed fast. In later years Island governors attempted their protection, but it was too late. In 1823 thirteen were reported still alive and the last of the race perished in 1829. They are believed to be in no way related to those Indians of mainland origin now on the Island and numbering approximately one thousand.

Much Island history lies buried along this coast, less of war perhaps than is discoverable back east. But plenty of tales are told hereabouts of piracy and of romance of the seas such as any homeland of seamen must gather over centuries. Mineral treasures there may be buried in surrounding rocks to be found in time, but pirate treasure's another thing, and if you believe all you hear, there's much of it tucked away in the depths of many a lonesome cove or island. There are no tales of any of it having been discovered.   It has been looked for—but not often, and few daring souls go hunting it.   Perhaps they're too busy, and anyway there are disquieting and discouraging stories of misadventure met with by those who have attempted the search.

Seemingly, pirates long since gone from this world are still very jealous of hidden stores of their ill-gotten wealth, and have a way of appearing on the scene showing every evidence of vindictive annoyance.   One story of many such tells of a fisherman who had a pretty good idea of the location of such a hoard and set out to find it.   As he started to dig, his dog frantically called attention to a great ship of ancient line and rig standing off-shore dimly observable in the evening mists, and from it came a boat swiftly rowed by what appeared to be exceedingly vigorous and determined characters intent upon anything but friendly relations towards such as might cross their path.   Disconcerting this, and calling for speedy retreat, particularly as the dog was displaying every terror bravest of domestic animals are supposed to experience in presence of the supernatural.   From safe distance the man looked back petrified in horror as the boat rowed on and on over the beach and disappeared into the black cliff wall.   They say that man never again went treasure-hunting, and one would not be astonished to learn that every hair on the dog's body turned white that single night.   At any rate, chances of meeting with that sort of thing are far from encouraging to search for pirate gold, and latest reports would indicate that not much of it is being done.   But, there you are—phantom ships, ghostly visitations as well as heart-stirring tales of the sea, its mysteries and its tragedies are the folk-lore of these people. They tell of them around the fire at night and sing of them in their ballads, and it all goes to add colour and fantasy to a manner of life that happily is not lacking in either.

Along the west shore of Notre Dame Bay are mountain range cliffs and many more hamlets with names that touch the imagination—Rattling Brook, Nippers Cove, Snooks Arm, Shoe Cove and Tilt Cove where copper deposits were worked for years.   Each of them are splashes of white, yellow or red habitations with fish-barns and cod-drying flakes standing vividly against the dark rock and ever looking seawards only from where communication with the rest of the world can come. Cape St. John is at its north end, and twenty-five or thirty miles out in the ocean is Horse Island, one of many off this coast, a few hundred acres of rock or scrub forest, each one home to a few people brought into life there by a fate against which they make no complaint. The shore-line is fantastic, at times marked by weird rock formations and never without interest.

The next great sheet of land-sheltered water is White Bay, where settlements are farther apart than ever. Almost fifty miles inland it runs, and green hills and wooded valleys sometimes break the line of elsewhere rockbound shore. The Great Wars touched life in these isolated settlements no less than it did in more populous centres of the American mainland. Here in the tiny outport of Seal Cove is a modern school-building dedicated to commemorate the valour of T. G. Ricketts, who in 1918 at age of seventeen became youngest British soldier to have won the Victoria Cross. Of the hundreds of settlements all round this Island coast, there were few from which neither man nor woman went when war sounded its call to service.

Farther down the shore is Western Arm, running far into the land between high tree-clad walls and forming loveliest of settings for the village of that name. Lumbering is done here, and pulpwood and mine-props float in the harbour ready to go out by ship. The long western shore of White Bay runs far to Newfoundland's most northern tip and the Straits of Belle Isle. Towards the north French names appear as frequently they do along the Island's west shore, suggesting that the French Canadian from Quebec has not failed to carry his hunt for fur and fish eastward to this Island. It seems probable that the village of Englee in earliest days was known as Anglais. Along here shore-lines are more precipitous than ever, and in most directions hills behind are bereft of verdure as though forest fires had cleared the trees away and subsequent erosion had left the rocks bare of every trace of soil. But the fiords are deep and wide and in most cases their valleys are sufficiently tree covered to offer some seasonal employment to woodsmen.

The most important place on this northern shore and best known to all the world is St. Anthony, headquarters of the Grenfell Labrador Mission. Here are the central hospital and administration offices through which the International Grenfell Association has exerted a profoundly humanizing influence upon lives of dwellers in the isolated communities scattered about these sub-arctic waters and northward far up the Labrador coast. This is not the place to tell at length of Grenfell achievement. Time and again the story has been told until there exists a library of information on its work almost as comprehensive as that covering Newfoundland's entire history.

Son of an English rectory and in early manhood a London physician, Dr. Wilfred Grenfell, along about the turn of the century, became interested in the British Royal Mission to Deep-sea Fishermen and was sent to survey conditions in northern Newfoundland and Labrador waters. Dire need for medical help was everywhere evident, and on his recommendation two summertime hospitals were established on the Labrador coast, and later the British mission built the first year-round hospital at St. Anthony and broadened its work throughout its area of influence.

As work progressed along lines of general social service as well as medical, Dr. Grenfell came to realize that his activities were outgrowing those of the British Mission, and he set about organizing the Grenfell Association with its contributory centres on two continents. His genius for organization proved to be no less inspired and dynamic than that which marked him as an outstanding humanitarian. By 1913 the International Grenfell Association included five organizations, those of Great Britain, Ireland, America (New York), New England, Newfoundland and Canada, and each of these made annual contribution to the work.

It would take an ocean of words several times the volume of that which has been published on the subject to tell the whole story of what this institution has done. By hospital ship in summer and dog-team in winter it has carried doctors, nurses and medicines into hamlets where such things were unknown. It has taught sanitation and rules of health and has established home industries that have given profitable employment for long months when fishing was not possible. At present Labrador's health services are almost completely in charge of the association which maintains four nursing stations on the coast, three twenty-five-bed hospitals and a small hospital ship. It also operates boarding and day schools at several places and an orphanage at St. Anthony. The Newfoundland Government makes an annual grant towards meeting costs.

The census report of 1945 gives the total permanent Labrador population as 5,525, and chances are that it has not since greatly increased. Of this number 1,124 are Eskimo, Indian or half-breed. During the summer fishing season, the population is largely increased when work of the association is considerably enlarged. Its sphere of active influence extends over Newfoundland's most northerly peninsula and outlying islands where another ten thousand or so people have their homes. In earlier days work along these lines was practically non-existent and the Grenfell Association gave lead to greatly increased government effort in this direction which has been expanded so that the entire Newfoundland coast has the services its communities require. In 1927 Dr. Grenfell became a knight of the order of St. Michael and St. George. One biographer describes him as navigator, healer, teacher, law-giver and industrial leader, and it should be added that he was author of many books dealing with Labrador and the work of his association.

The Grenfell organization carried forward its work in a thoroughly modern manner and made strong appeal to the charitably disposed, so that over many years it seemed that little information about Newfoundland and its people reached world newspaper and periodical press, and particularly that of the United States, other than that which concerned the Grenfell Association and conditions existing along the Labrador coast which it was designed to ameliorate. These often were presented in vigorous and realistic terms most acceptable to American journalism, with result that there came into being a very generally held idea that such unhappy conditions existed more or less throughout all Newfoundland, and that for most of its people life was set at about the lowest subnormal standard extreme isolation and dire poverty might be expected to induce—all of which, of course, was hopelessly and grotesquely contrary to fact and not at all pleasing to Newfoundlanders who are nothing if not independent, self-reliant, energetic and resourceful and who ask for nothing more than a chance to develop their own land, and who, by the way, are first to honour the International Grenfell Association and its founder for what they have accomplished.

Around the top of the peninsula and through the Straits of Belle Isle are more widely scattered hamlets and down the western shore runs a coast-line that for forbidding ruggedness and wild mountain scenery has no equal anywhere on this Island. The Long Range Mountains extend practically through the peninsula's length, sometimes rising over two thousand feet, and in places they come close to the shore to form a coast-line overpoweringly awesome. The centre of the peninsula is practically unmapped and inhabited only by bears, caribou, moose and other wild animals. Fast-falling rivers teem with game fish and rush to the sea through richly wooded valleys, and what human habitation there is lies along St. Lawrence Gulf shores. In summertime the regularly arriving steamship from St. John's or returning north brings touch with the outer world and such passengers as may offer themselves for so thrilling and varied a journey. The steamer concludes its southward trip at Bay of Islands and Corner Brook.

# 14

*Southwards We Go along the Avalon Peninsula—The
Land of Fairies—On to Renews—The Forgotten
Fortress—Wrecks and Wreckers—Ferryland and the
Calvert Settlement—Bay Bulls and Bread and Cheese.*

DEAR OLD ST. JOHN'S, friendly, homely, busy in an amiable,
leisurely way, not uncomfortably clean and not distastefully
dirty—a plain, honest sort of town with few if any false shop-
fronts of shining, stainless steel or uncompromisingly straight-
lined structures of the so-called modern functional type whose
builders must be humourless men having no taste at all for
pleasant wayward vagaries in building design. A delightful
place in which to loiter and uncover, one by one, fascinating
pictures of more colourful days. We return there; but time
presses and this is not all of Newfoundland.

Question is, where to go now. Steamship and railway
officials here have all knowledge of where to go, what to see,
and how to set about getting there, and they give of their time
and advice as though no other call so pleased them.

"Most certainly the South Shore should be seen," they said.
"You don't know Newfoundland if you haven't seen that."
Since I had read of some of its villages and wanted to see them,
that settled it, despite mild discouragement from others.

"What d'ye want to go there for?" asked one. "It's a queer
country—the people down there believe in fairies."

"Splendid," I said. "So do I, and I like that kind of

people." So I went, but on the matter of fairies could get not a word. Mere mention brought tight-jawed silence or marked willingness to talk of other things, thus awakening a strong suspicion that, if they don't believe in fairies, disbelief is not strong enough to allow careless talk about the "little people" who well are known, in fairy-dwelling lands, to be actively resentful of that sort of thing.

The midday sunshine brightened the most time-worn part of the town where starts the bus for the South Shore, which in no way at all is the south shore of the Island. It is the eastern shore of the Avalon Peninsula, and runs south from St. John's, reason enough, if you're not too particular, for calling it South Shore. No railway now runs in that direction, and if you don't like the looks of the bus clattering up to the starting spot, you'd better find a taxi—the term applied to large cars or station wagons irregularly plying the road and on which fares, like those of the bus, are quite reasonable.

A small bus this, of early vintage with a slightly disturbing look of having spent many years grinding its way over rough and troublesome roads. But we climb aboard cheerily enough, a fair load of bag, baggage and basket-laden passengers all pleasantly agreed that it's a "fine marnin' " and a spot or two of rain wouldn't hurt the country a bit. Very shortly afterwards we have climbed out of the city to bowl along a well-built over-land road passing farm lands, the occasional market-garden, and the modern-looking houses of those who favour half-town, half-country living. Then, with astonishing suddenness, we are running across as barren appearing and lonesome a land as any yet seen. Rock, scrub forest and stretches of peaty soil dotted with sky-blue ponds—sizable lakes some of them—merge far off it into purple hills—a land where daylight softening towards evening casts a sombre melancholy over the scene, and fades moodfully through long gloaming into starlit night. Who wouldn't expect to meet a fairy, or maybe a whole ring of them, in such a land on such a night as this!

The good road is behind us. Ahead is a stony path with many a bump and jar, a terror to light springs but offering little threat to those on this bus, which pass shocks on to passengers with carefree generosity. Along the road our party changes— a few drop off here and there and others get on—and friendly greetings at brief stops are general. There are parcels to be left off, too. Returning town visitors have neighbourly errands on their hands and if one bundle handed out to a couple of delighted countrymen contains not a large and weighty flagon of the wine of the country, the old flair for detection is sadly weakening.

This is a winding road, and often it takes sudden dips down steep hills to cross a little river or to visit one of the many pretty villages lying all glamorous in the afternoon sun at the end of its own deep arm of the sea. Turning and twisting with unexpected frequency, it thinks nothing of disappearing round a corner into an S-curve in the middle of a climb attacked with roaring snorts from the exhaust of our vehicle, while on one side there's a sheer drop of twenty or forty feet and a cliff on the other. There's adventure in every mile of this road—but it's a fine evening and everybody's happy, so we enjoy it with lively expectation of reaching the end soon.

Our hope was to find a comfortable staying place at Ferry-land, perhaps the most historic spot on all this richly historic shore. We were not too sure in our hope, for earlier inquiry in St. John's had no promising results. Indeed a phone call by a helpful friend to one of the priests here had brought assurance that no such thing was available. Our bus driver thought otherwise. Sure—there'd be lots of people glad to take me in. He'd find a place. He did not. Every inquiry met with complete lack of interest in the stranger, even when put forward with what was calculated to be a most engaging manner and registration of despair at prospect of spending the night on the stony beach, until, as with the man three times thrown out of a pub, regrettable suspicion arose that the room of visiting foreigners here was considered preferable to their company. But there's comfort in the thought that better people than I have been denied refuge in worse places than Ferryland affords. So—accepting renewed assurance from the friendly bus driver, and more than one of the passengers still with us, that there would be accommodation at the end of the run, we scurry back up the hill into black darkness now covering this solemn land, and safely passing we know not what dangers, in half an hour or so I find myself in the bright, cheery kitchen of a fisherman's home with a kettle merrily singing on a hot stove, and before me on the table that kind of a comforting meal that makes past worries and fancied dangers things of no importance whatsoever. There's pleasant talk around the lamp. And after that a bed as induce to restful slumber as might be found in the best of hotels—or even at home.

The village of Renews next morning appears all the more cheerful in contrast to impenetrable darkness of last night's arrival. Its many-coloured houses are widely scattered, and paths winding between its picket fences—sometimes white-washed—wander in no particular direction except that they go from door to door and always up to the handsome frame Roman Catholic Church standing in newly painted splendour back on the hill. A long dock with a few fish-houses about it reaches out into the harbour where fishing schooners and small boats cast black shadows on the still water. A Sunday morning scene, and motionless, except for whiffs of blue smoke floating idly away from chimneys, telling of preparations for breakfast, and that time of day when the entire population will be sauntering churchwards.

Renews is not at the end of the road. It goes farther down the peninsula towards Cape Race, southeastern tip of the Island. It passes through the village of Portugal Cove, a name recalling early explorers and fishing ships coming yearly for cod and, no doubt, establishing some sort of fishing station there. Then it goes on to Trepassey, apparently named from French word "trepas" and roughly translated as "place of dead men"—presumably commemorating one of those tragedies of sea or war found on almost every page of south shore history. An important harbour this once was, and scene of one of those early attempts at colonization doomed to fail wretchedly by reason of worst possible management and later because of England's determination to allow no permanent settlement on the Island. James I had given Sir William Vaughan and his associates a charter to take over great territories here, and he made headquarters at Trespassey. About the same time Lord Falkland started two colonies, mostly of Welshmen, one farther west on Trinity Bay and the other in the southern part of the peninsula, probably including Renews. Despite later devastating ban on land holding and home building, these two tiny outposts of humanity managed to survive. Robbed of all they had, some of the people must have taken to the woods or moved out along the shore where the living was half savage but plentiful enough, and where emissaries of West of England merchants could not follow. When the ban on settlement was removed or dictates of humane common sense forced it to become inoperative, the hamlets re-emerged as bulbs come up in springtime and now, like many others up and down the coast, they look back on prosperous times that were later their lot and to which, at the moment, there seems little prospect of an early return.

Origin of the name Renews was forgotten long ago. Likeliest guess makes it a colloquialism from "Renois," the name of some early Breton settler before Jacques Cartier entered St. Lawrence waters. If the French were ever a considerable factor in the population herabouts that was in forgotten days and their stay was short. Avalon Peninsula below St. John's is largely an Irish country, particularly so along this shore where forty of the fifty outports have a total population of between six and seven thousand, of which over four thousand are of Irish origin, two thousand English, some forty French, thirty Scottish and ten Welsh—this according to the census of 1945 and relatively little changed since. Irish manner of speech, living and, above all, religion have been retained. Of total population over six thousand are Roman Catholics. Trepassey's six hundred souls includes not one Protestant, and many other villages are similarly united in matters of faith.

"Did ever ye see the like of that?" asked the elderly gentleman peering through field-glasses over a wide spread of excellent hay and on up to a hilltop far beyond where three or four ponies lazed in the sun.

"I do believe that's him," he added, and after another long look, " 'Tis a little horse I bought over at Trepassey last year and had him in the shed all winter. I let him loose in the spring with the other town ponies soon as there was any grass to the ground, and never a sight of him have I had from that day to this. You'd think he'd come to the house once in a while the way the others do, beggin' for a slice of bread or a bit of sugar. But no. He stays away 'til I'm thinkin' he's gone back to Trepassey or fallen over a cliff—the little devil. Ah well—mebbe mosquitoes or flies'll drive him in a bit later. They get pretty bad on them woody hills, and all the ponies'll be glad enough to come down to shore then." A speech which reflected towards a matter of seeming importance, a philosophical attitude rather typical of the average Newfoundlander towards life in general, though perhaps one should add outside of politics, which never was a matter for easygoing thinking or speaking in this land.

"Nice crop of hay there," I said.

"Not bad. I've seen better. In a good year it'll grow twice as high as that—but there's plenty there for the little use we have for it."

"Not much interest in farming hereabouts?" I asked.

"No, and why would there be? Not much good land, and it's hard work getting it into shape. The young men stick to the fishing they're bred to, or they go off to find work back in Canada or the States. For many the fishing's too hard and the pay too poor these days."

"But there were farms along this shore once," I suggested.

"I'm told so. My grandfather used to talk about that sort of thing and he thought there should be more of it. Some of them that came from Ireland long ago went in for it and made a living—but there was lots of fish them days and prices were good and the sons forgot all about farming. You can't fish and farm, too. They used to grow a lot of potatoes in my time, but it don't pay now—they're cheaper coming from Prince Edward Island. They kept pigs, too, but feed has to come all the way from Canada and it's too dear. When fishin's good the men are too busy, and when it's not they keep at it anyhow, hoping for better times. Things were mighty good when war was on, and," he added reflectively, "I think many of them were spoiled them days. Money came easy, and it's hard to come back to days like these."

He struck a happier note. "Mind you," he said, "it'll come back again. The world needs our fish. And another thing— there's a lot of them saved when they had it. Back north there a few miles a woman had eighteen hundred dollars stolen out of her house, and I read in the paper the other day where a man lost two thousand the same way. I wouldn't be surprised, now, if you'd find a nice bit of money tucked away in most of the houses up and down this shore."

With this and much talk of a more general nature I left him and, having the harbour on my right, followed a path around the headland. A narrow path it was—mostly travelled by sheep, and at one or two places so narrow as to call for caution against slipping twenty or thirty feet down into the surf. At its end it opened out into a grass-covered, rock-sheltered nook overlooking the harbour entrance and open sea, and here was startling evidence of how little they bother about history in these parts. I had stumbled across another of those spots where, all uncared for, lay mute memorials of days when mastery of this Island and what it stood for as the North Atlantic's mightiest citadel was being fought for halfway round the world through three centuries of time.

Several beautiful old cannon lay half-buried in the springy sheep-clipt sod, and round its edge, though hardly discernible, was the outline of ancient earthworks. These were not heavy, clumsy guns marked with the Georgian monogram and crown that are found in mainland memorial parks where British fighting men set up the flag and planted seeds of Empire. Long and comparatively slender, their beauty of line and proportion was notable, and they bore as a mark of ownership the Tudor rose and a crown of shape never worn by Georgian king.

Here had been a fortification guarding the harbour of Renews, and by all accounts it must have witnessed stout fighting when French warships, privateering rovers or the ordinary, everyday sort of pirates dropped in on this part of the coast, as they often did.  But who planted these guns, and when, seems to be quite forgotten.  Nowhere is there written a definite story of any one valorous battle of the many in which they must have played a part.  What a stirring scene to recreate when some great murdersome galleon bore down on a favouring wind, or when in later years, perhaps, a ponderous square-rigged French ship essayed to force entrance to the harbour, sole landing spot offering an opportunity for rapine and plunder in many a mile of unapproachable rock.  From farm, fishing boat, home and tavern, anger-determined Englishmen, Irishmen and others had rushed to man them through the day in stinging clouds of burnt saltpetre fumes.  Their every bark had a bite, and there seems to be no record of their having been outfought; nor ever can there be tablet bearing names of those who died, or were wounded—and many there must have been on such a day. Wide open to the sea, the spot offered too fair a target to have escaped hits from enemy guns.

Here the cannon now lie, cast of some splendid metal upon which time and weather has bestowed only a warm russet patine like that of a lady's suede glove—no sign of rust or corrosion.  Pride of their makers, no doubt, when new, or perhaps even a "secret weapon" as terrifyingly important then as those threatening this unhappy age.  And they will lie there until rescued by government commission or public-spirited citizens to be set up again in a reconstruction of the primitive fortification they defended—if meanwhile they are not carted away to become meaningless ornaments of some place with which they have no historic association.

The largest house of the village is home of a branch of the Goodridge family which for over a century and a half has been one of the dominating merchant factors in this part of the Island. A visit brought forth a rich store of talk on Renews, past and present.  It was interesting even to sit in his comfortable office with furniture and fittings making a Dickens story picture.  A huge desk and comfortable chairs stand about a large fireplace. The walls are shelved with ledgers containing, no doubt, the

economic history of Renews and most of its families over years
of rising prosperity and decline.   An interesting flash of light is
thrown on the kind of co-operative association that must have
existed between such merchant firms as this and the fishermen,
by the fact that when time came in 1945 to select a national
convention for consideration of the future form of government,
it was Fred Goodridge they sent to St. John's to represent
Renews, despite his being the only eligible Protestant in town.

Long before General Wolfe took Quebec, Renews was a busy
place; and less than a century ago warehouses, fish-drying flakes
and homes crowded the shore.   Fires have destroyed most of
their timbers or they have gone into buildings of lesser importance
now standing.   It was well out at sea they fished then, where
fishing for cod was the world's best—not so today.   Fish are less
plentiful, and "jigging," or sometimes netting are methods
employed.   No light, pleasant job is jigging, most of the time.
For a couple of men out in a small dory on the lonesome and
almost always unquiet ocean, jigging a hundred feet or so of
heavily baited line, up and down for hours with full-arm motion,
has nothing of sport or child's play about it, particularly when
much of the time one is wet from flying spray.   A bit of fire on
the dory's floor boils a midday kettle and cooks a piece of newly
caught fish or slice of salt pork, unless luck is in and the fish come
fast.   With afternoon comes the return home, carrying anything
between a fair load of fish or only two or three.   The market for
fish at time of writing is not good.   One and a half or two cents a
pound, or at the most two and a half cents is a fisherman's cash
return, and even a good catch means modest payment for the
day's work.   At the moment, I am told, fishing earnings run
from $200 to $400 a year, or perhaps $500.   Back in war-
times they would go up to $1,400.   In 1945, as wartime trade
subsided, the average year's earnings of all trades and classes
up and down this South Shore is officially reported as $519 for
a total of 2,233 gainfully employed.   Of these, 987 earned $500
or less, 778 between that figure and $1,000, 228 went on up to
$2,000 and 113 up to $3,000, with 165 not stated.

In optimistic days when railroad building was going to lift

Newfoundland into new and better industrial expansion, a line was run well down this shore.   But like several other branch lines then constructed, it proved unsupportable by the amount of traffic carried and was one of those wisely discontinued under the realistic recognition of what traffic facilities the country needed and could maintain.   The road, which here and there skirts the disused right-of-way, is now being improved as are many others as part of the useful and progressive work now projected by the Provincial Government.   Before railroad days even summer traffic over this road was light.   Few people travelled anyway, and sailing probably was easier to most when a trip to another outport or even St. John's had to be made.   But even fifty years ago the road must have been in fair shape.   Mr. Goodridge tells of his mother having driven the fifty miles from St. John's to Renews in one twelve-hour day behind one pair of horses.

Strollers along Renews' pathways or road or two that enter the village now meet few traffic annoyances, and the walk offers frequent intimate glimpses into life here.   An open door or two reveal cheery and comfortable interiors.   In one I saw a spinning wheel.   The busy "woman o' the house" with a group of youngsters about her, all wonder-struck by a stranger's appearance in their midst, seemed amused by his interest in so commonplace an object.   Yes, she used it, sometimes in winter.   Her mother had used it much more.   Five sheep they now had and every year fleeces were washed and sent off to Codroy, over six hundred miles away, coming back carded ready for the wheel and ultimate knitting into socks, sweaters or whatever else might be needed.   Years ago home-grown wool was made up in nearly every family, but not so much now.   It is easier buying in the shops, or through mail-orders which bring the things almost to your door.   At one time some of the men did a bit of knitting too, but that's long since gone.   Women in those days looked after gardens, hoed potatoes and cabbages, helped in haying and fish drying.   They are too busy nowadays, and somehow comes the realization that times have changed here pretty much as they have world over and the prospect of backward turning in such things is dim indeed, even were it to be desired.

Another walk long to be remembered there was. Away up the hill behind the town and across rough land covered with spruce, pine and poplar to the edge of cliffs where nothing but sea lies between you and all Europe. The master of the house suggested it, an elderly fisherman, kindly and courteous, speaking with as cultured a voice as any from Dublin University, and wise in the ways of his country and his people—a man to be remembered as fairly representing the sound core of Newfoundland's most numerous and, up to recent years, most effective class.

Emphasized by a sheer drop to the sea of two to three hundred feet, the view from the cliff-edge was vast, and here one sees why Newfoundland could not, in days of primitive weapons and comparatively small forces, successfully be invaded and conquered from sea. This wall of rock surrounding most of the coast offers neither landing spot nor foothold except where broken by entrances to harbours and fiords, all more or less defensible by the people who got there first and built their settlements to stay.

Away to the right the headland runs seaward, in pre-radar days a treacherous neighbourhood to mariners not familiar with this coast. Many a ship has rounded this point in murky weather and, thinking it the southern tip, Cape Race, altered course westward, only to perish on rocks instead of finding safety in open sea. Tidal sweeps and ocean currents make navigation difficult. Off this point warm Gulf Stream waters meet those from the Arctic to swirl along both sides of this peninsula, incessant fog being one result. It would seem that ocean bottom along here and up into Trepassey and St. Mary's Bays must be floored with timbers and iron hulks that once were ships. The number of vessels that have perished here in recorded times is unknown, nor is there record of lives lost over the past fifty years—but their number must be great. Great, too, must be the number of those whose lives have been saved by heroic efforts of the people who live here. First call of a wreck was for the saving of those on board, their care when brought ashore, and reverent burial of the dead.    Up and down this coast an amazing number of Humane Society Medals have been awarded for the kind of bravery that dares danger to the limit of endurance and on fields of battle wins Victoria Crosses.

A notable instance of disaster in these waters was the loss of the *Anglo-Saxon* in 1863 with three hundred of her four hundred passengers and crew.    In November, 1816, the British transport *Harpooner*, carrying four hundred soldiers and their families from Quebec to England after the War of 1812, went ashore in a storm and only two hundred were saved.    Here is another good mark for the Newfoundland dog.    One of them swam through surf in which no boat could live, and carried a line to the rock shore where men were waiting to effect a rescue.    As late as 1942 the United States destroyer *Truxton* piled up on rocks nearby and a hundred and nineteen of her crew were lost.

Never was an inhabited seashore like this.    But stories of wreckings and wreckers persist through from times when a ship cast on shore was a heaven-sent benefaction to dwellers thereabouts.    No stories of ships lured ashore for plunder are repeated here as in other lands.    If ever such happened memory records it not, or perhaps, the reticence habitual to the Newfoundlander makes it one of those bygones best left as bygones.    Most likely it is that the nature of the coast offered little facility for exercise of such enterprise — or perhaps humane considerations and respect for law and order restrained up to a point.    What to do about a ship placed on the rocks by bad weather — clearly the hand of God—was something else again.    There's a story of the captain back in St. John's from wreck of his ship somewhere along this coast.

"How did the people down there treat you?" he was asked.

"Splendidly," he said.    "They pulled us out of the sea, took us into their homes, gave us food and dry clothing—couldn't have been kinder—and when I got back to the ship there wasn't a thing left in her that could be moved.    Even my cabin clock was gone."

There have been times when a hard winter or a period of

depression have been made easier for some one or other village by welcome comforts hastily snatched from a stranded ship before it vanished beneath the waves. It was a pious and trustful soul that answered inquiry with the statement that the community in which he lived would get through the coming winter all right, "with God's blessing and a wreck or two." And there's the story of the village that was greatly cheered one day by the sight of a large ship piled up on the nearby shore. But it was discovered with something less than joyful enthusiasm that she was laden with a ballast of red bricks. I am led to believe that a red brick church is now one of the features of the landscape. But all that was long long ago. Radioed weather reports, radar and instrument recording of the depth of water under the keel have made coastal navigation much less hazardous.

We walked home as night fell, sauntering down a path that was little else than a sheep-track. A good growth of young trees covered the rock here and there, and in open spaces a few not too prosperous sheep nibbled at odd patches of grass showing through the tundra. A couple of ponies or a lonely looking cow watched our passing with mild interest. Small plots of picket-fenced land bore crops of hay or potatoes, and healthy and promising enough both seemed to be, though as far as I could learn, any idea of spraying the latter for the discouragement of potato bugs or other enemies was nowhere given a thought. The plants bore little or no sign that such things are a problem in this land. As one man with a hoe said, "Mebbe it's the salt air and wet winters keeps 'em away." Wonderful if true—and mebbe it is.

Rocky as it may be and covered with muskeg as much of it is, this country is very kind to the blueberry, one native fruit that flourishes in abundance. Blueberry jam as made here is something worth making a long journey for. The berries are large and full flavoured and in more than one place they are picked, packed, given a quick freeze and shipped as far away as Boston and New York. As facilities improve, this could develop into one of the Island's important industries.

A pleasant place to stay is Renews, but the road calls and the bus demands dawn-rising, so we start away as the cold early light throws pastel shades over land and sea and the bus scurries about the village picking up adventurous souls bound for a day in St. John's, or a visit somewhere along the coast. Jimmie is coming—I never heard his last name—so we stop opposite his cottage standing a few yards off the road and lean on the horn until its angry scream fills the harbourside but brings no sign of life from Jimmie. "Look at his chimney," says one. "There's no smoke coming out at all. He hasn't had his breakfast yet. Let's go." And go we do while Jimmie likely rolls over in his bed with a happy smile, thinking that perhaps tomorrow will be a finer day than this for travelling all the way to St. John's. We rattle along over the highway in the happiest of moods and wonder what on earth worried us when we came over it in the dark of a few nights ago. All is plain sailing now, and as for sharp turns, well, we have a horn and we keep it as busy as if we were scooting through one of St. John's busiest streets. The driver is happy, too. When not discussing local affairs with passengers he sings to himself, and sings very nicely, and that sort of helps the general feeling that all's well with the ship—and anyhow, it's a fine day.

First stop is at the village of Aquaforte, and guesses seem to agree that the name means just what it suggests and is a relic of visitations of Spanish or Portuguese sailormen possessing as keen appreciation of the virtues of strong waters as seamen of any nationality. A tiny village this, but lovely as any on the coast. Lying at the end of one of the deeper fiords, it must have been hard to find and difficult to enter in early days. Emerging from somewhat nebulous clouds of historic lore concerning its highly colourful past is the story of arch-pirate Peter Easton having used the harbour as hideout, or more probably a snug spot from which he might dash out to plunder. There seems to have been little reason for a well-armed and valorous pirate to do much hiding those days. There are those living hereabouts who claim to have seen lying on harbour bottom the skeleton of one of his ships, burnt during a mutinous battle among his own people; and of course, there's pirate treasure hidden about here somewhere if only it could be found.

Another pirate appears in the history of these waters and to his memory I apologize for not having his name. He was a teetotaler—strictly so—and insisted that his men should practise that virtue even if they did not believe in it, and for certain crimes, including rape, he hanged members of his own crews. He turned up at Trepassey one day, burned and looted and took many prisoners whom he invited to join his forces. They would not, so he took what ships and spoil lay around and went on his way. One would like to know what eventually became of this interesting character.

Back over the hills we go and down into Ferryland, a scene so pleasant to look upon in the morning light that one regrets not having found a place in which to stay. When this Island goes forward with its plans for development of tourist traffic this is one spot where accommodation for the traveller should be provided. Broad white stone beach and its hundred or so houses with their gardens have an air of newly washed freshness made brighter by a background of treed and grass-covered hills. About six hundred people live here, and at the time of the 1945 census one of them was a Protestant who, no doubt, got along very well with his fellow townsmen. Two-thirds are of Irish origin and the remainder are English.

Here is the centre of South Shore history. When it began is not clear, but it seems to have been the yearly resort for the earliest overseas fish-gatherers. Spanish, Portuguese and Frenchmen knew it and came here as early as did West of England men. Here they fought their battles for the wealth offered by the inexhaustible cod banks. After that, fighting was hardly less fierce between Devonshiremen settled here and the authority that sought to drive them out. Shortly after John Guy started his ill-fated colony at Cupids, James I granted to Sir George Calvert a large area of land and a charter to establish a colony at this spot. He sent out colonists and agents to take over, which they did in face of something less than a warm welcome from settlers with homes already established after much hard labour and not a little hard fighting.

His agents robbed him, but built a large stone house for his later arrival for a short visit in 1627. A year later he brought out his family with every intention of building a prosperous and profitable community. Lady Calvert started for home early, the country not having suited her health, and died on the journey. French marauders made things difficult and no help came from any source. Appeals to Charles I, now enthroned, were wasted time. Charles had no interest in colonies. Calvert went home, was created first Lord Baltimore and, being completely discouraged regarding his Newfoundland adventure, applied for and received a grant of lands in Virginia which his son, second Lord Baltimore, proceeded to develop with some measure of success, thus helping to establish England's overseas Empire and giving his name to the city Baltimore.

The name Ferryland is supposed to be a colloquialism for Verulam, the Roman name of the Baltimore home near St. Albans, England. There are those who say the place was so called before Calvert's time, and Bishop Howley suggests that it originally was Floriland, a name given by earlier visitors for the beauty of its situation. Fail though the colony did, the name Baltimore is almost as firmly tied up with its history as it is with the Virginian city. Anything the first Lord Baltimore did for Newfoundland, including the spending of a huge fortune of some £200,000, was repaid by seizure of the colony in 1637 and turning of it over together with those established by Vaughan and Falkland and all the rest of the Island to Sir David Kirke and his group of exploiters. Kirke took over Baltimore's house and proceeded by taxation, restriction and general abuse of power to place himself in history as the worst Governor Newfoundland ever had. Under Star Chamber Rule of Charles I, Ferryland's people, like those of other settlements, were driven from their homes and scattered.

Cromwell's Commonwealth proved more kindly and, under Governor John Treworgay, a measure of peace and prosperity paid a seven-year visit until accession of Charles II and the influence of West of England merchants set back the clock and restored exaction and persecution as the main motives of government. Charles' venial surrender to France of two-thirds of the Island plus permission to establish a permanent fort at Placentia brought long years of woe and spasmodic ruin to this coast. As if that and uncontrolled piracy were not enough, the Dutch war brought hostile fleets, one of which ravaged Ferryland, killing many of the men and destroying the settlement despite stout resistance.

Predatory French warships were constant visitors, so that life for the Ferrylander those days included about as much fighting as it did fishing. This was a state of affairs existing all up and down the coast, lasting through the reigns of James II, William III and Queen Anne. In 1694, English prisoners who had escaped from Placentia brought news of an impending attack on Ferryland. At that time Captain William Holman had in the harbour the armed galley *William and Mary*. He pressed the inhabitants into service and erected defences. The French came, but after five hours of fighting scurried off for home in badly damaged ships, with a great loss of men and leaving their anchors and cables behind them. Such engagements happened time and again, and always the settlers and stout Devon sailormen gave blows better than they got, and if they were defeated, retired to come back and rebuild their town later on. D'Iberville paid a call here on his way to capture St. John's in 1662. Having been warned in time, the inhabitants had gone north to Bay Bulls where a stand was to be made, and once again they returned to set up new homes and fishing facilities. The wonder is that this grotesque travesty of British rule existed so long. One cannot but think that had the Newfoundlanders of those days been less stubborn and less doughty fighters, the ultimate fate of their country might have been very different from that which it has turned out to be.

More, perhaps, than anywhere else on the Island, Ferryland and its neighbourhood is fortunate in having relics and memorials of those stirring days. They have been preserved so far by happy chance rather than by any care on the part of the descendants of men and women who battled and suffered years ago, and there are many, despite Irish immigration of later years. The spot where Baltimore's stone house stood is well marked though little remains but a scanty suggestion of its outline.    The stones, they say, were used in building the church now overlooking the village, but clear cold water still runs through the stone drains built then.

Not far off the harbour entrance is Isle de Bois, and here the past literally speaks aloud.    By the year 1700 England was doing something about protecting her interests in these waters.    In 1705 another French visitation practically wiped out the town. Then Isle de Bois was fortified so that three years later a further French attempt at destruction was repulsed with crippling loss. Remains of earth-built emplacements still are there, and a few old walls and piles of brick and stone mark where fort and magazine once stood.    Half buried in the sod, several fine old British guns speak of the past as eloquently as they barked out defiance when an enemy threatened the soil they guarded. Altogether, Ferryland is a place to visit if you would know Newfoundland.

Back over the hills we go on our northward journey with many a dip down to the sea to look in on this or that village in passing.    South Shore dwellers are firm in their belief that the Island's loveliest scenery lies hereabouts, and I, for one, can see no reason to argue about it.    Tors Cove—a Devon name again—and the approach thereto are a delight to the eye.    Even the barren uplands, sea-wind swept and sunlit, have a vivid charm of colour splashed here and there across the sombre northland scene like gay songs sung in a twilight hour.

Bay Bulls once was called either "Bay Boulle," from the large round stones or bowls found on its shores, or "Baie de Bois." Neither name came easily to West of England tongues, while Bay Bulls did, and so it has remained.    No disrespect to the French language was necessarily implied.    They did that to English names, too.    We passed Witless Bay on the way up. Once it was "Whittles Bay," probably named for earliest of the settlers and changed for the facility of saying or remembering, not, one hopes, as an unkind reference to local mental equipment. Back down the coast is the tiny hamlet of Cappahayden, changed from Broad Cove in honour of a well-beloved parish priest of Renews who came from a place of that name in Ireland. When Irish immigration swarmed into these areas, their priests followed fast—fine scholarly men, some of them, and all Irishly human.

There's a story of one whose place in the hearts of his people was great. He was of them and spoke their language. From the pulpit at one Sunday mass he announced the need for a day's gathering of firewood "agin coming winter." "Now," he said, and emphatically rapped on the pulpit, "you'll bring me bright-burning wood. I want none o' your fartin' fir." Anyone who has burnt fir in a fireplace, at least, will credit the good man with fine sense of description. Wife of a local legislature candidate, knowing that her husband stood not high in the padre's estimation, came to him with request that if he could say nothing in favour of the candidate, he would not speak against him. The lady was a good, devout soul and the priest promised. So, after next Sunday's sermon he said, "You know that Patrick —— wants you to vote him into the legislature. I've promised to say nothing agin him and I'll keep my mouth shut." Here a sense of duty or conscience smote him, and he added, "But, if I opened it I could say a lot." The candidate was not elected.

Bay Bulls tempted a stopover and the accommodating bus rolled away, having deposited a pile of baggage at the roadside. A sign proclaimed a hotel built in the typical packing-case architecture of this part of the country, where fire has almost necessitated as frequent rebuilding as enemy assaults did earlier. Much door-knocking brought regrets from the ancient lady of the house, for crippling rheumatism and no help—the girls all being off to Canada for better jobs— meant no hotel operation. So—where to go? This took a little thinking. "Well, perhaps Mrs. White'll take you in—the yellow house round the corner past the church right under the big hill. There'll be a man fixin' the roof and mebbe a pony eatin' grass in the meadow in front—you can't miss it." Nor did I. After a discussion with the roof-fixer who for that purpose came to earth, and a long wait while he talked it over with his wife inside, I was agreeably accepted as a guest and housed as comfortably as one could wish, having made two warm half-mile trips back to the hotel for bothersome but necessary baggage. Reappearance of a little hot water and indoor plumbing was welcome.

A two-mile fiord running in from the sea forms magnificent Bay Bulls Harbour. High cliffsides are more than usually wooded and a road high up on its northern cliff passes through several good stands of pine and other trees. A dry dock and plant for repairing large ships tell of busy days during the two Great Wars, and about halfway down the fiord are the remains of great steel cable booms and buoys that prevented entry of enemy ships and submarines. All this is carefully tidied up and protected as though there might be a chance of its being used again some day. Those were prosperous days for Bay Bulls, and its people are as war-conscious as their forefathers must have been when the French paid too frequent visits here. They listen to radio and talk about disturbing world events with solemn but keen interest. Part of the plant now stores last year's unsold cod which is sunned and aired daily by a leisurely moving group of lads, each pair carrying a stretcher that bears no great load. The village is much quieter now that plant workers and naval ratings have gone back to peacetime occupations, but it remembers—perhaps a little regretfully.

Farther on along the road, past fish-drying stages flavouring the air with a not unpleasant smell of drying codfish, is the smallest named village yet visited, glorying in the most curious of names. Bread and Cheese would seem to be no name for any place—but there it is. Two or three cottages mark a spot that once may have been a busy fishing port but of its dozen or so inhabitants not one seemed to know how or why it came to be so called. An elderly citizen, the only human being in sight, was quite ready to rest from trundling his little pile of hay barnwards on a wheelbarrow and discuss the matter, but could offer no suggestion. He had been born there—so had his father and grandfather. Well over a hundred years back the latter had built a house up the hill a bit where the foundations still stand.

They had taken it down the other day because it looked as though about to fall. They needn't have bothered. When they came to take the timbers apart they found them so solid and so put together that it might have stood another century. The story was, he said, that the place originally was settled by an English family landed from a wreck. Anyway, the entire population, all twelve of them, are English and always have been.

Farther along the clifftop path is Gunsbridge, just such another place and about twice as large. The road rises and falls with the hills, ending in a thick growth of sturdy pine and a few houses and gardens overlooking the harbour far below, its silence broken only by the chatter of children and the occasional noisy passing of motor boats going to or from the nets at sea. Here again is an English group whose forebears were more or less thrown up by the sea, and still as English as were the first arrivals three or five generations back.

That explains the white Anglican church with its high-pitched roof, belfry and cross standing in a hundred-yard square churchyard cleared out of the forest. No ancient headstones are here. A century would date the oldest. The air is heavy with incense of roses, great purple-red single blooms on lusty dark-leaved bushes standing four or five feet high. Brought here long ago, perhaps by some English man or woman with a longing for a flavour of home in a new land, they now impress their grateful presence on the air of this and almost every village we have so far walked through.

Crowded, the church would hold about forty people. Walls, ceiling and benches are of natural pine. Under a three-lance stained glass window and bearing a brass cross, candlesticks and freshly cut flowers, stands the small altar with an evidently home-embroidered frontal drape of simple and effective design all ready for the parson's occasional visit and speaks plainly of the important part church plays in the lives of these people, be their persuasion of faith Roman, United or Anglican.

Along this road somewhere are said to be remains of an ancient battery, although undiscoverable at the time of this visit, and on the harbour's south shore are well-defined ramparts with more English guns embedded in the soil. Four of them have been rescued from what, to the "foreigner," seems almost contemptuous neglect and now serve as entrance gateposts to the Roman Catholic church grounds at Bay Bulls. On the upended muzzle of each stands a bronze figure beautifully executed and well designed as to size and form in relation to the graceful lines of the gun bearing it—altogether an imposing gateway that should be an inspiring reminder of past valorous days and price paid for possession of this land by those who lived through them.

Bay Bulls escaped none of the tribulation and savagery, and enjoyed all the prosperity that varying fortune has visited upon this coast. Enterprising D'Iberville all but destroyed it, and the last French devastation occurred in 1796 when the town once more became a smoking ruin. England under George III, busy fighting in European waters, had her hands exceedingly full; a French fleet one foggy day slipped through British navy lines and landed here once more to capture and destroy all the way up the coast as far as Carbonear. During the War of 1812 with the United States many a smart ship ran out of this port and others along the shore to harass and chase off American raiders and, by all reliable accounts, they acquitted themselves very well, winning considerable respect from enemy ships having the fortune to meet them at sea. Prize ships of one kind and another brought in to these ports made up a notable factor of Newfoundland wealth in those days. Hereabouts that war seems to have been considered much in the light of a family affair, leaving but little bitter feeling. That dreadful winter not many years later when fire had all but destroyed St. John's and, following upon the Battle of Waterloo and the end of the French war hard times had brought poverty and near starvation everywhere, Americans were the first to send food and comfort to their enemies of recent date. One ship from Boston carrying supplies got as far as Bay Bulls and no farther. The "Bay Bullies" apparently thought their empty stomachs ached as painfully as those elsewhere, so they took over the ship and cleaned it out—probably against little serious opposition since it was on a mercy mission anyhow, and who wants to stand between hunger and food.

Bay Bulls is only a short overland run to St. John's on excellent gravel road. A ten-minutes' wait at a road corner brings along an oversized station wagon comfortably packed except for one vacant seat immediately behind the driver— another cheery lad given to conversation and, like our southern-going busman, likely to fill in dull moments with quietly murmured song, all very pleasant if only he would drive on the right side of the road. But he seems to prefer the left—fair enough with a mile or so of empty road visible ahead but a bit wearing on the passenger's nerves when hustling around view-blocked corners. This may reflect a political quirk in his mind. Before Federation with Canada they followed the English practice, driving on the left always, and this could be his expression of disapproval of the new national tie-up. Now and then he showed a welcome tendency to compromise by taking the middle of the road, and it should be said, always turned off politely to let the other fellow go by just as one braced oneself against the seat for the threatened crash. Fascinated attention to this sort of driving is interrupted by the sudden discovery that we now are horning our way through St. John's bustling traffic, and very shortly we are back in the third-floor front room enjoying its wide view over the town's chimney-pots.

# 15

As SHORT as this stay in St. John's must be, happily there's time enough for a run out along the Marine Driveway which is as delightful an experience as lovers of natural beauty could desire. Grim bare cliffs of the city's harbour give no suggestion of lush meadows, tree-clad hills and snug, wooded coves opening out into the sea, all within short run of the city's centre. Here again one is reminded of the Pacific coast, Victoria and the Marine Drive there—a land of unforgettably fragrant memories. Quidi Vidi, five minutes from town, is no less an historic spot than a delight to the eye. On the last occasion of French destruction it was here that a force of troops from England and New England, after a cross-country march from Placentia and aided by British naval force, completely defeated the French, capturing Signal Hill and what was left of the city—which was not much.

Through soft blue mist, ghostly remnant of a fairly heavy fog, we bid friendly final farewell to station, harbour and dry-dock-hiding warehouses with tall ship masts reaching above them, and a church tower or two rising from the oldest and busiest part of the town, untidy, time-worn and lovably human-like.

Most of our western journey lies back over the main line, along the south shore of Conception Bay, to break off on a branch line at Placentia Junction and run over rock and tundra country past numberless lakes and ponds with summer and fishing camps about them. They say there's sporting fish to be caught here wherever you go. We make an odd stop or two where a lumber mill, a few cottages and perhaps a church make up a settlement. Beyond the junction, the character of the scene changes. Barrens give place to bush, and bush becomes forest as we roll on towards the sea and descend among impressive cloud-reaching, verdure-clad hills. Suddenly we are out of the forest and, far below, almost straight down, Placentia Harbour spreads itself like some great river flooding seaward from as far away as you can see into the blue. There may be lovelier fiords than this somewhere on this Island coast, but I have not seen them. Corner Brook's harbour seen from a hilltop on a summer's evening is a memory to be cherished—Placentia one could not forget if one would.

In a few moments we are at Placentia station, high on the hill overlooking the harbour entrance and town, and from here a waiting taxi soon runs us down to sea-level through a short street of wooden houses and a shop or two, and lands us at a dock beside a channel through which the sea swiftly ebbs and flows into the harbour. Ferrymen are waiting, and five minutes later I am standing alone on the Placentia town dock, fellow-passengers having hurried off on their several affairs. Where to find a place to stay, and how to get there?

Not for long does one stand alone in these parts. From everywhere and nowhere seven small boys appear, each beaming with politely restrained curiosity as they gaze on the helpless-looking stranger dropped on their town. Very vague they are about a hotel or anything like that—but one lad remembers Mrs. Cahill's and goes so far as to recommend it highly. No one seems quite sure where Mrs. Cahill's house is, but I gather it lies a mile or five miles beyond the other end of the town, and once again I view my pile of baggage with something less than friendly feeling. However, one can't stay here.

"Looks like a long walk," I said. "Anybody want to help?" They all did, and in a moment heavy suitcase, stuffed dunnage bag, fat portfolio and other odds and ends each had its bearer, and we set off on a safari through the town, our way brightened with much informative conversation about this and that.

Through village-like streets and rounding a corner or two, we come to a large automobile with a man tinkering at it. "That's the taxi-man," says one youngster casually, and walking ends there, but not the procession. Baggage, boys and all, get aboard. They are bound to see me safely housed. Some stood on the running-board so that further progress was like that of a United States president safely guarded against unkind demonstration from some misguided but perhaps quite patriotically inclined fellow-citizen. Mrs. Cahill's proved in every way to justify the recommendations—a pretty house with a wide view open to sun and air, every reasonable comfort and good, home-like meals. On our arrival bits of silver all round sent the boys away happy, and many a cheery smile I got from them when walking about the village over the next few days.

There is a special charm about Placentia. Its setting is delightful, and it is more gathered together into one spot than is any port yet visited. It lies low on a broad reach of stony beach where the fiord-like harbour otherwise would widen out into the tremendous expanse of Placentia Bay. Twice daily a mighty tide rolls in and out through the "gut" crossed by the ferry, but mostly it runs through a hundred-yard-wide channel skirting the village so closely that its pile-driven edge forms one side of a street. Something fascinating there is about this reversing surge of dark green water swiftly moving against a background of high overhanging tree-covered rock. At one spot dismembering skeletons of two wooden ships lie caught as though washed in and left there by some high tide not to be repeated. There's vast power in this ever-moving flood. Some day it will be harnessed and put to work running factories to make labour for a lot of people who would rather not work at all. But that is far in the future since there is no lack of available water-power in most parts of this Island.

Placentia's main street is like an English village lane, here and there lilac-shaded or made fragrant by nearby rose bushes.

A small shop or two supply all the needs. The tavern is the homey and intimate type, busy enough at evening-time, acting as the village club and house of entertainment for the surrounding district. The population is almost entirely Roman Catholic and much of its life centres around the large church, presbytery and convent dominating the town from an open square. One of the cottage hospitals, usual to such communities as this, stands facing the tideway and is equipped to serve this part of the country. Like all other outports we have visited, the village is fortunate in having an abundant supply of good, fresh water. At street hydrants they never bother to turn it off and no expensive pumping plant is required. Up in the surrounding hills are many lakes deep and cool. From one, water is piped down to the town—gravity does the work.

This is no longer a fishing port. It started as such, but war and preparation for war seems to have been its main business over much of its four hundred years of history. It is so now. Most of the men work at the United States naval station or airport three miles away at Argentia, and American money maintains an orderly prosperity hereabouts. The town was started about the year 1550, when some Portuguese picked on this as a comfortable and safe place in which to dry their catch before returning home. Later on Dutch, Basque and Spanish fishers set up stations here and it must have been a place of some importance since buccaneers are reported to have included it in their lists of ports profitable to visit. By 1645 the French had taken over in business-like fashion, for that year one hundred of their ships visited this port. They maintained their position here, meanwhile establishing claim to all the St. Lawrence watershed and any other part of the western world their explorers happened to visit. They did very well in this neighbourhood, occupying the area for well over a century. Charles II, ever generous to paymaster Louis of France, was quite agreeable and conceded rights to establish fortifications here. A sizable fort was erected at the channel entrance, and towards the year 1700 they built Fort St. Louis on top of Castle Hill, a three- to four-hundred-foot rock precipice completely commanding the harbour entrance and entire settlement. Very likely French Canada's Governor Frontenac was responsible for this since he had paid a visit here earlier. An impregnable fortress this—a Gibraltar of America second only to Quebec, and a nuisance to British claims throughout the Island. From here it was that D'Iberville and his little force of Frenchmen, French Canadians and Indians set out in 1692 on his grim march across this most forbidding land to carry devastation to St. John's and all the eastern coast. A gallant fellow, D'Iberville, serving his king and country well, and deserving to be so remembered. What a story there must have been in that march—if only someone had been there to put it down on paper.

By Queen Anne's time the French nuisance had become too troublesome for even British patience and twice the settlement and fortress were ineffectually attacked. In 1703 Admiral Greydon appeared off the harbour with fifteen ships, four thousand men and nine hundred guns and, looking the situation over, thought twice about going on with the enterprise. A council of war decided the best thing to do was go home—which they did. The admiral was promptly court martialed and degraded for cowardice. Ten years later the Treaty of Utrecht ceded Placentia and its fortifications to England, and the French sailed away with all their guns and with flags flying.

War or no war, fishing went on, though the sale of the catch often must have been a chancy business. When the French left, English and French settlers stayed on, and under government from Nova Scotia the place began to assume an air of a settled fishing community. The fort at the mouth of the channel was rebuilt and the harbour became something of a naval station. The faintest possible outline of earthworks with an old mortar and cannon half buried in the grass mark a field now used as pasture for ponies. Nearby is a more vocal relic of those days.

In the late sixteen-hundreds a Roman Catholic garrison chapel stood there, later to be augmented by a Franciscan convent. When the English took over they built a church on the chapel foundations, and there it now stands, restored once or twice, lastly as late as five years ago, and now probably looking very much as it did originally. A tiny wooden structure, much like that back at Gunsbridge, it now serves the community's seven Anglican families to whom the parson's periodical visit is ever an event to be looked forward to. The churchwarden is ex officio caretaker, and proves to be a friendly soul delighted to open the church for a visiting stranger. So we stroll from his home bearing an iron key large and heavy enough to turn the lock in the front door of any reasonably sized cathedral.

Here again the chancel speaks of continuous reverent care. Candlesticks and a brightly polished brass cross are on the altar graced by an embroidered frontal. Over it is a crude but effective painting of the Crucifixion, done, they say, by some sailor in days when tricorned hatted and be-wigged naval officers attended service here. Against the back wall stands a tombstone now undecipherable, but apparently Spanish and bearing 1676 as date. In the little vestry another does duty as a tabletop to commemorate "Sarah, wife of Joseph Blakburn who departed this life 20 January, A.D. 1782, aged 21—a faithful wife, a tender mother & a Sincere Christian." On the wall hangs a painting of the Royal Georgian Arms, rather a necessary item in a properly equipped garrison church.

A royal prince, Frederick William, Duke of Clarence and later King William IV, must have been among the naval officers doing devotional duties here. Much of his active naval time was spent in North Atlantic waters. He gave fifty guineas towards the church's building and a silver communion service now kept at St. John's Cathedral for safety's sake but brought down here for special occasions such as Easter and Christmas celebrations.

A breezy, boisterous sailorman, he is reported to have had a liking for Newfoundland and its sturdy sea-living people. One fine day he lined up a group of Placentia lads, talking to them, no doubt in a kindly, fatherly way. Suddenly he flashed a cane over their heads as though to crack a skull or two. One lad did not flinch. The duke took him to England, gave him an education and commission in the navy where he made his way to quite high rank, as a useful and dependable officer could in those fighting days—particularly if he had a bit of royal favour behind him.   Collins, his name was, and there are members of his family still in Placentia and round-about.   But, English politics hot and bitter as ever they were, ruined poor Collins.   At a dinner in Portsmouth or some such place, high spirits and free talking betrayed him into proposing a toast—"Long life to His Majesty and a greasy rope to Billie Pitt," which was no way in which a naval officer might talk about a popular Prime Minister.   So Collins was cashiered and sent back to Placentia where he languished and died two days before arrival of a pardon long and hard fought for by his English friends.

Surrounding the church is a small picket-fenced graveyard with a few almost unreadable headstones, the oldest bearing the date 1770.   Another cannon is here deep in the sod as though laid to rest among men who once served it.   A few flowers bloom here and there, and now, whenever the air I breathe bears fragrance of roses, again I view this scene, with its church, village and harbour, remembering first an ancient rose-bush, with purple-red bloom faintly flavouring the morning wind coming in from over a fog-hidden sea.

The cemetery used today, tree shaded and wind swept, tops a high hill far beyond the other end of the village.   The Sunday of my stay is the day of Memorial Mass.   Past my window, along the beachside road and up the hill strolls all the village dressed in Sunday-best.   There are hundreds of children, most of them bearing flowers and all chattering as though on a visit to distant friends.   Now a group of small shrill-voiced lads appears displaying none of the pious reverence they will put on for the Mass, together with crimson cassocks and white surplices swinging carelessly from their arms.   Now and then a motor car passes—one from the big church containing the parish priest and ecclesiastical superior.   A glint of purple on another costume proclaims the Monsignor.   Up on the hill is another bead to hang on memory's rosary—the temporary altar under a canopy of spruce-boughs, the crowd kneeling among tomb-stones in tree-cast shade, silent except for short murmurs of response to the priest's low-toned invocation, and an occasional burst of boy's voices in chant, all swiftly borne away on the wind. The expanse of blue cloud-broken sky, green meadows falling to the sea, and to the right, all Placentia, with its hills and misty blue harbour far below. Mass finished, graves are visited with much talk of past days and remembered friends, followed by the walk down hill to home.

The site of uncapturable Fort Louis should be visited, so back we go over by ferry to Jersey-side, a suburb of the main village where fishermen from the Channel Islands set up their fish-houses and drying stages, although perhaps not too welcome among the Englishmen across the gut. A short narrow street leads to the foot of the hill, and about a quarter of the way up is a grass-grown path going towards the sea, but no sign of a path or open passage upward through the trees. This calls for consideration—not greatly helped by a comfortable grassy seat, contemplative pipe and a pleasant view below of many homes snugly grouped together with many children playing joyously around them. Up-hill towards me strides an elderly man, a kindly, under-standing soul, who has guessed my desire and comes to guide me upwards. There is no path, only a stiffish climb up a tiny brook-course, in places almost a straight-drop waterfall. At top, a rest, and what a view—far out to sea and five miles back up the fiord. A small level platform this, not a hundred yards wide, with broken stone relics of buildings all pretty much as left by the French two centuries ago. Back from the sea the rock drops suddenly and the land falls gently to a lake. Looking it over, one wonders. Perhaps General Wolfe would have done better than Admiral Greydon—but it was all the same one hundred years thence, and more so now.

There are guns here, too, British guns nestling down into the sod. But why, since no British fort here was re-erected? My friend does not know, but he tells me of Mrs. Murphy, the local historian, who knows all there is to know about Placentia's past. When we get to the bottom of the hill he presents me to that well-informed and most helpful lady. In the old-world comfort of her sitting-room I learn much of Newfoundland's history—far more than space allows for retelling here. Years ago the guns lay at the foot of the hill where pounding sea-waves threatened their permanent burial. They were seen by officers from the United States station at Argentia who thought they would look very well set up as ornaments in front of the barrack-square buildings there and made strong efforts to that end. Town authorities made no objections—but Placentia has a Women's Historical Committee founded by Mrs. Murphy and a few friends, representing old families and interested in preserving such records and relics as often turn up in places like this where almost every family can trace its history back to very early days. The Committee had strong views on the matter. The guns were royal property in Placentia's keeping and would stay there. They did—even when the Newfoundland Commission Government suggested taking them to St. John's. The Committee fought this with town support, and as final settlement the government granted eighty dollars to pay for their removal to a place of safety. This was in the depression years of the nineteen-thirties, when eighty dollars went a long way, even as relief money. Bitter hard times were here then, as everywhere else. There was little American money in Placentia free for employment and no market for fish. Modest national economy could allow only six cents a day per person for relief—two dollars and fifty-two cents a week for a family of six was pretty narrow living. Food never could be cheap enough to make this reasonably comfortable. So labour was plentiful and willing. Lads of the village pried the guns from mud and rock and hoisted them up Castle Hill—though how they got them there is matter for wonder. The Women's Committee hopes, one suspects, that one day Fort Louis will be rebuilt as a national memorial, but to the visitor comes the thought that reconstruction of the British fort down by the village, and the old church, would be an easier and less costly job, and the resulting memorial would be more closely connected with the history of those now living here. An outline of the ramparts is still vaguely discernible, and I am told old drawings exist showing exactly how its buildings stood. Meanwhile, much credit is due the Historical Committee.

There are many places in Newfoundland where its example might be followed.

Evening in the village is made lively by the presence of airbase workers, soldiers and sailors from Argentia now and then dropping in at the tavern. There's a tavern, too, at Mrs. Cahill's, wisely set up in a separate building for sake of nighttime quiet. Callers here are mostly people passing through the town. The road all the way to St. John's has recently been improved and gravel surfaced to offer pleasant enough and safe driving. At every meal some passing commercial traveller, truck driver, official person or holiday maker joins us, so that we are well informed on news and gossip from faraway places. Over at Argentia a French warship is paying a courtesy call, and some of her sailors extend the courtesy as far as our tavern—bright, merry lads, not large, but vigorous, quick moving and much given to song. They know their own songs and sing them with strong-stomached enthusiasm. It's astonishing how they struggle to talk English in friendly chat with local beer-sippers. One comes to the service-counter asking for cigarettes which are out of stock at the moment.

"No cigarette!" he exclaims with hands extended in horror. "Ha, that is bad. Me, I am ver' on'appy. T'ank you ver' much." But he recovers and goes back to his friends now trying to sing "O Canada," and apparently knowing not many more of the words than do most Canadians. But they do know "Tipperary" and sing it very well indeed, suggesting, perhaps, happy wartime associations between fighting men of France and their British allies.

We meet no American sailors in town just now and rumour goes that they are less popular here than soldiers or airmen as the result of an unfortunate misunderstanding in which the town policeman was somewhat damaged. Placentia is out-of-bounds for the navy.

The word policeman reminds us of law enforcement, crime and jails. So seldom does one see an officer of the law—and there is no reason apparent to the visitor for his existence in these outports—that one wonders if they have a place of detention for evildoers should unexpected and unlikely need arise. The answer is the post office. For most outports they have one type of building, all erected from one set of plans, a central tower, the post office on one side and telegraph office on the other with dwelling quarters upstairs, tidily arranged and all painted green. Here, it stands out lonesome-like on a half-mile beach of stones. Against its rear an unusually high board fence with a small open gate arouses curiosity. It is the jailyard and a very small one. Two men exercising would have as much difficulty in keeping out of each other's way as would two unwilling boxers in a ring. An open door leads to a tiny cell with small iron-barred window and wooden bunk—altogether a considerably restricted area, and a place of which most of us soon would tire. Impressively heavy locks, hinges and bolts would discourage attempt at escape, but the whole place has a general air of having seldom been used, if ever, thus speaking well for local behaviour. In any case, perhaps, a prisoner does not stay here long. Maybe they stick a stamp on and send him by post to St. John's, there to undergo due process of law. This is purely a guess. If such was ever the practice it may be changed now that Mounties with motorcycles and cars are looking after Island policing.

It is time to say good-bye to Placentia—a well-named pleasant place. We ferry across the gut to Jersey-side and clamber aboard the bus waiting to take us up the hill and three miles over to Argentia and the ship that will carry us into the interesting harbours of great Placentia Bay. In a few moments we halt in front of a wooden hut before which flies a "Stars and Stripes" big and bright as a rising sun on a frosty morning. At this moment the largest United States army sergeant I have ever seen, and I've known several big ones and liked them, too, squeezes through the door and fills the forward end of the bus with the air of a man having a grim job to do, but going to do it right—and if you doubt it, note the gun hanging at his side so large and deadly looking that surely no man of ordinary size could use it.

"Got yer pass?" he demanded.

"Pass? What pass?"

"Airport."

"I don't want to go into your airport," I said.

"You're in it, and you gotta have a pass."

"But all I want is to get out of it, and on that ship waiting down at the dock."

Clearly, this was not quite the right thing to have said. One should have shown more kindly interest in his airport. He glared at the boat-ticket presented. "You gotta have a pass," he said, and went on down the bus as far as his bulk would let him. As he left he gave me a look—not what you'd call a particularly dirty one, mind you, but to this day I'm wondering did it mean, "You be careful, young fellow," or "I'll attend to you in a minute." Then he disappeared into the hut, doubtless to get a pair of handcuffs. Fortunately the bus started before he came out and in a few moments we stood at the ship's side. He might have known he wouldn't have needed those handcuffs. I'd have gone quietly with a three-foot midget carrying a gun as big as the young cannon he toted.

A smart ship is a lovely thing to look upon—be it sailer, steamer or what have you. The *Bar Haven* is that kind of a vessel. She is one of the fleet operating in connection with the Newfoundland railway and supplies year-round transportation for hundreds of outports scattered round the Island, most of whom have only the sea for a roadway to other parts of Newfoundland and the outside world. Trim, sturdy lines, bright new paint and a general air of power and efficiency offer the cheeriest kind of invitation to go aboard and settle down for the sea voyage ahead. She rates thirteen hundred tons of stout ship with sleeping accommodation for ninety passengers, and twenty-seven thousand feet of cargo capacity, some of it refrigerated, and will move along at a comfortable speed of twelve knots.

We are waiting for the St. John's train, and about sunset it arrives with as many passengers as can be comfortably packed away, and much freight for the holds below. Freight is as interesting as passengers. We learn what outport dwellers have to bring in for daily need. Foodstuffs are a large part of the load, vegetables, barrels of salt beef and pork, fresh meats. The lettering on bundles and boxes makes it plain that mail-order catalogues are serving their primary purpose throughout the land. There's a sewing machine coming aboard; and baby-carriages, furniture and household utensils present a revealing glimpse of intimate domestic affairs.

"You wouldn't have seen so many of these things going through before we joined up with Canada and got the baby bonus," says a fellow-passenger standing beside me at ship rail. "We're getting money from Canada, all right, but Canada's getting most of it back in business. Though, mind you," he adds, "business has been better on the Island ever since, and it looks to me as though it's going to work out all right." This was a commercial traveller with friends in every port we came to. He had opposed Federation, but now was not so sure. "One thing I know," he said, "if the vote were to be taken again there'd hardly be a woman in the country opposed to it."

Waiting for freight allowed a glimpse at Argentia and its bay. On a battleship here President Roosevelt and Prime Minister Churchill planned and drew up the Atlantic Pact—a document as pregnant with possibilities for world-peace and security as any ever designed, if nations honestly and steadfastly will stand by it. War may be over, but this station still is a busy place. Great barrack-like buildings extend in most directions and in the harbour a warship or two lie at anchor, among them the French cruiser all spick and span for party visiting. Moored nearby is a floating dry dock and an ex-aircraft carrier now a floating machine shop capable of any possible ship repairs. An important spot is this bit of the United States in Canada, convenient to the naval power keeping a sharp eye over all the North Atlantic Ocean.

As the last package of freight disappears into the hold, and last passenger leaves the dining saloon after an excellent evening meal, a typical Placentia Bay fog rolls in from off the southeast Banks, where fogs form with a volume and density attempted in other parts of the world but never exceeded. Distant harbour and ship lights disappear and near ones go out, while dockside buildings soften into deepening shades of blue, and vanish, and the ship's master wins a hearty—if unspoken—vote of thanks when he announces that until it clears, we stay by the dock which we believe is still there but cannot see. It would clear about midnight, he said. Awakened by the ship's motion, one saw harbour lights brilliantly gleaming as we moved past. It was one a.m. These Newfoundland skippers know their weather—a comforting thought brought home several times on this pleasant coastwise voyage.

Placentia Bay can offer samples of any and every kind of weather likely to be met with in these latitudes. But through June and July the behaviour of wind and sea is usually of the genial and reassuring variety awakening no apprehensions for the most timid travellers, but rather seeming to extend a gay and friendly welcome much as a charming hostess would prepare an afternoon tea-party for her friends. Bright dawn brought such a day as quietly we steamed along toward the eastern shore of rock rising abruptly out of the sea with Burin town and harbour hidden somewhere behind.

It is like that with many of these south coast outports. You see no sign of their existence until your ship has nosed her way through an apparently unbroken wall of rock opening up about the time the unaccustomed visitor expects to feel the keel beneath him grind against a shallowing sea bottom. It never does. Placidly the skipper walks the bridge gazing seaward, windward or seemingly anywhere but where he is going, passes a quiet word to the wheelsman now and then, and very soon we are at dockside in a snug landlocked harbour.

Burin's entrance is marked by queer, sugar-loaf islands and many more break the view up the winding bay running far back into the land. Well inside and round a wide corner, the town lies scattered along the shore and up the hill. There are not many trees on these hills. Here and there is a patch of cultivated land, but mostly bare, red-brown rock. A couple of churches lift spires skywards, and far away on what looks like a level green shelf white headstones mark a cemetery. Brilliantly painted homes in flowering gardens crowd together near the dock.

Whitewashed picket fences or stone walls line the winding gravel
road, which is narrow but freshly clean as the sea and distant
hills.  All the town is down to meet the boat, and a cheery,
colourful crowd it is.  Girls' summer costumes and bright
kerchiefs on their heads, and the noisy movement of freight
going ashore make a scene of bustling activity.  Times past it
must have been busier than this, for here stands a shipways where,
they tell me, many a fine vessel was built when trade was good
and fishing or wartime needs were great.

There's plenty of time for a walk ashore here.  When the
unhurried freight movement is finished, the ship moves to
another dock about half a mile away to fill its refrigerated space
with freshly frozen fish all nicely packed and cartoned just as
it will tempt your purchase from some ice-cold display case
perhaps a thousand miles from here.  Trolleys bring the
packages to shipside and leisurely they go below—just enough
to fill a refrigerated freight-car when the ship reaches mainland.

This is one of the modern fish-packing plants effecting an
important change in the economy of the whole Island.  Sun-
dried and salted cod has ceased to be a factor in trade hereabouts.
Five or six steam draggers work out of here on the Banks scooping
up their loads of cod and other fish from the sea's floor.  Other
smaller, diesel-driven boats, each with a crew of four or five
men and able to bring home twenty thousand pounds of cod
iced down, work closer, inshore waters.  The plant is not
impressively large, but going at full capacity when the market
demand makes it possible it is said to be able to turn out a
million pounds of filleted fish a month, and six tons of dehydrated
fish-meal a day, which would seem likely to account for a sizable
lessening in the fish population of these waters.  But the supply
keeps up somehow, and probably will so long as there's plenty
of food here to support it and encourage the admirable system
of reproduction to which fish seem to devote most of their efforts.
They say one female cod will produce eight or nine million eggs
a year—praise-worthy performance indeed, and one hopes,
highly reassuring to lovers of fish as food and to those who
catch and pack them.

From Burin a road goes westerly to Fortune Bay and it, like that going north and connecting with St. John's, is being improved so that in a short time the entire Burin peninsula will be open to comfortable motoring all round its coast. The population along this shore is predominantly English, Irish forming about one-seventh of the total. One-third are Roman Catholic and the rest Protestant of varying communions, among which the United Church is largest.

Living by the sea has its exciting moments even though one does not venture upon it, and Burin had a disastrous experience of that sort of thing November 18, 1929. About five o'clock on the afternoon of that day all eastern Newfoundland felt an earthquake. No great harm was done, but it was serious enough to startle people in St. John's, and perhaps frighten those where its manifestation was more violent—at Burin, for instance. It passed swiftly and soon would have been only a mildly thrilling memory. Then came the tidal wave. Somewhere south and east the ocean floor had moved in mighty convulsion, and two hours later most of Burin town was suddenly swept into the sea. Mack Ronayne, a writer in the St. John's *Telegram*, has described graphically what happened.

Households all along the coast were easing from the hustle and bustle of suppertime into the smooth rhythm of preparing children for bed and other day-end chores when disaster struck.

Its suddenness can be judged by the experience of men engaged in a game of auction shortly after seven p.m. aboard the old *S.S. Daisy* moored at the government pier. Suddenly a seaman burst into the cabin with the startling cry that the town was sinking.

Certainly that's what must have seemed, for there was the *Daisy* floating high over the wharf, water rushing in over the land to the accompaniment of buildings creaking, tearing from their foundations, falling apart, confused and frightened screams and frantic cries for help.

After about five unbelievable minutes, when it seemed that the world was to be swallowed up, the waves began to recede and the cold autumn moonlight shone on a scene of utter chaos and terror.

Stories of that day tell of waterside buildings and more than one home floating, apparently little damaged, out in the harbour, and of one with a mother and three children swept through the narrow entrance out to sea. The eldest daughter valiantly managed to swim ashore with the baby. The mother and other child perished in a similar attempt. Late that night the house was discovered still afloat with an oil lamp brightly burning in the kitchen. Total loss of life happily was small, most people having hurried to higher ground. There were many freak happenings. One large store moved to a vacant lot some hundreds of feet away without disturbing goods on the shelves. Heavy gales the next day completed the destruction of many floating buildings all up and down this shore. Telegraph wires were down, and the outside world knew nothing of the disaster for three days. When news did go forth, generous help flowed in from the rest of Newfoundland, England, Canada and the United States.

Ship loading finally ends and, making a wide circle in the harbour, we steam out again into the broader scene of Placentia Bay and south towards the Atlantic. Here the bay is forty to fifty miles wide, a noble sweep of sea running eighty to ninety miles back into the land. On its northern reaches, a thousand or so islands, some of curious and intriguing shape, give fascination to every view, and on many of them are tiny settlements whose founders generations back set up their homes and such rude fishing plants as were needed. Given a stout, small sailing boat with a reliable gas engine aboard, and comfortable accommodation for three or four, including a man knowing bay tides and currents, and here would be found every requisite for a perfect summertime holiday.

Rounding the cape and moving between formidable rocky hills, we enter a bay at the end of which lies the town of St. Lawrence. A different atmosphere here—no fishing, or very little. Nearby fluorspar mines employ all available labour and are an important adjunct to Island economy. Here ships load the crushed product of the mines brought by heavy trucks from back over the hills. The town has a prosperous and busy air and the crowd at the dock to meet us is larger than in most places and apparently as happy and carefree as any yet met with. A weighty load of freight goes off here, including the sewing machine and up-to-date-looking plumbing accessories, going, no doubt, into new homes now a-building out on town's edge.

Late afternoon sees us in Lawn, just such another harbour, but smaller and less rockbound. The shore rises gradually to bare hills once tree covered. Our ship's captain, Captain Rose, says that the way of human life here, and the scene itself, has changed entirely since fifty years ago when fishing prosperity was at its height. Where a few cows now browse down to the water's edge, fish-houses and merchants' stores lined the docks serving three-masted ships loading fish for European and West Indian ports.

As daylight fades and the rockbound shore turns a deeper red with violet shadows in the sunset, we slip into Lamaline Harbour after eighteen miles of whitecapped seaway with just enough swing and toss to make the ship a living creature playfully sea-borne. In that eighteen miles we have made two calls, at Lord's Cove and Point au Gaul, differing from others only in number of dwellings along the shore and height of massive surrounding cliffs and hills. Lamaline is different. We do not go dockside here—not enough water—so we drop anchor in mid-harbour, and ere the hook has taken solid hold far below, boats are alongside, some with a passenger or two to exchange for those going ashore, and others to take off freight. One interesting item being dropped here is a number of apparently long-used church pews picked up somewhere along the way. They pile up in the little motor boat until it seems she must roll over, but does not, so away they go, perhaps visible evidence of church extension in these parts, although the couple of churches we see on the hillside would appear to offer accommodation for all who dwell here. For the skipper's own good reasons we spend the night at anchor, a welcome thought to all, and particularly so to one or two whose well-suppered stomachs would rest more quietly here than outside where a fairly stiff breeze is tossing the ocean's surface about in a somewhat fretful way.   In here all is still.   It is late, almost bedtime when the last glimmer fades. Hills around are blacker than night itself.   We float suspended on the reflection of a starlit sky while village lights vanish one by one.   Soon the warmth and light of the ship's cabins call us below.

Whatever there may have been of romance and excitement in Lamaline's past history, and surely it must have had its share as has every other settlement along this stormy coast, it did not all die out with the coming of modern times.   Prohibition offered a challenge to adventurous spirits, no less adventurous because of hard times.   Within easy run of the tip of this peninsula lie the French islands of St. Pierre and Miquelon where prohibition would have been viewed with natural French scorn had it not proved a source of such wealth probably only dreamed of before. Here appeared inexhaustible stocks of every delectable beverage Mother Nature invited man to concoct and short-sighted, well-meaning moralists said must not be enjoyed.   Off every point of the compass from these isles lay the open sea-road to millions of Americans, Canadians and even some Newfoundlanders contemptuous of a law they believed hopelessly wrong and knew to be unworkable, and ready to pay handsomely for any opportunity of defeating it.   On the Islands, fifty cents or a dollar bought that which could be sold elsewhere for four or five dollars and sometimes much more.

The deep-sea fisherman takes chances every day of his working life, and running the gauntlet of revenue officers added only sporting zest to the effort.   There was need, too, for postwar depression had set in.   So no wonder there were doings up and down this coast that rivalled the best smuggling stories of the Old Land from whence these people came.   Pity it is that more of them are not remembered and told.   Perhaps those events are still too close to the present, too much concerned with living persons, and are bottled up for later enjoyment when, like the wares traded in, they will come forward greatly improved with age.

Revenue officers in these parts were about as unpopular then as they were in earlier days along the coasts of Devon and Cornwall. Many a deep-chested laugh goes round with tales such as the one about the officers having been tipped off that a sizable boat load of illegal importation was to arrive at a certain cove at four o'clock one November morning where they waited in vain in fog, rain and cold until daylight and the limit of bearable discomfort brought conviction that they had been fooled. They had. In their car a mile back on the road was found a note expressing the smugglers' regret at having missed the party, wind and tide having brought them in hours earlier. It also recommended liberal doses from a large bottle of the best, left lying beside the note, as a restorative from their bone-chilling labour of the night. Not often did such amenities pass between these adversaries.

Also, there was the man whose success in the trade and, more particularly his success in evading capture, made him a notable, perhaps even admirable figure up and down the coast. Finally, officialdom made a case against him so threatening to his liberty that he thought it wise to slip off to West Indies in a convenient south-going load of dried cod. But he came back to St. Pierre, answering, no doubt, the call of home and the desire to be near his friends. Anyway, what would a good Newfoundlander be doing in those soft southern latitudes when there's wind and cold to stir the blood at home. He could not live in Newfoundland or Canada where charges stood against him, so he stayed on the French islands. Then came the Second Great War, and later a split between the Free French and the Vichy governments. The French navy, for a time, stood mostly with the Vichy partisans, and St. Pierre was a frequent port of call for its ships so that much information interesting to the Allied Powers drifted that way. Our outlaw friend was a Britisher, and having heard something that seemed to him important, set out alone in a small boat on a two-hundred-mile journey over open ocean to the

Argentia naval station—United States territory and free land to him—where he told his useful and welcome story. They sent him back to St. Pierre where he proved a valuable source of information while war lasted. The inevitable answer to this was free pardon for all past misdemeanours, which pleased everyone concerned.

Open sea again, and this time you know it is sea. There's a stiff breeze, and waves are dancing ponderously, but the ship takes it beautifully, shoves her nose into it like a porpoise in full play and we surge along happily enough, except that attendance at one or two meals lacks the friendly presence of a few passengers whose minds are otherwise occupied than with thoughts of food. However, we soon round the peninsula into Fortune Bay and quieter waters. Our next call is at the town of Fortune, one of the more important places along this coast. Its presence is all unexpected until we round a point and enter its harbour. Schooners bound for the Banks are tied up here, and there's a freighter or two in. It's a scene of activity, bustling and colourful with all the town and its pretty girls to meet the boat. There's plenty of time for a walk in the town and chat with those whose amiable "Good day" invites gossip. They tell me Fortune originally was settled by men from Jersey, but never would one guess it since family names and tongues and everything about the place is as English as any part of the Island can be. There's fishing going on here now, and fish sun-drying in every direction. One schooner in the harbour has been banking forty-five years and looks good for as many more. The town is gathered around its huge United Church. Of a thousand or so inhabitants, over six hundred attend it, while three hundred gather for worship at the Salvation Army Temple and Anglicans number a dozen or two. This is a holiday, and the children are having a Sunday School picnic. From the United Church a host of flag-waving singing youngsters march through town making the kind of noise likely to be induced by bright prospects of buns, lemonade and goodness knows what else. If there be any children left over for the Salvation Army and Anglicans, this is a town with a future. Walking back to the ship, we meet one of the oldest inhabitants who has much to tell of past prosperity in these parts and of fortunes he has gained and lost in eighty years of good times and bad.

"It'll come back again," he says. "Five times I've seen it, and I'll live to see it again." Not easily daunted, these older Newfoundlanders. Varying fortunes have taught them patience, and they have a deep-founded faith in their land and the sea that gives them their living.

# 16

*Grand Bank, a Bit of Oldtime Newfoundland—Home of Deep-sea Fishing Fleets—The Ship that Made the Northwest Passage—They Play Soccer Here—The Buffett Records.*

FIVE MILES farther down the bay are the town and harbour of Grand Bank, suddenly presenting a delightful sight in the golden glow of late afternoon. Surely this is something like Newfoundland fifty years ago when wealth was measured only by the ability of men to reap an inexhaustible harvest of the sea and trade it for gold in hungry lands afar. A stout, stone mole protects the small harbour which looks hardly large enough for the crowd of ships it now holds. Small boats and big schooners fill every foot of dockside space, a lacery of masts and rigging standing high against the sky. Behind them a wall of tall warehouses, salting plants and stores mask the tidy, compact little town—a spot in a wide vista of brown and green hills.

This is a place to stay awhile and bid regretful farewell to the comfortable *Bar Haven* and her skipper who has done much to make a pleasant voyage happier. Where to "put up" is a problem soon settled. From the ship's deck we are directed to a fine old house fronting the sea, and in no time at all a waiting taxi has landed us at its door behind which we find excellent accommodation and satisfying meals. Hours later, having disposed of countless bundles, packages and several piles of lumber for trucks and pony carts to haul away, the *Bar Haven* backs out from the mole and disappears on her westward way.

234

A small town this as towns go over on the mainland, but back through history it has been the largest and busiest centre of south-coast fishing trade. South and east of here lie the Grand Banks, a vast submerged plateau where an abundance of food and suitable water temperatures favour codfish life. First settlers here were French, probably Channel Islanders. At any rate, it was one of their stations for salting and drying fish, and they called it Grand Banc. The town grew with the trade and the coming of Englishmen so that over years no longer remembered, ships have gone out from here bearing their ten or fifteen men and dories from which they fished with net or line through the days or weeks it took to gather a load. They still do it, and these smart schooners we see in the harbour spend most of their time on open ocean, coming in only to deliver their catch and replenish supplies of food, bait and ice. Perhaps this is a manner of fishing now passing away. The government is encouraging by subsidy the construction of larger ships for trawling or dragging, and there is a great deal of speculation regarding the possible establishment of a packing and freezing plant which the nearby town of Fortune says most certainly should be placed there, and not here.

This place was known three hundred years ago, and by mid-seventeen-hundreds it had grown into one of those sprawling, brawling fishing ports which laid the foundation of Newfoundland's future, looking as unlike as possible the quiet, well-behaved town it now is. Hills now bare were then forest covered, but by one hundred years ago much surrounding land had been cleared, and at least one farm was doing well enough, its few cultivated acres giving a crop of 1,308 barrels of potatoes and 108 tons of hay. The harbour never was easy to enter or the town would have grown larger. Settlers left for other ports upshore, but among the English coming in were educated and enterprising men to form a solid base for growth of the community.

As elsewhere, we find no buildings dating back to ancient and stirring days. Fifty or seventy-five years would seem to cover the lives of any now here, including dockside warehouses which have survived as in no other outport visited. The winding main street lies behind these warehouses with here and there a sizable store stocked with all the needs of a busy life.

Farther along is a blacksmith shop—the old-fashioned kind of blacksmith shop that has disappeared long ago from most communities. Staying to glance through its open half-door brings the cheery call to enter—and call by name, too. You can't stay in a town like this more than a day without everybody knowing you are there—and why. There is no thrusting forward for curiosity's sake, or breaking uninvited into conversation, but a friendly readiness to meet you halfway and be very pleasant about it. Long years it is since one has been in a blacksmith's shop like this, or in passing heard the merry ring of steel on hot iron taking useful shape under skilful blows. This is an old shop, for the master-blacksmith's father worked it many years before the son took it over. Ship's hardware is its chief product—the important iron pieces that go into building and rigging, and there has been much of both here in past times. Countryside ponies, and there are many, come here to be shod against the hard wear of flinty roads and stony beaches, and the tinyness of some of the shoes called for is astonishing. The blacksmith tells of a set of four recently mailed to another outport, comfortably packed in a cardboard box made to contain a pair of man's-size rubber heels, which conjures up the vision of a tough little pony about the size of a large Newfoundland dog bustling along ahead of a cart three times his bulk, and doing it as though he liked it.

The road continues over a stone bridge with a view of the harbour worth painting, particularly on a misty morning when ships and buildings stand ghostly blue-grey on still, shadow-deepened waters. There's a beach, too, wide, rainwashed, sun-swept and all pebbles, an ideal place for drying cod. By the time morning sun has warmed the stones, a flock of gossiping, laughing women, sun-bonneted and broad skirted, are covering acres with them taken from beehive-shaped piles where, canvas covered, they have passed the dew-wet night. On the shore fish-laden dories land their morning catch to be cleaned at long tables and piled like cordwood from where pony carts haul them to the salting in nearby sheds. Yes, the breeze carries a decided flavour of fish and salt, but it's a clean, healthy smell, and one imagines there's many a born Newfoundlander in foreign parts who now and then remembers it and wishes he might have it in his nostrils once again.

On over the hills to up-bay villages runs the road and thence on to St. John's. Atop the first hill it passes the town cemetery, but there are no records of long past times or of those who lived them. Before churches came to the land graveyards seem to have been but scantily cared for. A few old headstones now stand in orderly row in a plot back in the village, graves long lost and forgotten.

All round the town and through its cottage and garden-lined by-ways is not a long walk. About twenty-five hundred people live here with little diversity of opinion on matters of faith. A huge United Church has a membership of more than two-thirds of the population while a Salvation Army barracks satisfies the spiritual needs of most of those left. There's a Masonic Hall of imposing proportions and back in a small mid-town square stands a memorial to men who gave their lives in the First Great War. A bit startling this is on first sight. A granite pedestal rises from a bed of flowers to support a life-sized figure of a soldier painted a realistic khaki, face and all, except the boots which are black. One wonders why the face is not given life-colour and what the effect would be then.

Here is the public library as inviting and efficient looking a library as may well serve such community as this—a wide, generously windowed room with conveniently shelved books inviting all ages and tastes, even to that of anyone desiring detailed knowledge of the German war-criminal trials, thirty fat volumes of them. For those who like that sort of reading, they are just the thing with which to pass several years of long winter evenings. Children's books are here "in galore," with bright-looking youngsters busily engaged in sampling them. It is altogether a going concern and an encouraging factor in life here.

Main Street seems at its busiest on a summer evening. Young men talk together at corners and toss bright remarks to laughing girls passing in groups. Youngsters on bicycles flash by, and motor cars aplenty, some from as far away as St. John's, roll carefully along the narrow roadway. Elders gossip here and there, but most seem to stay at home. No taverns are found in this town under local option, and no beer is obtainable to lighten the social hour. The nearest thing is a beverage with two to three per cent alcoholic content, something like the so-called near-beer that fell far short of general popularity in prohibition days, nor does it seem greatly in favour here, or elsewhere on the Island.

No more fascinating scene presents itself to loitering eyes than does a busy dock with ships tied up alongside, particularly be they sailing ships with tall masts and bearing scars of battles with the seas and with histories of far-away voyages behind them. Grand Bank docks, small but busy, form just such a picture—not big ships with high overhanging sides to look up at as you pass, but trim, valiant schooners with decks hardly dock high so that you may gaze down on all the gear that makes a ship a living thing. Up for'ard are the stout, dependable anchors, back aft a brass-fitted, oaken wheel usually shining brightly in the sun, and between them a medley of half-coiled ropes, buckets of fishing lines, bait barrels, often a net or two and sails drying in the breeze. Perhaps, too, you can get a peep down below into narrow quarters where for weeks at a time the men sleep and eat and, perhaps, are happiest when with a hundred fathoms of moving water beneath them, they are swinging homewards over a white-capped sea before a favouring wind that lays the lee rail well down to take on flying crests of waves scurrying past. Nowadays the ships run on gas power most of the time, but masts and rigging are there, and a sad day for ship-lovers it will be when they all have gone.

Sailormen, mostly young, move about the decks, or leisurely mend a bit of rigging or bait hooks. Cloth caps and rough sea-going clothes help the picture except on hot days when it is bettered by the sight of broad sun-stained shoulders, deep chests and arms bared to the wind. But always the knee-high rubber boots are worn, even ashore on a hot day, and one wonders why, in later life, most of them are not crippled by rheumatic or other troubles.

But this is not the busiest of times here. There's a difference of opinion between fishermen and shipowners or merchants, and naturally enough it's about the price the lads are to get for their fish brought in. Prices have not been good for some time, and just now there's a tendency for them to go lower, so argument on both sides is stiff—not much bitterness, but a good deal of native stubbornness—and the men grumble together in little groups and, no doubt, the other side does the same thing elsewhere and in its own way. But some sort of compromise seems to be reached, and one hopes the men are better off thereby since the working income in these parts for most of them runs from four hundred to six hundred dollars a year, with many getting less and a very few slightly more. Cost of living soars here as elsewhere, and what is equally important, so does the cost of outfitting ships and keeping them sound and seaworthy. Anyway, an agreement is arrived at, the men complete preparations and one by one the ships disappear seaward toward the Banks.

Never were there busy docks with ships standing alongside and no interested loiterers enjoying the scene as one might enjoy a tasty meal. Several are here—oldtimers and sea veterans, weighing present-day doings with past, and sure in their minds that these young ship-handlers and fishermen have much to learn of their trade. There's one here looking like eighty years of age and probably is ninety. He leans heavily on a stick but his blue eyes are bright and his voice vigorous.

"No, fishin' ain't what it used to be," he says. "The fish ain't there—and d'ye know why? I'll tell ye." And he does so with much emphasis. "Fishin' on Sunday—that's what's done it. There's no luck in it. In my time a few did it and they're no better off today—worse, I think. I never did it or allowed it on my boats, and I've done well enough. Got a few thousands laid away. It's ag'in God and nature—don't give the fish a chance, and that's no good."

He's not very keen either on steam trawlers. For every

good saleable fish they bring up, says he, they dredge up others too small or the wrong kind—haddock, halibut and the like of that when they want only cod—and they throw them back dead or dying. "That won't last for ever," he murmurs as he walks away.

There's the man also, eager to talk about the men's demand for better pay and he has much sympathy with them. "It's a hard life at best," he says. "Easy enough fine weather like this—but what it'll be like tomorrow or next week you never can tell. But you do know that by time a month or two's gone by there'll be little fun in it. At sea they work from dawn to dark and often through the night. That's the fisherman's way of life—hard work when you're at it and easygoing when ashore, a lucky well-paying trip every now and then, and always pretty well their own masters. They're bred to that sort of thing and you can't change it. But today the lads won't work as their fathers did. They know about eight-hour days and wages in other trades, and they hear about the price the housekeeper pays for frozen fish in city shops, and they're doing a lot of thinking." All this, doubtless, is true. But they also have to face competition in world markets from Scottish, Norwegian and other fishermen equipped with the most modern ships and gear—a trade factor calling for a good deal of consideration.

Never does one foresee what interesting incident may be met with in the course of a stroll along busy wharves. That is the most fascinating feature of every deep-sea port. A strange ship came into Grand Bank one afternoon and tied up dockside with as little fuss and noise as one would make of walking into one's own room and sitting down. I looked at her bow nameplate— "R.C.M. Police *St. Roch*"—seagoing Mounties, no less, and something not often seen away from Arctic waters where their patrols carry law, order, and the mercies of civilization over polar wastes. The name was somehow familiar. Then memory awoke. Here was the ship that had made world history of the geographic kind by twice navigating the Northwest Passage, going from the Pacific to the Atlantic and back again westward around the top end of Canada—the first ship to

complete the passage from west to east, and the first to go from
east to west in one year.

The Northwest Passage around North America was a matter
that had puzzled and bothered mariners all through the years
back to Queen Elizabeth's days. European imagination had
been set afire by glittering tales of inexhaustible wealth awaiting
exploitation in the Orient. The Americas were less immediately
promising. To most they were a stumbling block in the way to
India, China or any other fabulously gold-laden lands that might
lie in their vicinity.

In the year 1567 Martin Frobisher, that gallant Elizabethan
sea-dog and Armada hero, made three voyages, getting as far as
the eastern end of Baffin Island. In 1600 Henry Hudson died
in Hudson Bay, the result of his attempt to find the Passage. Sir
John Franklin got part way through in 1845, but little trace
was ever found of either the ship or any of his party, though
sixteen different relief expeditions went searching. In 1854
Captain McClure went in from the Pacific, had to abandon ship
about one-third of the way east, pushed on by dogsled another
third where he joined a relief party in Lancaster Sound, and so
sailed home across the Atlantic, first man to have made the
journey, though not by ship. By that time there was no longer
an interest in the Northwest Passage as a road to the Indies, but
many navigators and geographers visited those waters, mapping
passages and islands and establishing the fact that if there were
an open seaway across it had little practical value for navigation.
That knowledge had been gained at the cost of many lives and
terrific hardships. In 1903 Roald Amundsen essayed the trip
from east to west and succeeded, taking three years to reach the
Pacific side.

On June 23, 1940, the *St. Roch*, commanded by Staff-Sergeant
Larsen and with crew of eight men, left Vancouver to arrive
twenty-seven and a half months later at St. John's in September,
1942, having spent two winters icebound in the Arctic. Sea and
weather conditions were bad from the beginning of the journey
around Alaska. In both the Bering Sea and the Arctic Ocean

came more than one threat of an ice-crush and the need for blasting a way to open water. Through here the ship carried supplies to Mounted Police western Arctic posts and later put in for winter at Walker Bay. Here they covered the ship with canvas for the sake of snugness and set about their job of patrolling any accessible area and visiting native settlements. A total of nine hundred and ninety miles they travelled by dogteam and sled, sleeping each night in snow houses. One patrol of six hundred miles to Banks Island took forty-one days. In leisure moments—so called—they scraped and painted and overhauled the engines, until on July 31st something like spring cleared the ice and allowed another start eastward. Held in ice farther on until August 24th, they reached Palsey Bay, sixteen hundred and sixty miles nearer the Atlantic, and anchored for another winter, the only apparently safe place being beside a shoal lying one and a half fathoms below water surface. Here crowding ice lifted the ship over the shoal, though why it didn't turn it over in so doing was a miracle. Winter lasted eleven busy months, the men doing dogsled patrols on the important job of visiting Eskimo villages and taking the census of native population throughout the area, one patrol lasting seventy-one days and covering eleven hundred and forty miles. On August 4, 1942, they were able to move out, but left one crew member behind. Constable Chartrand had died from a sudden heart attack and his cairn-covered grave lies in that lonely land.

The eastern journey was beset by grievous dangers. More than once ice lifted the ship almost out of the water and only blasting could save her. At one point another miracle occurred. An ice-jam formed ahead—they could not turn. As the ship was about to crash in an inevitable wreck, a smaller floe hit the larger one, breaking it in two, and the *St. Roch's* prow drifted forward in open water between the two. By September 10th they were off Baffin Island and heading down the Labrador coast towards Newfoundland—the Northwest Passage successfully made.

During the year 1943 the ship was busy on an eastern Arctic patrol. On July 22, 1944, she left Halifax bound for her return

Arctic journey to the Pacific. Off Baffin Island the new gyro-compass stopped working and the magnetic compass did the same shortly afterwards. Nothing but Admiralty charts and a sense of direction were left to navigate by. But they kept on through ice, bad weather and what the ship's master, Larsen, called "good luck" to enter Vancouver harbour October 16th with all flags flying, and a large white banner proudly proclaiming their successful trip—three hundred and sixty-eight years after Frobisher had first attempted to find the passage.

Well, here was the *St. Roch* tied up to a Grand Bank dock, looking as beautifully trim, alive and well groomed as any horse a "Mountie" ever rode—a small ship to look at, eighty tons and, by guess, seventy-five or a hundred feet long. They call her a schooner, two masts with fore and aft rigging and a high-powered diesel engine for regular use. A friendly lad aboard invited our inspection—bless him for that—and a delight it was to tread her deck and wander about down below. Up forward were sleeping quarters narrow at any time let alone an eleven-month winter. Amid-ship were the comfortable lounge and dining-saloon, well-fitted galley and an engine room. No good housewife's kitchen ever shone more brightly or looked more efficiently business-like than the latter. Elsewhere was wide accommodation for stores, freight, sled-dogs and whatever else Arctic travel demands. She was built in Vancouver in 1928—a wooden hull with an outer sheathing of Australian iron-wood and steel plates around the prow, all of which came undamaged through three years of grinding ice. She had now come from the Pacific through the Panama Canal for more years of work in Arctic waters.

Mounted Police authorities talk little about the *St. Roch* and her historic journeyings. To them Arctic patrols are all in the day's work, and if one happens to be longer and attended by more hardship and danger than others—well, it just so happens, that's all. But to say they are not proud of the little *St. Roch* and the records established by her valiant skipper and crew would do them an injustice. They have a neat pamphlet reproduction of an article from the *Canadian Geographical Journal* telling in terse detailed fashion of these two trips—which makes most interesting reading.

Another visiting ship comes into port, the *Rui Alberto*, fourteen days from Portugal, a link added to the unbroken chain of trade relations going back to Newfoundland's earliest days. As have her predecessors over many generations, she carries a load of salt to be emptied into warehouses here and will return with salted cod. A business-like capable-looking craft built in wartime of steel traded by England for badly needed Portuguese timber, she is as smartly maintained and manned as becomes a nation with a great sea history. Her captain, tall, lithe and dark, with iron-grey hair, looks like a movie hero. Officers and men are young, animated people with ready smiles and ingratiating manners. The sole unfriendly crew member is the ship's dog, a fuzzy sample of the spitz family about large enough to fill a quart jug. But she has three mouse-sized youngsters to guard and gives every assurance that visiting foreigners will be torn to pieces before touching one of them. She lives under a shelf in a spotless galley where cooking utensils shine on the wall like old silver.

The ship's cabin is a pleasant place. Over a glass of excellent wine we learn of a perfect outward journey and much of the homeland where living is cheap and, this time of year, climate and other considerations tempt one to stay aboard as a passenger for the return trip. They speak no English, but with us is a representative of the shipowners, for three days a fellow-sojourner at the hotel, and we get along very nicely. He tells me of the early Portuguese discovery of Newfoundland by Gaspar de Corte Real who visited what is now Portugal Cove in 1501, eight years after Cabot's arrival. Since then Portugal has depended on Newfoundland waters for a large part of her fish food. Even today her people require from here 1,200,000 quintals of 112 pounds each, and the ships of his company account for about 500,000.

Mild excitement prevails on the dock this evening. The local football team has returned across nine miles of sea from St. Pierre where they administered a beating to a French team.

The Mounted Police seem to suspect that they may have brought back with them something more exhilarating than pleasant memories of a well-won game, and are making a thorough search with doubtful help of kindly but pointedly ironic suggestions from footballers and a dockside crowd of townsfolk enjoying the event. One returning passenger most certainly has brought back a "package," but he has it safely stored where it can do the Mounties no good at all, and its effects are mostly observable in the rude form of wit with which he counters official inquiries and greatly delights bystanders. It's all very friendly, and in the spirit of good, clean fun.

Perhaps authority, and particularly that represented by revenue officers, has never completely been given a warm entry into the hearts of these people. It goes back a long way. When early settlers were being dispossessed and driven from their homes, doubtless this was one of the places to which they fled. Memory of this still lives, and it must have been still more alive in 1866 when in return for closing American markets to Newfoundland fish, the Legislature stopped United States fishermen from buying Newfoundland bait upon which their fishing depended, and thus brought another wave of depression over south and east coast outports. But the Americans had to have bait and paid ready gold for it, and Newfoundland ships were busy gathering herring, caplin and squid. When selling became illegal, they sailed to St. Pierre where Americans awaited them and eagerly bid for their cargoes.

The government had a hard time enforcing the law in the face of determined and universal opposition, even with revenue boats cruising up and down the coast. Stubborn fishermen ran the blockade and even went out boldly in fleets of up to forty vessels with revenue craft following on. Many were the arrests, convictions and terms in jail handed out, but equally many daring and resourceful law-breakers got by with considerable and much-needed profit. A tough, thankless job for revenue officers it must have been. There are tales of more than one of them being tossed into Grand Bank harbour to sink or swim as they could when their pursuit of duty seemed over-zealous to an exasperated community. Such memories were far from conducive to the obedience of law in later days when prohibition presented another opportunity for gathering illegal wealth.

You do not know a people unless you have seen them at their sports. Most welcome, then, is the opportunity to witness a game of soccer played by the Grand Bank team against one from Burin, sixty or so miles away across the peninsula. It is a fine summer evening, with the sun giving golden play to every flash of colour on land and sea. Along the road, over the bridge, up past the cemeteries saunter all the town's young people. Pony carts and a few motor cars carry groups of young men and brightly clad girls. But nearly all are afoot, for the walk out is part of the fun. Traffic moves easily, slightly impeded now and then by such things as the pretty girl herding home a flock of ten or a dozen goats nonchalantly taking the road as though well knowing their right to it. The playing field has a high board fence, and you learn why when, at the gate, you part with a small piece of silver as a contribution towards expenses. There are no seats, but a rail keeps the crowd in place and at start of the game there's little vacant space around it.

In due time a truckload of visiting players rolls down from over the hills and the teams are face to face on the field—well-built, active and keen young men as likely to be seen anywhere. Football uniforms display rugged, muscular physique and there's no lack of grace or vitality in their movements, or courtesy and goodwill between contenders. The game is a good one, smartly played and noisily encouraged by a good-humoured crowd with more than a little old-time Devonshire English in their speech. They cheer a fast-running ball carrier and joyously chaff his pursuer.

"Catch 'un, Bill, catch 'un," roars a bulky lad at my right. "Ah, 'e can't catch 'e," comments another, and he doesn't catch him either, though he tries manfully enough. And so the game goes on until Grand Bank is beaten by a small margin, and crowd and players mingle in what appears to be as happy a mood as might have followed a home-team victory.

A wet and stormy morning by the sea seems wetter, stormier

and more sullen than ever it could when viewed across some green and varied landscape or met with beating down on city roofs and streets. So we sat in the glassed-in hotel porch and watched the waves roll in to break in foam against the rocks and low sea-wall across the road. It's Sunday morning, but the weather is not too encouraging to church-going, and even when rain has ceased and watery sunlight flits now and then across the scene but few people move through lanes and paths leading to the big city-size frame church. Early afternoon brings a Salvation Army street meeting, with flag and drum, a few musical instruments and fifteen or so strong clear voices, mostly from young women and girls.

The religious history of Fortune Bay is not without interest. By 1800 the town had acquired commercial importance, but like other settlements about, the bay had no established church organization of any kind. Those so inclined met on the Lord's Day and read service from the *Church of England Prayer Book*, and those best qualified administered baptism, marriage and burial services as need arose. In 1816 St. John's Wesleyans heard, apparently with astonishment, that five thousand churchless and preacherless Protestants were scattered along the shores of Fortune Bay, and a missionary was sent to them. However, one man over so wide and hazardous a sea coast could do but little, and almost fifty years later, a missionary visited fifty-two harbour and cove settlements which neither school nor church had reached. Sunday was unobserved in many, and the general behaviour what might be expected under such conditions. Newfoundland's Protestant churches were no less impoverished than were the people, and help from British missionary societies, while generous, could reach but a fraction of Island settlements. Church came gradually, but resolutely, so that within memory of many now living, natural instinct and desire for better living asserted itself. In the year 1883 the Wesleyans became Methodists—perhaps with some reservations. The Reverend Superintendent of Circuit then stated that "Rules remain with us as they were collaborated by John Wesley himself one hundred and fifty years ago." At Grand Bank the church flourished and later voted strongly against Church Union when that proposal came up, but eventually joined in with the overwhelming Island majority. Of the town's 2,500 people, 1,350 are listed as United Church, 863 Salvationists and about 125 as Anglicans.

The friendly painter busy giving the big church hall a new coat, which it does not seem to need very badly, has a morning greeting for the inquisitive reader of ancient tombstones lined up in the plot below him. "If you want to know about the history of this town," he says, "you'd better go see Mr. Buffett over at the big store. He's got it all written down." Most welcome information—and at the big store, which is big enough and varied enough in its stock to appear to cover every purchasable human need, we find Mr. Buffett genially disposed to hunt up the precious document for the enlightenment of this unknown caller. It proves to be a hundred or so pages of record written by his father, Aaron F. Buffett, born in Grand Bank and dying here in 1948, aged seventy-one. A seagoing family the Buffetts, probably long before any of them saw Newfoundland. A Buffett took part in the Mutiny of the *Bounty* and first of that name to settle hereabouts was son of a British admiral.

The eighteenth century saw arrival of many English settlers and Jerseymen with French names who found homes all up and down the coast, but their names long ago ceased to be French. The widely spread Tibbo family, for instance, dropped the original Thibeau or Thibault. Welshmen, too, arrived, and you'll meet an Evans in most shore villages. Late in 1716, on board a British ship approaching Halifax, a young man and his wife were on their way to the new world. The husband fell into the ship's hold and died, and his wife gave premature birth to a boy. Surgical help aboard could not have been too bad since youngster Jonathan Hickman successfully came through six weeks of living in cotton-wool and managed to extend a hearty existence over a hundred years and five months. He died here in 1817, leaving a well-established family, the descendants of which have been prominent in Island affairs more or less ever since. His mother had gone to St. Pierre, then a British possession, as housekeeper to an army officer, and Jonathan must have been one of those who from that island's shore saw General Wolfe's fleet pass westward to the taking of Quebec. A man with whom I spoke here tells of having talked with a St. Pierre islander whose grandfather saw that same sight. Jonathan's tombstone is one of those still standing here. A Jonathan Hickman was pilot to James Cook when the latter surveyed Newfoundland's west coast and he named Hickman Harbour in his pilot's honour. The Forsey family, branches of which are to be met in most parts of Newfoundland and even in Canada, seem to have sprung from a seed planted here. An enterprising youth of that name heard a whisper that across the bay a capable and desirable lady had suddenly become a widow. As fast as the wind would urge his boat he sailed across and proved himself a swift and successful suitor, and is to be remembered as having thrown an interesting sidelight on social amenities of the times.

It was during the eighteenth century that people found their way into the coves and bays of this South Shore. Many were young men working aboard ships that came this way. They saw pleasant, food-producing, well-wooded land waiting to be fenced, built upon and owned at no cost other than labour—freedom and opportunity obtainable nowhere else. Doubtless some were deserters from ships; certainly others were refugees from unhappy conditions, perhaps tyranny, at home. They all had experience of the sea and found life in this country not too difficult. As restrictions on settlement expired and the fishing trade became prosperous, opportunity widened and their sons proved no less resourceful and hardy than their parents.

Ownership of a seagoing craft of some kind was the first step towards independence, and to most young men the trees standing in the forest offered the only available shipbuilding material. So when the fishing season was over they went to the woods and felled the trees best suited to the job. Next year they hauled them to the shore and with hand-saw and axe hewed out the timbers and set about building. Timbers on hand and a well-started vessel established credit for purchase of needed ironware, and quite often the sea brought in planks or logs from some wrecked lumber-carrying windjammer. A large ship loaded with dressed deals from England floundered off shore and nearby villages that year enjoyed unprecedented activity in both home and shipbuilding.   Two, three or even more years it took to finish a sizable schooner protected by a covering of boughs while its owner was earning money at sea, but when the job was done he was builder, master and owner of his ship, independent and on his way to fortune.

In later palmy days of schooner building, 1850 to 1890, fishing flourished and money was plentiful.   In 1886 seven ships were launched in Grand Bank and all available carpenters, blacksmiths and handymen were at work.   They fished for herring in the winter and built ships in summer.   Prosperity was general, but it had to be paid for in loss of life and shipping—winter fishing on the Banks was hardly less hazardous than sealing in the north.   Since the middle of the nineteenth century, according to the Buffett records, a score of Grand Bank ships have been lost with all their men, while three times as many from which crews were saved have never reached home port, and the number of men lost from dories is beyond memory or knowledge. The writer suggests, too, that men were more daring in those days than now and took greater chances.   Insurance was unknown or unused as being an invention working somehow in defiance of Providence, and loss of a ship usually meant ruin and poverty for a family.

But on the whole those were happy times, and dwellers in each outport developed a strong communal neighbourliness born out of a hard way of life and probably more comprehensive and effective, and certainly more friendly, than it could ever be in larger and more diversified communities.   Travel to other parts of Newfoundland seldom was thought of.   No one wanted to go to St. John's or elsewhere except on business—which bothered few.   Overland communication did not come until the eighteen-nineties, and irregular steamers or schooners provided the only means of transportation.   They lived to themselves all up and down three or four hundred miles of Fortune Bay shore, a widely scattered group of tiny communities.   Having little communication with the rest of the world, they hammered out their own destiny and developed a typical character of life and thought that stands up well in the broader life of modern times into which events of the last half century have impelled them.

A whole summer spent here and about Fortune Bay would be continuously delightful, but again home calls. For our last morning here, a walk through town, across fields and up a stiffish rock hill rewards us with a view of all the countryside and far south over the ocean to where two small dark blue blots mark the islands St. Pierre and Miquelon. Two or three hundred feet below, waves break against the rock wall, and back behind is all the town of Grand Bank looking small and a bit lonely in this wide expanse of rock and sea. You think that perhaps long after this place first was a fishing port, New York, or Boston, was very much like it in both size and appearance, maybe not so tidy and certainly not so brightly painted—more like Grand Bank must have been in busiest days.

On the way down hill there's the elderly man mowing his meadow and inviting a chat, while his pretty little granddaughter frocked in bluest blue and whitest white smiles a shy, winning welcome and eagerly takes in the foreigner's every word. This meadow is well up the hillside and far from flat, as you might expect a meadow to be. To walk across it is almost to climb, but the scythe swings in long, strong strokes and tall hay falls in a wide swathe. Eighty-three years he's lived here, except for a time when he went to Canada and the States and didn't like life in either. People and things were too fast and fussy. He found no friends and home was the best place for him. Well he remembers South Shore activity when selling bait to American fishermen kept the country prosperous. More than once he ran the revenuer's blockade to St. Pierre. On one occasion his schooner, the only one arriving there in several days, was met by an anxious group of skippers bidding for his load before he had docked. Excitement bustled one off the dock into the harbour, where he disappeared long enough for a shocked hush to fall over the scene to be broken by the bobbing up of his head and a spluttering shout, "Will you take forty-five?" Forty-five shillings a barrel was good money those days and he got the bait.

American skippers paid in gold and, says our friend, there was lots of it around.

His knee-high rubber boots looked ill-fitted for mowing a dry hillside on a warm day, but a suggestion that they might induce foot trouble or rheumatism was not acceptable.

"I had rheumatism once," he said. "It was bad—got so I could hardly walk. My brother-in-law told me I'd never be rid of it until I burned it out. So I put my feet up against the hot stove long as I could stand it—most of one night. It hurt terrible, but I never had rheumatism again."

Whatever other effective, if drastic, remedies he might have for human ills remains untold. Far out at sea a moving speck and a faint cloud of smoke announces the approach of the weekly steamer heading this way, and warns us of time to pack the baggage and start moving westward.

# 17

*Journey along the South Coast—From Belleoram to
Port aux Basques and into Twenty-one Harbours—Sea-
borne Pioneers in Rockbound Coves—Ramea, the Village
Out at Sea—And Finally, Back to Our Starting Point
and Good-bye to Newfoundland.*

THE *Baccalieu*, a somewhat larger sister-ship to the *Bar Haven*,
otherwise is as much like her as one could be like another, equally
smart, friendly and inviting. She carries a heavy load of freight
and all the passengers she can accommodate. This busy time of
the year Newfoundlanders are travelling about on business or
pleasure, and young men are setting out on annual trips to
lumbering jobs back in the bush accessible only from some of the
outports at which we are to touch. Every berth is occupied, and
when night comes sleepy forms fill salon chairs and couches.
It is early evening when the last deep blast of the ship's whistle
fills the town and rolls over the hills. We move seaward, viewing
diminishing Grand Bank with more than a little regret, as one
might say good-bye to an amiable friend met with on a lonesome
journey.

Ahead lie four days of sea travel with twenty-one harbours
to be entered, and twenty-one townlets and hamlets to be
visited—each having its own unusual setting in some ways
different to others, and yet basically alike in presenting a view of
life in this land pretty much as it has been lived since settlement
first took place. Until thirty-five or so years ago, living on

this western south coast must have varied but little from that of a century back. Along here there is no land communication with other places, in many spots not even between one village and the next, and in all of them are people who throughout a whole lifetime have had no occasion, perhaps no desire, to journey beyond the sight of their own village. Others there are who have been afar in the world, elsewhere in Newfoundland or overseas to other countries as sailors, and as sailors do, have come back to re-enter the life they knew before they went abroad.

Thirty-five years ago this certainly was more generally true than it is now. The arrival of regular coastwise communication made a difference, and most likely it was impact of the First Great War that brought about a stirring and a broadening in Newfoundland life and thought that has reached down into the tiniest and loneliest oceanside village. The primitive, isolated, almost viking-like existence in these outports met with rude shock when the country was swept into the maelstrom of world-war and became an active force therein. Their men gave worthy account of themselves in the navy and merchant marine, and under influence of travel and new world-wide associations became world-citizens as never before.

The Second World War accelerated the forward movement. Meanwhile other influences were at work. What education the Island could afford was regularized and spread out into areas hitherto unreached as were medical aid and other social services. Then came radio into the homes, opening up visions of the outside world, and thrusting these people into daily contact with it as imagination could not have foreseen when Marconi brought the first ocean-crossing message to Signal Hill back at St. John's. How deeply and how swiftly the entry into Canadian Federation will influence life and thought along this shore and throughout the land is not yet clearly seen. There are varied opinions about it, but certainly family allowances, old-age pensions and unemployment insurance have had their salutary effect observable in both family life and in general economic activity, and may be reasonably credited with a definite trend towards a renewed prosperity now making itself felt.

Belleoram, first stop after a pleasant run, is one of the more important outports on Fortune Bay's north shore to which we have crossed. Grand Bank may have been the earliest settled, but many more desirable harbours lie along this north shore than on the south, and each has its village sheltered down under the hills and presenting a picture that must have changed little over many generations. Belleoram's houses stand close together along pretty, winding lanes. A kindly land to flowers this— old-fashioned home-garden varieties bloom with astonishing brilliance and size, and lilacs still are fragrant though August fast approaches.

The view down the bay from here is very lovely—clouds hang low on the mainland and island hills, and soft waves of fog waft in from the sea between flashes of sunshine that paint the rock shores deep red and the hilltops all the shades of green there are. Up and down this shore the Church of England has taken over, spreading its work as its means will allow. I am told the parson here has thirty outports under his charge, most of them reached only by sea—surely a job calling for youthful and untiring energy even in summer weather, and for the remaining three-quarters of the year a test of physical endurance to be faced only by a seagoing Newfoundlander born and bred to it.

Through summer days and nights no lovelier coastwise ocean journey than this could easily be imagined. Every rugged mile of coast-line has charm, and every harbour has interest for those who like to see a different and, in many ways, an admirable way of life, and for whom the mood-provoking scenery of northern seas makes a special appeal, swift to change in endless variety with each unpredictable change of light. We enter harbour after harbour. St. Jacques is only about five miles from Belleo-ram, a harbour about big enough to allow a ship to turn and no more. Rounding a rock point unexpectedly you find yourself in the middle of it—another of those places into which the skipper smells his way. He's been doing it for years as nonchalantly as though he were in midocean with a hundred fathoms of water beneath him. All the same, as we approach unbroken shore at many points along here, it is comforting for the stranger to these waters to watch the indicator of the depth-recorder up on the bridge that tells exactly the distance between keel-bottom and ocean floor. Twenty to thirty fathoms are under us most of the way in here, and it's safe as can be. The skipper does not need it. He knows the way as he knows his own home and moves in and out just as easily. A whistle-blast from well outside tells of our approach, and by the time we arrive the entire population is at the dock, as warmly welcoming a crowd as you'd wish to meet, all eagerly looking for mail or packages or even friends. Quite an event, the ship's arrival.

And so we go from port to port, and on the way pass many villages snuggled down on the shore but not large enough to justify our calling. Little evidence of harbour or dock is seen from the sea, a few houses, perhaps only three or four, fish-drying flakes on hillsides, and almost always a church awaiting the parson's occasional call, bits of fields nearby and perhaps a few cattle, certainly goats, and one wonders how often these people get to the nearest larger port for mail and supplies. By sea is the only way, for behind them is a vast area of rock and forest reaching into the half-explored centre of the Island. One wonders, too, how they came to settle here and why. Unfortunately any information on this picked up on the way is highly inconclusive and probably guesswork. Interesting stories might be dug up here and there along this coast if one could but drop in and stay over a day or two.

The best guess seems to be that forebears of some sought refuge in these lonely spots when settlement anywhere within reach of authority was a crime, or perhaps, that some just moved out when older outports became too crowded for their taste. They say a family would find a desirable bay or cove and set up home there. Along would come another group. They too, would take a liking to the scene and settle down—on the same sheltered water, but over on the other side, as far away from the others as possible. It was wide open space they wanted, and no gossiping, inquisitive neighbours to mess up a peaceful life.

Anyway, there they are, and how to give them schooling, medical attention, church and all other things they should have is a major problem among the many Newfoundland is facing. Common sense says these people should be moved to centres where such things are available, but that may not be easily done. Home is home be it ever so unattractive and its surroundings repellent to other people. After your family for two or three generations has followed a way of life, in a spot you are used to and like, to move into strange scenes where a vastly different manner of living will be dictated by strangers with whom you can foresee neither common interest nor mutual understanding is likely to seem terrifying, and it is natural that a forced move would take on in prospect much the same aspect of tyranny as did that which originally drove the forebears of some out into solitude. Time and changing conditions, without doubt, are bringing about a change in this respect, and a generation now growing up will be looking towards an easier and more satisfying existence found in closer association with the rest of the world.

In exactly the same way did civilization spread through all North America. The pioneer built his home in the wilderness, but the spread of population and the development of industry speedily surrounded him so that isolation and solitude were gone for ever. These Newfoundland shore-dwellers are unfortunate in that their country's population has not increased to spread down their way, and the type of land on which a hard fate has thrown them, in no way invites further settlement.

Regrettably, the longest of sunlit midsummer days comes to its end, all the more swiftly when filled with passing scenes that charm, and surrounded by the bustle of interesting fellow-travellers each busy doing nothing much more than chatting or watching other passengers, turning up regularly for meals but being very active about it all. This is a ship load of Newfoundlanders. A couple of tourists have slipped in, but they matter little except as objects of polite and quite friendly curiosity. The ship's crew, lads headed for the woods, merchants on business trips or holidaying with their wives, a parson or two now and then, and an ever-changing crowd of amiable Newfoundlanders, old and young, make the trip a holiday and enjoy every moment of it. Not for a moment does any one of them intrude on the "foreigner." There's a quiet reserve about them that may easily be mistaken for stand-offishness. Nothing of the kind—it has its base in decent self-respect and good manners. But when the stranger offers conversation or even puts a question, he meets with the same frank willingness to exchange ideas as he may have the wisdom or grace to extend. Only by talking to them do you get to know a people.

Through the day half a dozen harbours are visited. Pass Island is different. Here thirty or forty homes are clustered together on the side of a mountainous rocky isle of perhaps two hundred acres extent, set in a quiet winding, island-studded bay and very lovely indeed to look at. Dock, Anglican Church, school-house, and one or two other like buildings complete the settlement. No going up dockside here—not water enough, so we drop anchor and for an hour or two ship's cranes are busy passing freight to boats lying alongside. You wonder what so small a community would do with it all, but learn that some will be reshipped in these same small boats to other villages along the coast.

As westward we move, coves we enter seem even more guarded by rock, and smaller. We steam through walls of tree-clad rock into Gaultois, pronounced Englishly, as it is spelt, and once inside there's less than room enough to turn ship in the ordinary way. But turn we must, and that before tying up at the dock. So we move well forward to drop anchor—no use dropping it a ship's length out towards the middle of the harbour, the water is far too deep. Down it goes almost within a stone's throw of land, and in a neat piece of manouevering, slowly turning engines swing the ship around on straining hawsers as a minute hand moves on a clock and brings us snugly alongside as evening shadows fall across the hills.

The scene is a bit unusual here. Most of the town rises abruptly from the waters edge and houses look down on each other from three or four levels. To go to the town's centre is a climb of many steps, and the one street is a ledge in the rock. Part of the town is a mile or so away at the end of the harbour and more of it lies on the other side.   Lumbering and the pulp industry are carried on hereabouts, and farther back in the hills are swiftly running streams where trout and salmon abound— but getting to them is not easy.   An interesting incident is the arrival of a stoutly built motor cruiser about forty feet in length swinging down the harbour in a business-like way.   As it ties up, an efficient looking and active man of middle age steps ashore carrying a small black bag and moves briskly townwards across the dock acknowledging greetings from all.   He is the medical officer on a regular round of visits and his boat a travelling dispensary and surgery for emergency operations.   Up and down the coast he goes at all seasons and in all weathers on regular rounds or wherever telephone or telegraph calls—part of the system that includes cottage hospitals at larger ports and fully equipped medical ships supplying them   Here we spend the night until a deep grunt or two from the whistle announces dawn and says good-bye to Gaultois.

Through island-studded, land-girt channels all pearly blue in morning mist, we steam for hours until entering the broad waters of Bay Despair.   That is what generations of Newfoundlanders have insisted on calling it despite the fact that original Jersey settlers named it Bay d'Espoir and modern maps so mark it. Frenchman's hope or Englishman's despair, a less despairful appearing or more inviting, sheltered waterway would be hard to find.   There's many a beautifully situated hamlet along its shores that run back forty or fifty miles into the Island.   Up near its end is Milltown—just what its name denotes.   No fish-houses or drying flakes here.   All the men work in the mills or back in the woods.   Again we drop anchor and lighters carry off what freight there is as well as the young men going into the woods.

Here again is a different scene.   The hills are lower and are wooded, and in the valleys, says one who has been there, lies good, ploughable clay soil, perhaps not enough for a widely extended farming industry, but plenty to supply good rich living for many a family.   Homes are scattered all around the wide bay, and far across is the village of St. Albans, written "St.

Halbans" on one large packing case going ashore, doubtless by some lad who believes in spelling as he talks.

Back down the bay we come to Pushthrough, a narrow opening out to sea. An answer to the question as to why it was so named seems quite lost. Some say a whale got itself stranded on the way in or out long years ago, while others attribute it to a narrow, shallow waterway beside the village through which small boats could be half-floated, half-portaged, out to sea, saving a few miles run around the peninsula. Now that gasoline engines push the boats along the "push-through" is disused and bridged. The village is scattered over bare rock. Its main features are the church and wandering sheep, though what they find here to eat is a puzzle to anyone whose view of the surrounding terrain is limited to a short over-hill walk to the store in search of unobtainable pipe tobacco. But sheep and goats seem to thrive, and if they can do that here, surely they would do well anywhere on the Island.

Since leaving Gaultois and up and down Bay d'Espoir, the shores have been less precipitous. Land, not all of it rock, runs down to the shore and much of it is tree-laden. Towards the end of a day-long run from Pushthrough the scene changes again. Tops of a small range of mountains appear and the shoreline reassumes forbidding heights so that as we approach Recontre West the ship and all aboard it seem dwarfed in inconsequential littleness. Entering the narrow harbour, the passenger on the bridge mentally assumes the magnitude of a bee finding its way through some wide open cathedral door. Fourteen hundred feet the rocks go up in more than one place, and since the ship's mast tops are probably less than a hundred feet above water-line, the overtowering effect is terrific. The harbour is small and the depth of its dark green water is said to be equal to shoreline heights. There's an awesome eeriness about this deep bowl-like place. Early in the afternoon when the sun has passed over its rim, dusk rises as water rises in a glass, and with night comes a sense of closed-in darkness that might be terrifying to one not used to it. And yet the village seems happy enough, presumably enjoying a feeling of security it would not find in a less guarded spot open to all the world.

An hour or two later we come to Francois, just such another place and hardly less impressive in setting. By the chart, the hills behind rise nine hundred to a thousand feet. At one side, close to the village, is a moraine of fallen rock, and in almost every direction there seems to be danger of more coming down at any moment. Not long since a mass of rock fell, carrying away a fisherman's home so that no splinter remained to show that once it had been there. The absence of the entire family at the time is taken as a special working of Providence and, no doubt, is greatly encouraging to the three hundred or so men, women and children content to dwell amid such possibilities rather than leave the place where their forefathers lived and lie buried.

Similar majesty marks Cape la Hune, our next port of call, but the village has a different setting. The homes of its less than two hundred inhabitants cluster together on a few low-lying acres of stony beach between mountainous rock—on one side the harbour and on the other open sea—twenty or forty wooden cottages and a church just about large enough to hold those who live in them, comfortably crowded. Small boats are hauled on shore and two or three larger ones are anchored in the bay. So close to sea level does the village seem to sit, that one wonders what happened when the tidal wave of 1929 carried destruction all across Placentia Bay. It reached this far, but so diminished in volume as to cause little damage. We drop anchor in mid-harbour and a scurry of boats comes alongside. One is heavily laden with a family moving out—a youngish couple, three children and a dog—the little dog nailed up in a crate which, judging by whimpered protests, is not at all to his liking. A few bundles and household effects, including a stove, are hauled to the deck, and the family forms a lonely looking group, apparently not much happier than the dog sounds. Later on when we turn and steam away, the group stands at the ship's stern silently gazing at the village on the beach now fast disappearing round harbour bend. One understands their thoughts of friends and relatives left behind. No easy thing this moving out of known shelter into a new world.

Now out over open ocean we go until high rock cliffs fade behind us to a low blue line on the horizon. A glorious day for sea-going, sunshine, a fair wind, lazy-like white caps rolling by and the ship dipping her nose into a mild splutter of foam and spray as though playing at riding a storm. Away ahead lie a couple of bits of rock sticking up out of the sea, and not very high. Ramea Islands, two of them, supporting the clustered homes of six or seven hundred people, their school, cottage hospital and a highly important fish packing plant. A church for its more than five hundred Anglicans is there as matter of course, as also are a couple of public halls and two lighthouses and nothing much else, not even one tree. Less than a thousand acres would cover the two islands and the smaller ones crowded around to form a well protected harbour. Trees were here before early settlers started building and burning them for warmth's sake, and when the trees went the soil followed—swept away by wind and water. They burn coal from Nova Scotia now, though oil heaters in homes are becoming general. This is an important fishing centre and has been so for a hundred years. In 1822, it is recorded, two families lived here. A man and woman had moved here from Port aux Basques. Later on another family came to settle on the harbour's other side. By the eighteen fifties, when fishing was at its best, the place became a community. Its nearness to most productive fishing grounds was attractive. Nothing else mattered. By then, probably the original settlers had begun to complain bitterly of over-crowding and even talked among themselves of moving away to some place where a little peace might be enjoyed. But everybody seems very happy about it now, and the crowd meeting the boat is as jolly, children as plentiful, and the girls as pretty and smartly dressed as any to be met with on the main island.

Ten miles of ocean lie between them and the nearest coastal town, but they are no more cut off from the world than many a hamlet we have visited over the past few days. Time seems not to hang heavily on their hands. Almost always the fish plant is busy, and for amusement they have sports and even a movie three times a week—though if the films shown be anything like the one seen at Grand Bank they are something less than better off on that account. What a splendid challenge each town or village like this offers the government for the presentation of interesting and educative films—at least something better than the fifth-rate canned melodramas and vulgar thrillers now forming the taste of youngsters that crowd to see them. Perhaps this is too big a job for the National Film Board—but surely it calls loudly for an attempt.

This packing plant is another of those promising to revolutionize all Newfoundland's fishing industry. The day of our visit it is closed for a periodical cleaning, and if ever a food producing plant is thoroughly scoured and manicured, here is where it happens. Probably no more prolific fishing grounds exist in the North Atlantic than those within a fifty or hundred mile radius of these islands. Cod, haddock, ocean perch or red fish are brought in by trawlers, draggers and line fishermen in such quantities that the plant sends out three or four million pounds of filleted fish yearly and most of it goes in full shiploads to American cities down the Atlantic coast.

One ship in summer-time carries loads up the Great Lakes to Buffalo, and in winter serves the fish-hungry inhabitants of Atlantic City. Canadian cities receive little or none of this river of food flowing from here. Apparently their demand does not justify economic delivery in full shiploads. Time was when all fishing was done from dories taken to sea on schooners, but young men no longer are interested in that way of earning a living. It is not that they lack the stamina or courage of their fathers, but the big iron steam or diesel-driven ship offers a more comfortable, less hazardous and more economic way of doing the job—and that's the way it's being done.

The busiest place on the day of ship arrival is the post office, and if you have mail to send, better get there early if you wish it included in the outgoing bag. One learned that unforgettably at one of the post offices far back in the journey when trying to post one of those letters too long delayed in the writing, and for which, one hopes, post office efficiency and speed will cover up the writer's neglect or laziness—sometimes it works. Behind a wire caged counter an elderly gentleman, the postmaster no doubt, having a determined air and a somewhat uncompromising cast of countenance, was unhurriedly busy, while one or two others seemed no less leisurely employed in the distance. A visitor's presence at the counter created such evidence of no interest that one seemed to have acquired the power of invisibility. "Mail's closed, sir," was the answer to a request for stamps, and "Mail's closed, sir," was the best obtainable on any phase of that subject.

An almost tearful appeal for the inclusion of one more letter in a pile of those being sorted brought the same reply with an added suggestion, for comfort, that there was no hurry, there'd be another mail day after tomorrow—this spoken with a firmness indicating final closure of the incident. I retreated, exactly as D'Iberville had retired from before Carbonear Island— defeated. "Stuberne fellows," these Newfoundlanders. But part owner of a postal system and a regular paying patron of its services had a right to frustration's rage. The postmaster had been firm, mark you, but very polite—a "sir" in every sentence, and that, of course, was disarming to one unaccustomed, as it were. So, after all, no letter went to Ottawa firing the Postmaster General. But still there's a wish that some day he might learn how nearly he came to losing his job that day.

From Ramea to Burgeo, back on the Newfoundland shore, is an hour and a half's run. A big place is Burgeo, says one fellow-traveller, but as we draw near, you look in vain for corroboration of his statement. So scattered over the scenery are its homes and other buildings as to suggest a suburban approach to a town to be entered later—but this is Burgeo. Another packing plant is busily working here, and we stop at its wharf to take on a load of its product before moving a few ship lengths to the town dock for the usual public reception, this time quite large enough to convince one that a town does exist somewhere hereabouts, and a place of some importance too, the largest on this south coast between Grand Bank and Port aux Basques. The population is about one and a half times that of Ramea, and one of its buildings is a hospital serving many miles of shore area. Whatever its historic and busy past, a packing plant and a few shops today comprise its business activities. Here is an air of resignedly waiting for better times sure to come in the not too far distant future. Meanwhile, the packing plant is doing very well and the town prospers accordingly.

Our stay here is short, and soon we are back on our western course where other hamlets are looking forward to the ship's visit. There's an overnight run here. The number of passengers has dwindled considerably and there are beds for all. It's curious how welcome bed can be after a day of effortless ease at sea. By early night the decks are deserted. Opportunity and desire for conversation has left us, the majestic shoreline has disappeared and the best thing to do is turn in where the gentle swing of the ship hastens slumber, all the more welcome, perhaps, from being unearned, like an unexpected present from a friend who owes you nothing.

Along this south shore from Gaultois to Port aux Basques, a matter of a hundred and fifty miles, ten thousand people are thinly scattered. Nine thousand eight hundred are of English origin with Basically English characteristics yet moulded into something different by several generations of living the unescapable manner of life Newfoundland has forced upon them. Or it may be, that sheltered from the direct influence of world events and change, they have retained original characteristics no longer dominant among English people elsewhere. About one hundred of the total are of Norman-French origin, all that is left of a Jersey invasion and now so absorbed into the general mass as to retain little suggestion of French origin. The remaining hundred or so are about equally divided between Scotch and Irish. If it were not for their names and Newfoundland pride in family history, all evidence of their origins would have disappeared long since.

The placidity of life here can be little disturbed by religious differences. The Anglican Church points the way for eight of the ten thousand, while about fifteen hundred are United

Church in faith but widely divided as to habitat. Roman Catholics run to about one hundred, and the census gives the whole area to one Presbyterian whose Sabbaths may be lonely, but who at least has the advantage of complete unanimity on questions of doctrine and faith which, it has been said, not always has been noticeable among some larger congregations elsewhere.

As we move along over a friendly sea, cliffs glowing in the morning sun and washed by a line of never-ceasing white breakers, vary in height, and not a mile is without interest in startling formations or because of tiny groups of fishermen's homes, even single dwellings, snuggled down to the water line with miles of rugged shore intervening between it and the next. In the ship's company are one or two who have been ashore here and know something of the people.

One is a business man, representative of the younger, forward-looking type of Newfoundlander who wants Island industry and commerce to leap forward with record-breaking speed into place alongside those people who for generations have been in front line of material progression. He doesn't say that, but you know it is in his mind. He is not greatly sympathetic towards these people—says they are backward-in their thinking, unambitious, stubbornly conservative, even superstitious and an easy prey for self-seeking political sharp-shooters, and will not be moved out of their present way of life. When asked what chance the past has given them to be anything else, he has no worthy reply. A good fellow this, and many there are like him—all vitally interested in the welfare of their land and the furthering it with imagination and energy. They will do well for the country if reason and experience are allowed some control over their efforts.

But the merchant with us thinks differently. He has moved amongst these people more frequently and knows them, perhaps, more intimately. Older and of somewhat conservative type, he represents solid citizenry, the class whose fathers and grandfathers built what trade Newfoundland has had and carried it through prosperity and the reverse. He knows the qualities of these shore-dwellers and has admiration for them. Also, he knows the limitations to which they have been subjected. If, in days gone by, illiteracy and ignorance were general, it was because schools did not exist. Island revenues could not possibly establish and maintain them through these lonely areas. Their school learning was meagre, but the world over, no men were better schooled in their trade as seamen, and as such they made a worthy contribution to national life in peace and war as opportunity demanded. Religion has been a guiding force with them and decent living a habit. He reminds us that the latin motto on Newfoundland's coat-of-arms may be translated—"Seek ye first the Kingdom of God," and insists that the age-old admonition has been more than a pious piece of heraldic decoration. Their disabilities are swiftly passing, says our merchant friend. The generation now oncoming will be vastly different. They are seizing offered opportunities and with reasonable help will go forward into better things as, he believes, all Newfoundland now is moving. To the listening bystander who recently has talked with Newfoundlanders of all kinds and classes about their country's future, this sounds like fairly good logic.

Earliest days must have seen fishing along here dominated by Jerseymen. There's hardly a cove, harbour or outport but bears a French name; La Poile, curiously translated frying-pan, no one knows why; Grand Bruit, the big commotion or quarrel; Rose Blanche and Isle aux Morts. At each of these we make a short call passing by many more smaller and of less consequence, and not in one of them will you find a suggestion or trace of French origin other than its name.

The Jerseymen came first, says one local gossip. English came next as merchants and business men. They employed the French as clerks, and it was not long before the French, being bright people, owned the businesses. In time, having learned their lesson, English clerks took over again and have managed to hold on until now. He seemed to think that things might somehow have been different had the population included a fair number of Scots—but that, probably, was because he for a time had lived in Nova Scotia where many of them flourish.

Villages differ only in size and scenic setting, and the latter continues to offer variety enough to satisfy any reasonable traveller. There's a church for every one, some seemingly small enough to be crowded by a dozen or two worshippers. "It's easy to understand why church and religion are very real things to these people," says another fellow-passenger. "They live close to nature." Their life is a battle with natural forces, and in times of direst extremity they find no help in man. Dangers of the sea always are with them. Through generations threat of sudden death has been companion to their daily toil, and that will give thought to the most courageous.

"No," says my friend quite warmly, "I wouldn't call them superstitious. Ghosts? Well—yes—some of them'll tell you there's ghosts all up and down this coast." And the way this bright young man tells it you know he doesn't believe in ghosts, but you suspect there might be places he wouldn't willingly visit on a dark night—or if he did you'd expect to hear his whistle as he went along.

Ghosts or no ghosts, they have profound respect for the dead, and the last dying wishes of the departed are obeyed punctiliously and without question. To do otherwise would appear scandalous in neighbourly eyes. Furthermore, they are all for having the dead rest in peace and not walking around working bad-luck tricks in revenge for neglect.

There's a story of the man who, preparing for death, picked out half a dozen fellow villagers who at one time or another had won his long-lasting displeasure. Perhaps he had been a bit mean himself to have so many unfriendly neighbours. At any rate the six were to be his pall-bearers, and he stipulated that no horse-drawn vehicle was to carry his mortal remains over the two-mile steep road to the hilltop cemetery. The pall-bearers were to do the carrying, and they did—all the way. Tradition says that he was a large man and that one or two of his victims were long in recovering from that day's work. I am told too, that of all those present, it is generally agreed that he alone could

have got much fun out of that funeral.   This is another story
you do not have to believe.   I prefer to.   There's a grim humour
about it that could exist only among a people accustomed to
looking grim things fairly in the face, and dealing with them
forthrightly, and not without a laugh, grim though the laugh
may be.   The Newfoundlander's readiness to laughter is one of
their engaging traits—nothing boisterous or extrovertish about it,
but a quiet expression of enjoyment having a ring of honesty that
makes it good to hear.

From port to port we move on to another night at sea, a
smaller group, and more conversationally inclined now that
tomorrow's Sunday dawning brings us close to our journey's
end.   A hundred and fifty or so miles we have come from Grand
Bank, the distance a plane could leap in half an hour.   In and
out of bays and coves and round broad capes we have wandered
until we have something like four hundred miles behind us.
But when, far ahead, the church tower and the clustered homes
of Port aux Basques glimmer in morning sun, the interest-crowded
past few days seem a period of time far too short to have included
all that we have seen and experienced.   Was it less than weeks
back that Grand Bank faded out in blue distance?   Surely not
—and what a great number of weeks must have passed since our
Newfoundland holiday began, a thousand miles back right here
in Port aux Basques.   Only two and a half months really, but
every day of them rich in experiences and contacts such as a
traveller cherishes so long as the blessed gift of memory remains
with him.   The town looks somewhat larger now, more crowded
with homes than it did when first seen, and since it cannot have
grown much in that time, this must be by unconscious comparison
with countless smaller outports seen on our way.

Being Sunday, there's no crowd to greet our arrival, and anyway, the daily train from St. John's is much more important
than a weekly ship.   Sunday or not, there's freight to be landed
here, and much more that our energetic little friend the railroad
has brought to go with us to the mainland.   Plenty of time for
a walk ashore for a parting glimpse of the town which really

hasn't changed much since last we saw it, and probably very little indeed over the past forty or fifty years.

The path back to the ship leads through the long shed where freight cars are receiving loads of goods an earlier ship has brought to the Island. Among them are bags of potatoes, cabbages, and cases of other vegetables, even packages of bread, and one wonders if so large a part of the country's limited store of wealth must always go abroad to pay for those things which, in large measure, its own land could produce.

About noon, the ship's warning whistle startles the Sunday-quiet town, and we back out of the harbour, turn, and head towards Nova Scotia over a dancing, sparkling sea, and for hours a school of porpoises gambols along on either side of our bow keeping pace as though forming a farewell guard of honour. Far behind, all deep red and purple in mellow sunlight, Newfoundland dissolves into a vivid memory.

A few hours later, between lush, green, low-lying shores we swing up the channel into North Sydney. Vastly different scene this—coal mines just over there, busy coal docks along the shore, and across the harbour great blast furnaces belching flame and smoke.

"Yes," agress a Newfoundlander standing beside me, "a different land—busier, maybe, but sometimes I wonder if always it's very much happier than ours. Troubles we have—but one thing we have learned and remember. Life is for living —not getting."

"Put that in your book," he adds—and there it is.

# INDEX

271

NEWFOUNDLAND HOLIDAY * NEWFOUNDLAND HOLIDAY * NEWFOUNDLAND HOLIDAY * NEWFOUNDLAND HOLIDAY *
NEWFOUNDLAND
holiday